RECLAIMING LESSON OBSERVATION

Reclaiming Lesson Observation explores the latest practice, thinking and research in lesson observation, putting teacher learning at its heart. Illustrated throughout with practical examples from a range of education settings, each chapter contains a rich variety of state-of-the-art, evidence-based case studies to demonstrate how new approaches to observation can be applied in practice.

The book is split into four easily accessible parts:

- making the transition to ungraded models of lesson observation
- recent research studies in lesson observation
- peer observation, coaching and mentoring
- innovations in observing classroom practice.

With a carefully chosen team of contributors, from senior leaders and managers to classroom practitioners and education researchers, this book provides an informed perspective on how to maximise the use of observation, and most importantly, implement proven successful schemes to improve the quality of teaching in the classroom.

Reclaiming Lesson Observation is for all practising educators who want to break free from the constraints of performative lesson observation to redefine and reclaim it as a powerful tool for teacher growth, on which to build sustainable, collaborative communities of teacher learning.

Matt O'Leary is Reader in Education at Birmingham City University, UK. He is also the author of *Classroom Observation: A guide to the effective observation of teaching and learning*, published by Routledge in 2013.

RECLAIMING LESSON OBSERVATION

Supporting excellence in teacher learning

Edited by Matt O'Leary

Routledge
Taylor & Francis Group

LONDON AND NEW YORK

First published 2017
by Routledge
2 Park Square, Milton Park, Abingdon, Oxon OX14 4RN

and by Routledge
711 Third Avenue, New York, NY 10017

Routledge is an imprint of the Taylor & Francis Group, an informa business

British Library Cataloguing in Publication Data
A catalogue record for this book is available from the British Library

Library of Congress Cataloging in Publication Data
Names: O'Leary, Matt, editor.
Title: Reclaiming lesson observation: supporting excellence in teacher learning/ edited by Matt O'Leary.
Description: New York, NY: Routledge, 2016. | Includes bibliographical references.
Identifiers: LCCN 2016018992 | ISBN 9781138656598 (hardback) | ISBN 9781138656604 (pbk.) | ISBN 9781315621838 (ebook)
Subjects: LCSH: Observation (Educational method) | Teachers–Training of.
Classification: LCC LB1731.6.R45 2016 | DDC 370.71/1–dc23
LC record available at https://lccn.loc.gov/2016018992

ISBN: 978-1-138-65659-8 (hbk)
ISBN: 978-1-138-65660-4 (pbk)
ISBN: 978-1-315-62183-8 (ebk)

Typeset in Bembo
by Deanta Global Publishing Services, Chennai, India

CONTENTS

FIGURES

TABLES

CONTRIBUTORS

Emily Barrell M. Ed (Leadership and Management) has worked in the further education and skills sector for 19 years. She is a Quality Improvement Manager for Teaching, Learning and Assessment in an adult community learning provider in Suffolk. Emily is known for her expertise in consultancy and project management in collaborative professional development for teachers, and supporting high performance management cultural practices. Emily has led on a range of highly successful local and regional projects to support teacher-led collaboration, as well as speaking at local and national conferences on teacher professionalism, coaching and ungraded observations.

Sally Challis-Manning is Assistant Principal for Quality at Chichester College. She has responsibility for quality, professional development, maths and English and teaching and learning across the college. She has worked in the FE sector for 30 years and began her teaching career at the London College of Fashion. Prior to her time in FE Sally worked as a writer for *Woman's Own* magazine and set up a successful business. Sally is passionate about teaching and learning and works relentlessly to promote a culture where innovation flourishes and teachers are inspired in a supportive and developmental environment.

Jon Haines is Course Leader for Secondary Science Initial Teacher Training (ITT) and Lecturer in Education at Newcastle University. He has recent experience as a classroom teacher and as Head of Department /Curriculum Leader for Science in a large urban community college. Jon has a passion for improving learning outcomes and teaching through the effective application of technology, and is co-founder of VEO – Video Enhanced Observation, a low-cost app integrating video technology with graphical and text-based feedback for recording classroom practice for use in CPD.

Ann Lahiff has been a teacher educator in further education (FE) for more than 20 years. Prior to moving into higher education, Ann worked in FE for 15 years. Her involvement in FE teacher education began in FE and continued at the Universities of Greenwich and Anglia

Ruskin. Currently a Lecturer in Education at UCL Institute of Education, Ann's teaching and research centres on the ways in which learning in and for the workplace can be understood and enhanced. Her specific focus on the role and significance of teaching observation for vocational teachers was the subject of her PhD research.

Jane Martin is the Professional Development Manager at Shrewsbury College. She has recently been responsible for creating and implementing a framework of curriculum-based Professional Learning Communities at Shrewsbury College and works closely with a team of Learning Coaches to support professional development through this initiative. Jane has also recently introduced a peer review process which draws on the principles of coaching and mentoring to inform professional dialogue.

Joanne Miles has worked in education for the last 20 years, in both teaching and training roles. She spent ten years in Professional Development as a teacher trainer, quality observer and CPD Lead, setting up development programmes and coaching networks in further education. Joanne was also a managing consultant at the Learning Skills Network for several years and worked with colleges and schools to improve their CPD, observation cycles and coaching delivery. She is now a freelance trainer, consultant and coach interested in whole organisation approaches to developing teaching and learning and creating improvements through solution focused coaching.

Paul Miller is co-founder and the CEO of Video Enhanced Observation Ltd. He is also a guest researcher at Newcastle University, where he is studying for an EdD. Alongside his business partner Jon Haines, Paul has overseen the development of the VEO concept from the idea's inception through to its launch. Paul's career has spanned business, education and research. Recent consultancy for Newcastle University has involved designing and delivering both large-scale teacher CPD programmes and educational research across slum areas in West Africa. His interests lie in creating sustainable and scalable platforms for learning to flourish in challenging environments.

Matt O'Leary is a Reader in Education at Birmingham City University. Prior to this he was the co-founder of the Centre for Research and Development in Lifelong Education (CRADLE) and a principal lecturer in post-compulsory education at the University of Wolverhampton. He has worked as a teacher, teacher educator, head of department, principal lecturer and educational researcher for over 20 years in colleges, schools and universities in England, Mexico and Spain. He is well known internationally for his work on classroom observation and is the author of the highly acclaimed book *Classroom Observation: A guide to the effective observation of teaching and learning* (London: Routledge 2014).

Lorna Page has worked in education since 1995, initially working with Deaf students and teaching British Sign Language for Further and Adult Education programmes. Having been fortunate to travel extensively, Lorna has also worked as a secondary school teacher in both UK state and independent schools; furthermore, she has taught at international schools in Europe and enjoyed a role as a school governor. Having completed her PhD at Lincoln University, she has worked as a course leader and teacher trainer in the further education sector and has been involved in a number of teacher education programmes.

Terry Pearson began his teaching career as a vocational lecturer in 1985. Since then he has held senior positions in further education and higher education with responsibilities for staff development, teacher education and quality enhancement. He has designed and implemented a broad range of lesson observation schemes and conducted more than one thousand observations of teachers at work in a wide variety of educational settings. Terry is passionate about research-informed and evidence-supported practice and now works independently as an education researcher and consultant. He is a chartered member of the Chartered Institute of Personnel and Development.

Dean Price is the Standards and Performance Manager at Dudley College where he leads and manages a highly creative and staff-driven approach to developing teaching and learning through collaborative communities of practice. He has worked in the further education sector in England since arriving from Australia in 1996. During that time, he has held posts as a lecturer, advanced practitioner, coordinator of teacher training programmes, as well as recently completing a secondment as Vice Principal at Al-Qatif College in Saudi Arabia. He has a master's degree in Education and is a strong opponent of formalised lesson observations.

Rachael Stevens has taught English for 23 years, in Shropshire, Birmingham and now Worcester. She is a Specialist Leader of Education and Assistant Headteacher at Christopher Whitehead Language College and Sixth Form where she leads the Teaching and Learning group. She is a keen advocate of evidence-based educational research and practice, and collaborative approaches to school improvement and professional development.

Louise Taylor is an educational consultant and Teaching and Learning Strategic Advisor at Harrow College. She has worked in further and higher education in the UK, Greece, Thailand, Portugal and France for over 20 years. She has held a wide range of roles from teaching and teacher training to senior management. She has worked on a range of UK national projects and research and was awarded a University of Westminster Fellowship for excellence in teaching and learning. She has recently introduced teaching and learning strategies featuring non-graded observation processes with professional dialogue and reflection at the core in two London Colleges.

Sheila Thorpe is the Professional Development Manager at Chichester College. She began her career in 1973 training as a registered nurse. In the latter part of her 29-year NHS career, Sheila managed the education, support and development of Health Visitors. She wrote and set up the highly acclaimed Beacon Award, winning 'Licence to Observe' training package – a programme designed to develop skilled observers of teaching, learning and assessment and promote lesson observation as a unique opportunity for CPD. She is currently the chair of the 157 Teaching and Learning group and a passionate advocate of developing staff using a coaching approach.

Phil Wood taught secondary-level geography in Lincolnshire for ten years before moving to the School of Education at the University of Leicester, where he initially worked on the Secondary PGCE team. He then went on to help develop both campus-based and distance-learning Masters' degree programmes. He has a long-term interest in researching pedagogy through action research and lesson study and interprets the insights gained through the use of complexity theory. Together with Joan Smith, he is the co-author of the recently published *Educational Research: Taking the plunge* (Independent Thinking Press).

Victoria Wright is a Senior Lecturer in Post-Compulsory Education at the University of Wolverhampton. Before this, she worked in further education colleges as a lecturer, Programme Manager and Advanced Practitioner. Before moving into the field of teacher education, she was an English teacher. Her chapter in this book draws on research she carried out for Doctorate in Education, which she completed at the University of Birmingham in 2016 and as part of which she developed an autoethnographic account of giving lesson observation feedback.

PREFACE

This book is made up of a collection of chapters from educators working in further education (FE) colleges, schools, universities and adult education providers across the UK. Ranging from senior leaders and managers to classroom practitioners, consultants, education researchers and teacher educators, what each author has in common is a shared interest in exploring, explaining and exemplifying how lesson observation can be used to support excellence in teacher learning.

What originally started as a casual conversation between two of the book's contributors quickly progressed to the staging of a large national conference in June 2015 dedicated solely to the topic of lesson observation and ultimately culminated in the writing of this book. Throughout this journey the key aim has always been to provide a platform for practitioners, researchers and thinkers in the field of observation and the wider education community at large to discuss and share the latest practice, thinking and research relating to the use of observation in an educational context.

One of the notable strengths of this book is the diversity of its contributors. The different contexts in which they work, their differing roles, involvement and experience with observation means that each contributor brings a unique set of skills and knowledge to their respective chapters. For some contributors, academic writing is not necessarily something that they have experience of or are familiar with. Unless they work in higher education, and even then expectations vary according to roles and contexts, it is unlikely that they would be expected to engage in academic writing. Thus for some contributors, this is their first experience of writing for general publication purposes. Though some have written for public audiences before via online platforms such as blogs, writing a book chapter has been a new and challenging experience. Yet the plurality of their perspectives along with the passion and authenticity of their voices as writers only adds to the richness of this work, while also extending its appeal and relevance to a wide readership.

That each contributor is involved with observation in differing capacities in an applied context is another key strength of the book in terms of its authenticity and credibility as a piece of work. All the authors are practising education professionals who occupy that interface between policy and practice. They are involved in the very real, grounded work of mediating and making sense of policy and translating it into practice. The importance of this cannot be underestimated as their knowledge and experience of working with observation in a strategic and logistical sense means that each of the book's chapters is written from an informed, situated perspective.

Finally, what the chapters in this book have in common is that they tell a story, often of a journey and the experiences of those involved in that journey of reimagining and redefining the way in which they interact with observation as a form of practice. These are the stories of educators who have decided to break free from the shackles of performative lesson observations that have contaminated many people's conceptualisation of the practice for decades and have begun to redefine and reclaim observation as a powerful tool for teacher growth and on which to build sustainable, collaborative communities of teacher learning. These are the stories of real people who are engaged in real, meaningful work with alternative approaches to traditional models of observation; people who realise that worthwhile, sustainable improvements in teaching and learning take time. Their stories offer hope of how, when used supportively, observation can become a powerful tool for teacher learning.

Matt O'Leary, April 2016

INTRODUCTION

Reclaiming lesson observation as a tool for teacher learning

Matt O'Leary

Introduction

Lesson observation continues to be one of the most widely discussed and hotly debated areas of practice amongst those involved in the teaching profession. In recent years much of this debate has centred on its use as a performance management mechanism with which to evaluate the quality of teaching and teacher effectiveness. In England, the removal of graded lesson observations from Ofsted's inspection framework marked a significant milestone in policy development, which heightened interest further and opened up new possibilities for the ways in which the teaching profession conceptualises and engages with observation. Yet this shift in policy has not necessarily been matched by a parallel shift in practice in many circles. Despite Ofsted's recent change in stance, there is concern amongst teachers that it is unlikely to lead to a change in the mindsets and working practices of some senior managers/leaders in education. This is unsurprising given how engrained the normalised practice of graded observations has become in many institutions over the last few decades. But what does this tell us about the role that observation has traditionally played in the lives of teachers and the role it could play in the future?

There are three key points that I wish to cover during the course of this chapter. The first is to share with you my views as to where I think we are at present with the use of observation in the education system in the UK. The second is to say where I think we need to be and what this implies for the teaching profession as a whole. The third is to provide an overview of the book by indicating the focus of each of its four parts and reflecting on how each contributes to this ongoing debate.

Japanese knotweed and the use of observation in the UK

Japanese knotweed was originally introduced into Britain from Japan as an ornamental plant in the early nineteenth century. Although it may look like a harmless plant, it has actually become a menace to many homeowners across the UK in a very short space of time. So invasive a plant is the Japanese knotweed that it has even been known to burrow under the very concrete foundations of buildings, appear under the floorboards and penetrate the walls.

Once Japanese knotweed establishes itself, it is notoriously difficult to get rid of. Like any stubborn weed, unless you are able get to its roots, it is impossible to eradicate it completely and it simply continues to regrow and resurface.

I realise that at this point you might be wondering what on earth does a weed from Japan that has become the scourge of gardeners and homeowners across the UK have to do with the central focus of this book, *lesson observation*? Allow me to explain what I see as the link between the two. I see the Japanese knotweed as a metaphor for the way in which observation has been conceptualised and applied in the British education system over the last few decades. For me there are parallels between the destructive growth of the knotweed and the use of observation as a high-stakes summative assessment with which to rate teachers' classroom performance. It is this performative use in particular that is responsible for generating such strong emotions and negative associations with observation among teachers. Since the 1990s, observation has come to be used as a means of exercising power and control over what teachers do and how their professional worth is evaluated and subsequently valued. Through the lens of observation, teachers have been repeatedly asked to perform to show their worth in the classroom.

Performance-driven models of observation have therefore come to symbolise the all-encompassing colonisation of the Japanese knotweed. Such performative models of observation seek to reduce the complex processes of classroom interaction to a superficial set of skills and behaviours. However, they are the manifestation of a much more deeply rooted, chronic problem that underpins the very foundations of the British education system, and has done so for years. A problem that Hall and O'Shea (2013) refer to as 'common-sense neoliberalism' and Stephen Ball (2015) as 'necessarian logic', which has resulted in the reallocation of authority away from classroom teachers and local authorities, for example, to policy makers, education technocrats and senior managers and leaders. This necessarian logic has championed a form of competitive, market-driven individualism in education.

It is a logic that is repeatedly echoed in the speeches of politicians and policy makers when discussing education policy. For example, in June 2015, the Office for Standards in Education's (Ofsted) Chief Inspector, Sir Michael Wilshaw, delivered a so-called radical speech outlining the changes to the Common Inspection Framework (Wilshaw, 2015). If you closed your eyes and listened to it without knowing who it was, you could very easily have mistaken it for a speech by a high-profile business leader. In his speech, there are lots of references to leaders: 'good leaders', 'great leaders' and 'exceptional leaders', but very little mention of teachers, learning support assistants or anyone else for that matter who make an important contribution to the educational attainment of students. The overriding message being that all you need to be a successful college/school is to have a great leader at the helm and everything else will fall into place. There is a part of me that wonders why Sir Michael did not follow his thinking through to its logical conclusion and simply do away with observing and evaluating teachers and students altogether and just focus on evaluating the quality of leadership. Now that certainly would have been a radical policy development!

The removal of graded lesson observations from inspections: a new dawn or false hope?

It is no exaggeration to say that when Ofsted decided to remove grading from individual observations in inspections, this was met with widespread approval by teachers and was generally perceived as a step in the right direction. In many ways, this reaction was to be expected as graded observations had become one of the most polemical areas of practice for the profession in recent years (e.g. O'Leary, 2014). For someone who has spent the last decade of my career exposing the shortcomings of reductionist practices like graded observations and highlighting their counterproductive effects on the professional lives of teachers, not to mention the massive question marks surrounding the validity and reliability of such practice from an assessment perspective, Ofsted's policy shift was a welcome development. How individual institutions have chosen to interpret and respond to this is another matter for discussion, but Ofsted should at least be commended for listening and responding to the views and experiences of practitioners and the compelling evidence presented during the course of this debate. Yet, at the same time, I believe that their change in positioning has not been thought through carefully, nor does it go far enough.

Let us just reflect for a moment on Ofsted's current position when it comes to evaluating the quality of educational provision. What we know is that inspectors are not supposed to give grades to any of the lessons they observe during inspections, but – and it is a big but – they should still allocate an overall grade for the quality of Teaching, Learning and Assessment, though recent announcements in the 2016 White Paper suggest this may change in the future. When it comes to deciding this grade, inspectors are expected to do so by drawing on a range of sources of evidence, e.g. student achievement rates, the written feedback on student's work, speaking to students during the inspection, etc., rather than simply pooling grades from individual observations and arriving at an aggregate. Whether this is actually happening, the question of how systematic and reliable the inspectorate's approach is in applying this remains unknown as it is impossible to examine closely the data analysis and decision-making skills of its inspectors.

When I met with Mike Cladingbowl (Ofsted's National Director for Schools 2012–14) in May 2014 and he told me that Ofsted were planning to remove graded observations from school inspections, I asked him how he intended to prepare inspectors for the change in policy and what he thought the wider repercussions would be for Ofsted's assessment framework. His response highlighted this was not something that had been carefully considered. What I was getting at with these questions was, firstly, a change in procedure does not necessarily equate to a change in practice. In other words, simply asking observers not to grade lessons any more does not deal with the wider issue of how they conceptualise their role. And secondly, the decision to remove individual lesson grades from the inspection process has much more far-reaching consequences for the way in which Ofsted, or any other organisation, seeks to assess the quality of educational provision. If, as Cladingbowl argued in his position paper that attaching a grade to a one-off, episodic event like a lesson observation was no longer deemed fit for purpose (Cladingbowl, 2014), then this inevitably raises the question of why stop at lesson observations? Why should the same logic not be extended to the removal of grades from the inspection process as a whole? If grading individual lesson observations was no longer fit for purpose, then why should the grading of educational providers per se according to its 4-point scale be deemed any different? As an organisation whose principal remit is that of a regulator of standards, surely there is a case for it to move towards an assessment framework that simply operates on a 'meets standards/doesn't meet standards' or 'good enough/not good enough' basis?

A positive outcome of Ofsted's recent shift on grading is that it provides a valuable lesson for practitioners and policy makers alike about how powerful a teacher's voice can be when captured and communicated effectively. And how, despite decades of continuous government intervention, there are messages of hope and windows of opportunity for the profession to wrestle back some of the professional autonomy and authority that has so steadily been stripped away from teachers since the 1980s. Teachers' knowledge, experience and expertise is all too often undervalued or even ignored when it comes to education policy. But it is important for all educators to continue to challenge policy makers and resist policy that we know is not in the common good of the profession or the people we teach.

Without wanting to underplay the significance of Ofsted's policy shift, I would argue that it is only the beginning; a small victory in a much bigger battle that faces teachers across all sectors of education. I have argued for some time now that simply removing grades from the observation process is not in itself a panacea. The mere act of doing away with lesson observation grades does not suddenly result in it becoming a transformative tool that wipes clean the lived experiences and mindsets of those staff who have come to view its use cautiously – and with some justification – as a punitive, disciplinary mechanism. The reality is that, like two mature adults embarking on a new relationship later on in life, for many teachers, observation carries with it a certain degree of emotional baggage. And once that baggage is opened up, a pattern starts to emerge that does not just tell the story of one individual's experiences, but a collective narrative of more systemic issues concerning cultures of teaching and learning, power, trust and control. And the findings from the University and College Union (UCU) research project into the use and impact of observation on the professional lives of those working in FE are a compelling illustration of this (O'Leary, 2013).

Over two years have now passed since the publication of the UCU research report. The UCU research captured the views of thousands of FE staff and still represents the largest and most extensive account of the topic in the English education system as a whole to date. The report raised serious questions about the fitness for purpose of graded observation systems. The overriding message was that not only were they failing to assure and improve teaching quality, but the reductive and punitive ways in which observations were often used was responsible for a catalogue of detrimental effects that were impeding improvements in teacher learning. The report played a key role in influencing Ofsted's shift in policy on lesson observations in inspections and triggered debates about the continued use of observation across education, as well as resulting in a growing number of institutions changing their practice. Yet despite all of this, many teachers contend that such developments have still not changed how many senior managers and leaders view the use and purpose(s) of observation.

There is a concern amongst many teachers that Ofsted's decision to scrap grading in lesson observations has not or is unlikely to lead to a change in the mindsets and working practices of some senior managers and leaders who, returning to the earlier reference to Ball's argument about the reallocation of authority, in some cases have become institutionalised to see part of their role as internal Ofsted teams. 'Old habits die hard' as the saying goes, and the reliance of some on the grading of teachers' classroom practice on an annual basis has become firmly engrained in the performance management systems of many institutions.

From a management perspective, there is undoubtedly an allure about the quick and easy nature of attaching a number to a teacher's performance that may ultimately prove a stubborn practice to change. *How do we measure and monitor quality if we're not going to grade anymore?* This is a question I hear all the time from senior managers and leaders. But it is actually the wrong question; it is a question based on circular reasoning. The premise on which this question is built is just as devoid of proof as the outcome itself. It is a question that is built on the premise that the phenomena you are purporting to measure in the first place is actually measurable and that it can be measured in a consistently reliable way. The allocation of a grade to classroom observations has never been, nor will it ever be a practice that is consistently reliable. There are very good reasons for that and no amount of tinkering is going to make it more reliable, which is why educational providers and researchers are barking up the wrong tree focusing efforts on developing standardised observation instruments or attempting to improve things such as inter-rater reliability. Such interventions amount to little more than tinkering with a flawed system and an unproductive use of precious time and resources.

Another recent example of tinkering with the system in terms of the observation of practice is the introduction of exercises like 'Learning walks'. Learning walks first appeared following Ofsted's decision to introduce no-notice inspections. But what exactly are learning walks? Some senior leaders and managers justify them as being an important exercise in capturing the 'reality' of classroom teaching because, as the argument goes, by not giving teachers time to prepare in advance, etc., then you are more likely to get a realistic picture of classroom practice. In an institution that boasts a proven culture of collaboration, where there is an open and collegial working environment and where observations are seen as a genuinely supportive exercise this may indeed be the case, as Rachael Stevens (Chapter 11) explores in her chapter when discussing the use of 'walk-throughs'. But in other less collegial contexts, there is evidence of them being used as another exercise in performance management. Whatever the context in which they are being used, exploring the complexities of the classroom in a ten-minute snapshot raises questions about what can be observed in such a short time frame and the value of such practice.

Switching the lens of observation: looking ahead

For decades there have been debates around the quality of teaching and attempts to capture what it means to be an excellent teacher. In recent years, the desire to 'measure' what excellence and/or effectiveness in teaching might mean has seen the rise of a catalogue of research studies internationally, often equipped with quantitative instruments that purport to be able to capture this. Yet the reality is not one of them has been able to do so. Not because these tools are necessarily flawed in themselves, but more importantly because teaching is not an exact science that lends itself to transparent measurement. Teaching, and education as a whole, is a human system not a mechanical system. It is a complex system that is about people! As Shulman (2004: 258) reminds us, '… classroom teaching is perhaps the most complex, most challenging, and most demanding, subtle, nuanced, and frightening activity that our species has ever invented'.

If we accept classrooms and teaching and learning as an example of a complex, non-linear system, we can see that they are made up of different elements (e.g. students, teachers, resources, environment etc.) that are largely defined by their iterative connections, which makes them unsuitable for studying or measuring by traditional linear systems of scientific analysis as, unlike phenomena in the natural world measured by calibrated instruments like thermometers, there are no transparent cause and effect connections. So to use a concrete example, student achievement is not solely dependent on the quality of teaching, despite politicians and policy makers trying to convince us otherwise. All these elements are part of a dynamic system that can only be properly understood in terms of their interactions and relations with other elements in and beyond the system, and not in isolation. In other words, the model of classrooms as complex adaptive systems is relational.

For decades, the main lens through which many people have experienced observation has been a summative lens; a lens which has used observation as a ranking device, a tool for evaluating and sorting teachers. My argument and indeed that of this book's contributors is that it is time to switch lenses. I accept that there is an argument for the use of observation for both summative, and formative purposes, and indeed, when intelligently combined, these two can complement each other well. I am a firm believer and supporter of the intelligent use of observation. Observation has great potential as a medium for teacher learning, but to date, it has rarely been given the room to grow as the common-sense neoliberal performance management agenda, like the invasion of Japanese knotweed referred to earlier, has colonised the space in which it operates and with that its ability to foster teacher learning and growth.

Until underlying political and epistemological issues surrounding the use of observation as a method of assessment and ultimately as a means of managing teachers' work are confronted, and by that I mean issues relating to professional autonomy, judgement and how we attempt to capture the complexities of teaching and learning in the context of teacher evaluation, then the removal of grades runs the risk of being little more than a superficial change that is unlikely to have a lasting and sustainable impact on practice in the workplace.

One of the biggest challenges that lies ahead concerns the way in which the profession conceptualises the use of a mechanism like observation. Grades or no grades, the next stage of the debate needs to confront the long standing issue of how the profession breaks free from the assessment straitjacket that has conceptually constrained the way in which it has engaged with observation for decades.

For too long the emphasis on the use of observation has prioritised the *sorting* of teachers rather than *supporting* them. It is where every previous policy has gone wrong. Now is the time for rebalancing those scales. If as educators we want to make a real, sustainable difference to improving the quality of teaching through the lens of observation, then supporting rather than sorting teachers is where our energies need to be focused. It is time therefore to reclaim observation as a medium on which to build sustainable, collaborative communities of teacher learning, united by a collective pursuit to further our understanding of the complexities of teaching and learning and with it a renewed sense of professionalism. I really hope this book can act as a catalyst for us all to be part of that pursuit by beginning to share and discuss our work and interest in this important area of practice.

Structure of the book

The book is divided into four parts:

Part I – Making the transition to ungraded models of lesson observation
Part II – Recent research studies in lesson observation
Part III – Peer observation, coaching and mentoring
Part IV – Innovations in observing classroom practice

Through three distinct case studies, Part I explores the journeys of four differing organisations in making the transition to adopting an ungraded model of lesson observation. Each chapter provides a detailed account of the context and rationale for their transition to different models of observation, the considerations and challenges encountered during the period of transition, the practical implementation of these models, what they look like in practice and concludes by reflecting on the impact and effectiveness on their staff and their respective organisations as a whole.

In Chapter 1, Louise Taylor explores the rationales and approaches taken by two different FE colleges in their transition to an ungraded model of observation. She unpicks some of the pitfalls, challenges and solutions experienced when transitioning from graded to ungraded observation models and provides tips and strategies to support the effective implementation of an ungraded scheme. As she comments in the opening of her chapter, 'the thinking is fuelled by a belief that … there are models of observation which stimulate deeper teacher engagement and reflection on and innovation in their practice'.

In Chapter 2, Emily Barrell tells the story of an adult and community learning provider in the East of England and how, over a three-year period, it replaced a regime of graded observations with a grass roots approach to developing its staff through the use of ungraded observation. She reveals the thinking behind this longitudinal change, the reasons as to why her organisation chose to transform their policy, the considerations that accompanied that choice and how it has impacted on their staff and ultimately their learners. She issues a word of warning, however, for anyone thinking of embarking on such fundamental policy and organisational change that they should not do so unless they are totally committed to the journey and the obstacles as well as the opportunities that it is likely to throw up. Yet, as Emily argues, perseverance brings its own rewards that can be liberating for all involved and lay the foundations for sustainable improvement for years to come.

Chapter 3, by Sally Challis-Manning and Sheila Thorpe, explores how an award winning college has successfully introduced and developed a model of ungraded lesson observation. The chapter focuses on the rationale for change, how this change was communicated and introduced to staff, the support systems put in place to ensure the successful implementation of the new scheme, how it was monitored and evaluated by staff involved and a discussion of its impact on teaching and learning across the college.

Part II focuses on three recent research studies carried out in the field of lesson observation in the UK. All three studies formed part of the authors' doctoral research and were situated in the English FE sector.

In Chapter 4, Ann Lahiff draws on recent case study research investigating the use and value of teaching observations conducted with vocational staff following in-service initial teacher training (ITT) programmes in England. In presenting the study's findings, the chapter explores the value attached to ITT observations by those involved in the process and identifies the conditions under which vocational teachers' learning can be maximised. It ends with a clear set of recommendations for future practice.

In Chapter 5, Lorna Page shares segmented findings from a six-year FE single institution case study, examining the perspectives, experiences and engagement of a range of teachers with being observed teaching. Through the unmasking of teachers' voices, a new model for conducting observations emerges. This model acknowledges that observation still has a place in the English education system, but it is a model that takes into account teachers' professionalism, experience and development needs.

In Chapter 6, Victoria Wright shares her doctoral research on observation feedback. The chapter seeks to discuss experiences of observing and being observed in an exploration of the ways in which context, attitude, values and expectations are evident in those practices. Drawing on Foucauldian theory, it delves deeper into the psyche of those involved in the observation process by interrogating the relations between power (i.e. the institutional and policy contexts), the subject (the writer as tutor observer, and her students on an ITT PGCE programme) and truth (the nature of observation feedback, its forms of knowledge and ways of being and behaving). She concludes by sharing some suggestions for both observers and observees in negotiating and managing observation feedback.

Part III comprises three chapters focusing on the role of coaching and mentoring in observation as well as peer-based models of observation.

In Chapter 7, Joanne Miles puts forward the case for the importance of embedding coaching into the observation process and outlines ways to address some of the challenges involved. Drawing on a series of case study colleges that have introduced ungraded models of observation, she highlights how this has led to a greater focus on coaching and mentoring skills for observers as part of the professional dialogue and action-planning meetings. The chapter concludes with some practical suggestions for embedding coaching approaches into observation cycles and provides contextualised examples to assist in that process.

In Chapter 8, Jane Martin focuses on a single case study college and explores the impact of a peer review strategy into which the principles of coaching have been embedded and which is supported by a framework of Professional Learning Communities (PLCs). Her chapter explores the concept of observation and peer observation, discussing the characteristics of different approaches and identifying the advantages and disadvantages and impact on professional development. The chapter concludes by reflecting on the impact of the peer review process and proposes ways in which to shape future developments.

In Chapter 9, Matt O'Leary and Dean Price pose the questions: What do peer-based models of observation look like? How do they differ to their dominant, performance management counterparts? How do they work in practice? And what is their impact? The chapter seeks to answer these questions by discussing some of the core elements of peer observation, sharing recent research evidence from the FE sector and hearing about the introduction of a new peer observation policy in a case study college.

Part IV includes an eclectic mix of chapters all under the broad umbrella of 'innovations in observing classroom practice'. Each of these chapters explores observation through a number of different lenses, ranging from the use of a specially designed mobile app for videoing classroom practice, to the creation of an observation classroom and accompanying viewing room, walk-throughs, the relationship between observations and teacher self-efficacy and lesson study.

In Chapter 10, Jon Haines and Paul Miller explore an alternative approach to paper-based observations via the use of digital video technology and the creation of a specific app VEO. With the development of Video Enhanced Observation (VEO), their aim is to enable teachers to take control of their own professional practice, developing and sharing the things they are good at, while improving in areas they recognise as less effective. This chapter charts their journey of how VEO came about, introduces the thinking behind it, how it works, the contexts in which it is and can be used and their future hopes for its continued development.

In Chapter 11, Rachael Stevens discusses the experience of observing and being observed from two particular angles. The first examines the impact of a dedicated 'observation classroom' in a school with a built-in viewing room. It explores how this classroom has facilitated the sharing and collaborative development of innovative approaches to lesson observation amongst the school's staff, using instant feedback from practising teachers in 'live' lessons. It highlights how this experience has helped colleagues to focus on evidence-based practice, on real classrooms and on student and teacher learning. The second angle she explores is the use of 'walk-throughs' as a means of developing an open-door policy amongst staff when it comes to observing and sharing ideas about practice.

In Chapter 12, Terry Pearson uses the lens of teacher self-efficacy to examine lesson observation. Terry argues that exploring lesson observation from the perspective of teacher self-efficacy highlights the potential of lesson observations to generate valuable information to support teacher professional learning which in turn can foster the development of their self-efficacy. A framework is presented and explained as a means of stimulating thinking and encouraging discussion of how lesson observation may be used effectively to develop teachers' perceptions of their self-efficacy.

In Chapter 13, Phil Wood outlines the basic principles and procedures behind the adoption of a lesson study approach. He then goes on to consider the role and issues surrounding the use of observation as a methodology for understanding and developing support for learning. He makes a number of suggestions as to how conventional models of lesson study might be added to, which can help to extend its potential for questioning and understanding the process of learning in relation to classroom practice.

References

Ball, S. J. (2015) 'Back to Basics: Repoliticising education'. *Forum*, 57(1), 7–10.

Cladingbowl, M. (2014) *Why I Want to Try Inspecting Without Grading Teaching in Each Individual Lesson*, June 2014, No. 140101, Ofsted. Available online at: www.ofsted.gov.uk/resources/why-i-want-try-inspecting-without-grading-teaching-each-individual-lesson. Accessed 23 August 2014. Last accessed 11 June 2015.

Hall, S. and O'Shea, A. (2013) 'Common-sense neoliberalism', chapter 4, *Kilburn Manifesto*. London: *Soundings*. Available at: www.lwbooks.co.uk/journals/soundings/pdfs/Manifesto_commonsense_neoliberalism.pdf Accessed 21 May 2015.

O'Leary, M. (2013) *Developing a National Framework for the Effective Use of Lesson Observation in Further Education*. Project report for the University and College Union, November 2013. DOI: 10.13140/RG.2.1.1751.7286. Available at: www.ucu.org.uk/media/6714/Developing-a-national-framework-for-the-effective-use-of-lesson-observation-in-FE-Dr-Matt-OLeary-Nov-13/pdf/ucu_lessonobsproject_nov13.pdf. Last accessed 30 March 2016.

O'Leary, M. (2014) 'Power, Policy and Performance: Learning lessons about lesson observation from England's further education colleges'. *Forum*, 56(2), 209–222.

Shulman, L. S. (2004) *The Wisdom of Practice: Essays on teaching, learning, and learning to teach*. San Francisco, CA: Jossey-Bass.

Wilshaw, M. (2015) *Speech at the Future of Education Inspection launch*, Central Hall, Westminster, 15 June 2015. Available at: www.gov.uk/government/speeches/speech-at-the-future-of-education-inspection-launch. Last accessed 30 March 2016.

PART I

Making the transition to ungraded models of lesson observation

1

SOMEWHERE OVER THE RAINBOW

Transitioning from performative to informative models of observation

Louise Taylor

Introduction

Scenario one

The year 2000: 8.15am at 'Green School', a medium-sized language and business school in London. It was a misty Monday morning in west London. Sara was excited as she had been reading an article about independent learning and was anxious to try out some of the strategies with her class. She wanted to get in early to grab Stuart, the school's academic advisor, before the start to ask him to pop in and give some feedback on the session. She particularly wanted him to focus on Ali and Stefan as she knew they might struggle with one of the tasks. Stuart always had brilliant insights to offer, particularly at noticing the impact on individual learners.

Scenario two

The year 2010: 7.45am at Purple College, a large further education (FE) college. It was a grey Wednesday morning and Amy arrived at work with a feeling of dread. Her annual observation was scheduled for 9.00am and she rushed around gathering all her materials, the cut-up text envelopes, the differentiated worksheets, the detailed plan, the mini-white boards, the post-it notes and, of course, fumbled in her bag for her USB stick. Would the computers work? In the last observation she was told she had not used enough technology, even though the levels of learner engagement were commented as 'high'. She never really felt the feedback was useful. It was so formulaic and there was always that dreaded question 'So how do you think it went?', but she just had to tick all the boxes, as having another 'requires improvement' judgement would have implications for the whole year …

Do these scenarios sound familiar? Which of the approaches do you think would stimulate teacher learning and improved learning experiences and outcomes for students?

In the first scenario I was Sara, working as a language teacher in a highly successful language school which had continuously exceeded quality standards in all areas of British Council inspections over many years. The observation approach in the school was informal, feedback in the form of discussion and qualitative and informative in nature. Observations were on an *invited* basis from teachers. Observers were either the academic advisor or colleagues and were usually triggered by the teacher experimenting and wanting a critical friend's view on the experimentation. Teachers at Green School were energised by their observations and used these to refine and interrogate their practice. In contrast, the second scenario has been described on numerous occasions by those working in further education (FE) colleges where they have experienced and interpreted observation largely as a tool to quality assure, using an Ofsted 1–4 grading scheme (Hatzipanagos and Lygo-Baker 2006: 421). Their observations were formal, followed written policies and were carried out by their line managers or a member of the quality team. Feedback related to specific sets of criteria linked to a mixture of pedagogic practice and impact on student learning and achievement.

This chapter seeks to contribute to the observation debate by taking the reader on a short journey along a metaphorical 'yellow brick road', which two FE colleges have taken to transition from the performative type observation practice experienced by Amy at Purple College to the more informative observation approach experienced by Sara at the Green School. The thinking is fuelled by a belief that 'somewhere over the rainbow' there are models of observation which stimulate deeper teacher engagement and reflection on and innovation in their practice. Drawing on the perspective of two case study FE colleges, The Rainbow College and The Yellow Brick College, the chapter will explore the context and rationale for their transition to different models of observation, how these models have been implemented, what they look like and reflect on their impact and effectiveness.

Context and the rationale for transitioning to different models of observation

Many of the teachers at institutions such as Purple College told a similar tale as to how ineffective the impact of their observations was on their own learning as teachers (Taylor *et al.* 2009). Rather than refining practice, at times it led to a distortion of practice as they sought to follow what they believed their observers required from them or the criteria demanded. This can lead to the normalisation of practice in observation, as highlighted by O'Leary (2013a), which is based on prescribed notions of *excellent* or *good* teaching and can lead to teachers playing the game of observations, becoming 'compliant tutors', 'taking no risks in their teaching', 'retreating to safe methods of teaching, transmitting via handouts and PowerPoint presentations' (Coffield *et al.* 2014: 3). The desire of many colleges to interpret or enshrine the dominant discourses of Ofsted and 'best practice' toolkits can lead to a passive approach to pedagogy. This has been fuelled by tick-box observation criteria which can undermine teacher learning and development, thus serving to detract from the development of knowledge and skills within a specific, contextualised situation. The tick-box observation approach often seeps further through the system to appraisal and inaccurate and unhelpful teacher 'labelling by number' which over-simplifies teacher performance and potential and can result in an unrealistic picture of teaching and learning quality.

The hegemonic practice of grading observations as a central initiative to develop quality has continued despite a number of voices identifying the negative backwash of graded observations on the quality of teaching and learning (e.g. Coffield *et al.* 2014; O'Leary 2013a, 2013b, 2014; Washer 2006; Wragg *et al.* 1997). Many graded observation models also appear to be confused or contradictory in purpose. Is the purpose to promote quality improvement (which would necessitate a process which is supportive and developmental and encourages teacher learning) or quality assurance (which would seek to simply assure against particular standards)? Many practitioners view observation as a managerial response bound up with the accountability agenda where, 'rather than being seen as a constructive tool that engages with practice it becomes viewed as a management tool' (Hatzipanagos and Lygo-Baker 2006: 421). This has left many teachers, like Amy in the second scenario, feeling judged, criticised and disengaged from the process (Taylor *et al.* 2009). Observation models which imply that if we can 'fix the teacher' all will be well ignore many other influences and conditions for student progress outside the control of the individual teacher (Hattie 2015: 5). This, in turn, relates to a deficit model of teacher competence stemming significantly from political and public concerns that poor teaching and poor institutions are not improving and can detract and divert institutions away from wider issues in educational provision. This has implications for the way in which the teaching role is being defined, developed and supported and also 'functions to pre-empt or silence alternative answers to the question of what causes low standards in FE' (Wallace 2002: 81). The practice in colleges of using a graded observation profile to define the quality of teaching and learning can lead to a cul-de-sac if other factors are ignored.

There has been a seeming inability within performative graded observation practice to grasp the notion that an initiative which alienates a significant body of people upon whom its practices impact is doomed to fail. The flawed aim of many educational organisations striving to observe and capture outstanding teaching and learning in one-off observations, whilst perhaps emanating from a lofty ambition of quality improvement, frequently falters and becomes distorted in the messy and complex practice that lies beneath. Assessing teaching and learning practices based on a tiny fraction of a teacher's annual working hours (approximately 0.00079 per cent) can only engender superficial judgements or snapshots of quality at best, and can mask both poor and good practice, detracting from the efficacy of overall strategies for improvement. The tiny fraction of work activity observed in annual observations can often lead to a plethora of processes proclaiming to engender effective development but, due to a weak evidence base and lack of in-depth analysis, only serve to promote surface learning rather than the sticky and challenging unpicking of practice needed to support deeper learning.

O'Leary describes lesson observation as 'one of the most widely debated and hotly contested initiatives to affect teaching staff in the FE sector' (O'Leary 2013b: 6). The 'heat' of the debate is underpinned by the perception of many teachers, like Amy in scenario two, that graded observations fuel de-professionalisation and innovation inertia. The 'normalisation' (O'Leary 2013a) of graded models of observation over the last two decades within an educational context has deep within it many elements of what Shore (2008) describes as 'cognition traps', leading to a series of institutional or national 'blunders'. These blunders stem from: (a) 'Infomania'; the trap of maintaining an obsessive relationship to information (clinging to inaccurate and scientifically suspect observation profile data); (b) 'Static Cling'; the trap of failing to accept that circumstances have changed (ignoring widely cited evidence against graded observation as an effective assurance or improvement tool) and (c) 'Exposure Anxiety'; the fear of being seen as weak or of being risk adverse, (the trap of colleges fearing inspection and the high-stakes nature of inspection outcomes). This can lead to a collision between the 'business' of colleges and the 'business' of inspection. The fall-out from this collision is experienced through observation models set to ape perceived expectations of Ofsted serving in some cases to subvert the very standards inspection was seeking to raise.

Colleges are highly complex organisations, often with fragmentary physical contexts due to multiple sites of delivery and have been subjected to continuous change, funding cuts and restructuring in response to the hyperactivity of changing government priorities and policy (Coffield 2008: 44–45). This has impacted significantly on staff morale and has served to contribute to a 'two-college' divide Coffield describes between senior managers and staff in many organisations (2014: 158–161). Sennett's question posed in *The Corrosion of Character* is particularly apposite for colleges: 'How can mutual loyalties and commitments be sustained in institutions which are constantly breaking apart or continually being redefined?' (Sennett 1998: 10). One response is for colleges to creatively review and realign their observation processes to situate these within a context that will be more informative at individual and institutional levels, address the cognition traps many colleges have fallen into, ignite teacher curiosity in their craft and inform overarching strategies. This may serve to reduce the alienation and innovation inertia experienced by teachers and ameliorate the two college divide or dysfunctional tensions and contradictions (James and Biesta 2007: 158) thus supporting a more engaged workforce.

Drawing on the national research study he conducted on behalf of the University and College Union (UCU), O'Leary suggests there is an 'increasing appetite for change in many institutions across the sector' (O'Leary 2013b: 6). For both case study colleges (Rainbow College and Yellow Brick College), concerns with a graded observation process and flirtations with different approaches began in 2011.

The appetite and desire for change in Rainbow and Yellow Brick emanated from many of the factors outlined above and emerged out of a clear sense in both colleges that their current systems were not having the desired impact in either: (a) developing teachers and improving the quality of teaching and learning or (b) providing a robust and reliable assessment of quality. There was also a recognition in these colleges that their observation models were elevating a focus on teachers as the central controllers of student achievement (Hattie 2015: 5).

How were the new models at Rainbow College and Yellow Brick College implemented? And what do they look like?

In two medium-sized general further education colleges, Rainbow and Yellow Brick colleges, similar processes were adopted in terms of developing a refreshed teaching and learning strategy, undertaking staff consultation, research and literature reviews, setting up a change group to steer the new strategy, developing and realigning the observation scheme, providing training and assessing and evaluating its impact. Both colleges recognised the need for clear communications, branded their strategies and held staff information/dissemination events. In the Yellow Brick College, the implementation of a new teaching and learning strategy was captured through a video made by a team of students in the college and recorded teacher views, learner views, manager views and was shared with staff at the end of the first year of implementation to capture the impact of the new approach in a visual format.

The Rainbow College having introduced a new teaching and learning strategy entitled 'Moving from Teaching to Learning' began by looking at observation. The first step was to ensure that the key stakeholders – teachers – had their say and a survey was created and circulated at a whole college staff development day to maximise completion. The consultation highlighted that whilst a significant number of teachers felt that the observation process had helped to improve their practice, this was highly dependent on the way in which feedback was given. They felt there was too much weight given to paperwork which detracted from a focus on learning; learners needed to be more involved in the process, there should be greater frequency of less formal observation and a considerable number felt that grading was unhelpful and undermined the efficacy of the process, detracting from innovation and improvement in their teaching and discouraging their own learning.

Following the consultation, desk-based research was conducted into alternative models of observation. This resulted in the development of a model which was set to support four key elements of the college's initiative to move from teaching to learning entitled 'ESCP' (Engage, Support, Challenge and Progress). The model was posed to emphasise learning, to develop learning conversations, to embed observations within general practice rather than one-off performances, encourage innovation and self-reflection and to be a supportive and developmental process with no link to formal capability processes. The initiative was supported by a range of continuous professional development (CPD) events to develop teacher practice with input from external trainers and CPD sessions run by learners on what the core characteristics are of effective learning.

A revised set of standards for teaching and learning was developed and the observation approach included a pre-observation discussion between observer and teacher, an observation and feedback dialogue followed by a further discussion one month later to reflect on the process and to include the possibility of additional observations. The pre-observation discussion gave the teacher an opportunity to discuss what they would like to gain from the observation, areas of focus for the feedback and to stimulate innovation and experimentation. Observers still had a set of agreed criteria to review under the engage, support, challenge and progress elements closely linked to the Common Inspection Framework (CIF), each criterion was noted by observers as strengths or areas for development within a session but no numerical grading or overall grading was applied.

Similar discussions were taking place amongst teachers and their managers in the Yellow Brick College and there was a two-stage transition to implement a refreshed observation approach. Stage one included moving from numerical grading of overall sessions to a rating of elements of practice within an observation using a colour system (gold, silver, bronze). This was an initial move away from the graded approach and whilst making a significant transition from 'feeling like a number' was still perceived by many staff to be a form of 'numbers by colours'. Following inspection in 2013 where the college was graded 'good', the Head of Quality and Learning started to think about what the college would need to do to be outstanding. He felt that it was important for the college to have their own standards of aspiration aligned to the entire learner journey. This led to a whole-organisational approach to develop a set of gold standards which articulated the impact on learners. In line with this approach, the Head of Quality and Learning felt that the teaching and learning systems and processes, including observation, needed to be much more developmental in order to stimulate improved teaching and the desired impacts on learners.

The revised strategy and observation process was branded under the acronym 'LEAP' (Learning, Engagement, Attributes and Progress) to outstanding and began with staff consultation on how they felt teaching, learning and assessment should be evaluated and developed, and their input was sought in shaping the standards. The Learning Development Manager described that what underpinned the revised approach was a freeing up of teachers from any prescribed pedagogy or method, as the focus in the gold standards was on the impact of teaching on learning, for example developing students to become more independent in their learning. This, she felt, would enable teachers to be more innovative and experimental as there was no prescription as to how this should be achieved. Like the Rainbow College, crucial to the model at Yellow Brick was the introduction of a pre-observation professional discussion, alongside which was the implementation of professional learning plans for all teachers in which they articulated their areas for development, exploration and innovation for the year. The professional learning plan asked for teachers to reflect on the impact of their development including commentary from their learners. Observations focused on information rather than judgement or prescribed pedagogy and reports simply recorded what happened in the session with observer reflections. Yellow Brick College also introduced the option for teachers to elect to have 'live feedback' in the form of support given during the observation itself. Many teachers opted for this and observers were able to make suggestions unobtrusively and in collaboration with the teacher during sessions which had immediate impact on student learning. Observations were, again, followed by discussion and teacher reflection in their professional learning plans and followed up through later discussions on practice. The questions asked in feedback discussions typically focused on the learning process rather than the practice of teaching. For example, 'When did we feel moments of learning occurred most effectively?' 'Why was that?' 'What supported this?'

How effective have these observation models been and what impact have they had in these two colleges?

There were a number of challenges experienced by both colleges in transitioning to a more developmental approach to observations, the first of which centred on the clarity of purpose of the observation process. In Rainbow College and the first iteration of a revised model at Yellow Brick, there was still some confusion as to whether the observation process was to evaluate or develop teaching and learning, and the conflation of these purposes led to greater debate as to whether the two can be effectively subsumed into one process. There was a sense that they were 'jacks of both trades and masters of none' and that they were not happy bedfellows. Assigning 'strength' or 'area for development' to elements of individual practice within sessions perpetuated the sense of observation as an evaluative rather than developmental tool.

Revising and developing new approaches is no quick fix and there was a need for strong, persistent and supportive leadership of the processes in addition to constant monitoring, balancing and redefining the process and avoiding 'derailment' due to external influences. Both colleges had supportive and innovative principals and senior management teams willing to take risks and embrace different approaches to development and quality improvement. This was a crucial factor.

It was also noted that whilst there may be 'buy-in' from observers at the context of influence (Bowe et al. 1992), this could be undermined in the context of practice by observers continuing to use a performative discourse of evaluation and formulaic feedback, focusing on prescribed pedagogy rather than engaging in an informative dialogue about the impact of the teaching on learners and their progress. In other words, the policy may have changed but not necessarily the practice. In some cases, observers continued with a tick-box approach, focusing on whether, for example, objectives were provided on the board or there was sufficient use of technology as opposed to whether learners were clear in general about the purpose and outcomes of the session, whether there was a need for technology to support learning and how it could be incorporated to enhance learning. There was also a struggle to move away from the habits of observer-led feedback discussions, which centred on the observer giving a blow-by-blow evaluation of the teacher's practice, to the more informative dialogue of what learners were doing, how they were processing information and on the impact of the teaching strategies on learner outcomes.

Observations are positioned within a political context which has been debated and contested and is rife with staff negativity and scepticism – overcoming this and making refreshed approaches feel different for all was challenging and required persistence, transparency and continuous adaptation of underpinning processes to support the development of trust in observers and in the process itself.

The intense weight of bureaucracy and work-loads for teachers and managers in FE also brings a heavy influence to bear on adopting processes which require time (e.g. adding in a pre-observation discussion, managing diaries to enable the teacher to choose the observation slot) and this can again lead to the process being undermined. There were also challenges raised by a number of stakeholders about how teachers could be assessed if there were no grades given. Hayes *et al.* (2007: 178) have a simple response to this, 'Don't. Don't measure them. They have knowledge. Get to know them and you will improve your understanding of what teaching in FE or any sector of education is about'. Both Yellow Brick and Rainbow colleges sought to put in place appraisal and review systems which moved away from relying on one-off assessments to inform judgements of teachers and teaching and learning, seeking to look more holistically at a range of measures to provide more evidence-based assessment of quality linked to learner feedback, achievement and teacher learning. At Yellow Brick College, this included staff feeding into what these measures should be and revising the appraisal scheme.

The observation models experienced in both Rainbow and Yellow Brick, despite the challenges outlined above, succeeded to stimulate a journey towards more authentic exchanges between professionals which subsequently led to further discussions beyond the confines of a one-off observation and into comparisons of how things were done in other classes; this was felt to be both confirming and affirming and enriched communication about learners, approaches, strategies and planning. When this worked particularly well, a debate and exchange on practice continued long after the initial observation. The approach of critical shared reflection on real-class teaching also led to some changing perspectives and practices and an increase in experimentation and risk-taking. This was shared in Bell's (2001) study of peer observation in which participants reported making immediate changes to their teaching practice.

What did teachers say about the developmental observation process in observation surveys following implementation of the new model at Yellow Brick College?

- It encouraged me to develop some new ideas that I had been mulling over but would not have 'risked' in the old-style observations.
- I am more encouraged to regard observation as a less threatening process which will allow me to experiment more with delivery.
- Observation will be less intrusive on the relationship between teacher and students. Teachers will have more freedom to develop new approaches to delivery without having a particular style imposed on them which may not suit the subject or group nor allow them to play to their own strengths and style.

- The discussions were very useful as they helped me identify any gaps and ethical issues that I hadn't thought of. Good to share my passion within a community of practice.
- It was very useful to go over the lesson and the objectives, and to get advice over practical issues such as to do with resources before being observed.
- Professional support rather than a judgement.
- It was like a breath of fresh air really.

Whilst neither model has quite reached the 'promised land', both have made a significant move away from the frequently superficial and subjective practices of grading teacher performance by number based on a tiny fraction of their working year and of having criteria which are heavily dependent on prescribed pedagogy, often loosely linked to decontextualized good and best practice. They have moved away from a conflation of purposes embedded within their observation models and the purpose of supporting teacher learning is becoming clearer. The approaches have shifted towards reviewing learning in situations and have encouraged deeper joint practice development (Coffield *et al.* 2014) which has helped reignite teacher curiosity about their practice, a key component of craftsmanship (Sennett 2008). There is a gradual and conscious change to developing informative and more analytical unpicking of practice within a specific context.

At Yellow Brick College there is also a culture slowly evolving of increased trust between observers and teachers and enhanced motivation to innovate and not to play safe with an observer in the room. Collaboration amongst colleagues to develop their own set of standards, coupled with the focus on observation as a CPD tool has also helped to reduce the dysfunctional divide Coffield *et al.* (2014: 158–161) discuss between managers and staff.

Alongside the developmental aspects of the observation approach, a more rounded view of teaching and learning quality is developing outside the model through revised methods of teacher evaluation and appraisal, which has led to more evidenced identification of poor quality and support interventions to ameliorate this for the learners. The Rainbow College was recently inspected by Ofsted and its report highlighted that the 'well-managed observation process ensures that practice is improving'. It is also interesting to note that following the implementation of revised teaching and learning strategies and observation models, both colleges experienced a significant increase in overall success rates and The Rainbow College moved to a good grading from Ofsted. The correlation of this to the revised approaches has not been studied and no claims could be made as many other factors inevitably impact on learner achievement. However, there was certainly no negative impact on student or institutional success as a result of the implementation of these two new approaches to observation.

Where do we go from here?

Any observation approach seeking to develop a more expansive learning and development culture needs to reclaim the territory of the classroom as a rich and informative learning environment rather than a replication of the inspection arena. The progression to enhanced professional practice needs to empower teachers to both manage their own learning but also be responsible for this in the best interests of their learners. One way of making this happen is through their professional learning plans (Yellow Brick College). Where teachers do not or cannot engage in these processes and their teaching quality and learner outcomes are poor, other systems need to be aligned to address this or, as Coffield *et al.* (2014: 167) states, they 'will be, with dignity and respect for their employment rights, removed from the profession'.

The fact that observations are situated within a contested context also suggests that there may be a need to change the language associated with its use to affect changes to underpinning practice. In order to ameliorate the negative legacy of observation as a *doing to* rather than a *doing with* approach, there is a need to carefully consider the language applied within the policies and strategies used to outline processes, the processes themselves (feedback and follow up) and the meta discourse adopted in professional discussions about observations. It is interesting to note that even in discourse aiming to transition to a supportive and developmental approach observation is referred to as a 'form of intervention' (O'Leary 2013b: 9) which has connotations for the 'intervened' and the 'intervener'. Rainbow College has changed the terminology from 'observation' to 'developmental practice', which may serve to shift the negative connotations linked to having an 'observation'. One of the practices of observation has been traditionally to supply the teacher with a feedback report. Once again, this is rife for discourse analysis in terms of how information and judgements are framed, recorded and received. At Yellow Brick College, there was a move away from a criteria-based observation form to a less prescriptive approach that simply recorded what happened during the observation alongside observer questions and reflections. The filtering of perceptions by the observer and observer authorship of any record can, however, be a barrier to developing a more open and collegial approach. Yellow Brick College is piloting removing any form of written observation report from the process replacing this with teacher reflections and actions recorded in their professional learning plan and audio recorded feedback for future reference.

Many teachers at Yellow Brick and Rainbow colleges commented on both the relevance of the revised models to their own development and the fact that they had never been involved in CPD which was directly linked to their own teaching and learning contexts with their own learners. This has implications for the nature and impact of what CPD colleges currently offer teaching staff and is an opportunity to position observation within a teacher learning framework. As Ewens (2003: 9) advises, 'staff development should not be considered as a discrete activity somehow linked to day-to-day experiences and responsibilities'.

Ofsted (2008) identified how the most improved colleges in their review had an effective programme of staff development informed by the outcomes of lesson observation. Yellow Brick College has sought to locate observation within a CPD rather than quality assurance framework by making the observation model informative rather than performative. Extending the 'live' feedback element of the observation could lead to a more participatory or collaborative approach to observation and provide the foundations for a staff development programme which is located in the heart of the learning context (the classroom).

The heavy administrative work-load and work intensification experienced in colleges discussed by Garner and Harper (2003) and Wallace (2002) is a very real obstacle for engagement in the type of approaches adopted at Rainbow and Yellow Brick. The most challenging factor for both teachers and observers was arranging when to meet. Timetables were often incompatible, meetings clashed, participants worked across sites and other priorities took over. For this approach to really have any impact, ways of prioritising time for engagement and integrating this within the annual institutional calendar need to be found.

Over the last few years, debate around observation processes within the sector has led, inevitably, to the question of whether observations of teaching and learning have any place at all and whether observations could be replaced by an increased emphasis on reflective prac- tice. There is certainly a need for further discussion about the direction in which observation models evolve and an appetite to refresh and renew observation for teacher learning. The notion of reflective practice outside any critical debate and discussion on real classroom based practice could, however, lead to solipsistic thinking and may be insufficient to support many teachers in developing their practice. The sustained review of literature, analysis of theory and evidenced research together with informative insights and genuine questions from an observer to inform debate, dialogue and experimentation can enrich the craft of teaching and the lived experience of teachers and their learners. To throw out observation in any form may be to throw away the proverbial baby with the bathwater and so lose a powerful tool for analysing, challenging and evolving the exciting practice of teaching.

Conclusion

This chapter has explored both the needs for and the practice of changing observation approaches to support teacher learning with reference to two case study colleges. It argues that for any initiative set to improve quality in teaching and learning to have impact there must, at the heart, be trust in and nurturing of those who can make the difference. The model that Sara experienced in scenario one, outlined in the introduction to this chapter, both motivated and inspired her to experiment and to utilise her trusted and respected observer to provide insight and challenge. Perhaps as colleges transition along the yellow brick road, like Dorothy seeking to return to Kansas, we need to return back to look forward to a refreshed era in teacher learning. A government 'Handbook of Suggestions for the Consideration of Teachers' presented in an era of hope for education (1947) stated, 'The only uniformity of practice that the Board of Education desire to see in ... teaching ... is that each teacher shall think for himself, and work out for himself such methods of teaching as may use his pow- ers to the best advantage and be best suited to the particular needs of the school' (Board of Education 1947: 3). A critical friend/observer could support teacher learning through a form of multimodal classroom analysis (Jewitt *et al.* 2001: 6) to analyse and enhance the methods to best suit their classroom context, unlocking their powers to the best advantage of their students.

The current era of accountability and targets in which graded observation has been firmly situated has, perhaps unwittingly, served to undermine the sense of many teachers believing they can think for themselves. The key question for colleges now is how far they should respond to the expressed needs of individual teachers and learners (often highly personal- ised and place specific) rather than simply preparing teachers for the increasingly regular and sharply defined inspectorial evaluations and institutional status quo? There has been a fear that encouraging independence and initiative in the face of challenging learning situa- tions can actually militate against individual and institutional success as judged by external regulators. The argument for increasing the range and efficacy of observation as a model to support teacher learning is rooted in the view that this can support the enabling of teachers. Freeing teachers from performative models to challenge the prevailing external orthodoxy may better stimulate moments of innovative and inspiring practices emanating from a mix of theory, research, shared knowledge and an informed and sustained encounter with the actual learning situation. The alternative is simply to respond to the politically contrived and inevitably superficial judgements of 'experts' who may subjectively eschew particular learning approaches and cultures and the unique array of talent expressed by a specific body of teachers.

References

Bell, M. (2001) 'Supported Reflective Practice: A programme of peer observation and feedback for academic teaching development'. *The International Journal for Academic Development*, 6(1), 29–39.

Board of Education. (1947) *Handbook of Suggestions for the Consideration of Teachers and Others Concerned in the Work of Public Elementary Schools*. London: Crown.

Bowe, R., Ball, S. and Gold, A. (1992) *Reforming Education and Changing Schools: Case studies in policy sociology*. London: Routledge.

Coffield, F. (2008) *Just Suppose Teaching and Learning became a Real Priority*. Learning and Skills Network.

Coffield, F., with Costa, C., Muller, W. and Webber, J. (2014) *Beyond Bulimic Learning: Improving teaching in further education*. London: Institute of Education Press.

Ewens, D. (2003) *Managing Staff Development in Adult and Community Learning: Reflection to practice*. Dorset: LSDA/NIACE, Blackmore Ltd.

Garner, L. and Harper, H. (2003) 'Teaching, Learning and a New Profession: Perceptions of trainee teachers in the post-compulsory sectors in Russia and England'. *Research in Post-Compulsory Education*, 8(2), 141–152.

Hattie, J. (2015) *What Works Best in Education: The politics of collaborative expertise*. Pearson. Available: www.pearson.com/content/dam/corporate/global/pearson-dot-com/files/hattie/150526_ExpertiseWEB_V1.pdf. Accessed 23 June 2015.

Hatzipanagos, S. and Lygo-Baker, S. (2006) 'Teaching Observations: Promoting development through critical reflection'. *Journal of Further and Higher Education*, 30(4), 421–431.

Hayes, D., Marshall, T. and Turner, A. (ed.) (2007) *A Lecturer's Guide to Further Education*. Berkshire: Open University Press.

James, D. and Biesta, G. (2007) *Improving Learning Cultures in Further Education*. London: Routledge.

Jewitt, C., Kress, G., Ogborn, J. and Tsatsarelis, C. (2001) 'Exploring Learning Through Visual, Actional and Linguistic Communication: The multimodal environment of a science classroom', *Educational Review*, 53(1), 6–18, Institute of Education, London University, London, UK. On-line http://techstyle.lmc.gatech.edu/wp-content/uploads/2012/08/Jewitt-et-al.-2001.pdf Accessed 18 September 2015.

Ofsted. (2008) *How Colleges Improve – A review of effective practice*: London: Crown.

O'Leary, M. (2013a) Surveillance, 'Performativity and Normalised Practice: The use and impact of graded lesson observations in further education colleges'. *Journal of Further and Higher Education*, 37(5), 694–714.

O'Leary, M. (2013b) *Developing a National Framework for the Effective Use of Lesson Observation in Further Education*. Project report for the University and College Union, November 2013. DOI: 10.13140/RG.2.1.1751.7286. Available at: www.ucu.org.uk/media/6714/Developing-a-national-framework-for-the-effective-use-of-lesson-observation-in-FE-Dr-Matt-OLeary-Nov-13/pdf/ucu_lessonobsproject_nov13.pdf.

O'Leary, M. (2014) *Classroom Observation: A guide to the effective observation of teaching and learning*. London: Routledge.

Sennett, R. (1998) *The Corrosion of Character*. New York: W.W. Norton & Company Ltd.

Sennett, R. (2008) *The Craftsman*. London: Penguin.

Shore, Z. (2008) *Blunder: Why smart people make bad decisions*. New York: Bloomsbury.

Taylor, L., Dee, S., Richardson, J., Richardson, B., Bayliss, P. and Kill, T. (2009) *Engagement. Promoting the development of teaching and learning through a participatory observation process*. The Westminster Partnership CETT.

Wallace, S. (2001) *Teaching and Supporting Learning in Further Education*. Essex: Learning Matters Ltd.

Wallace, S. (2002) 'No Good Surprises: Intending lecturers' preconceptions and initial experiences of further education'. *British Educational Research Journal*, 28(1), 79–93.

Washer, P. (2006) 'Designing a System for Observation of Teaching'. *Quality Assurance in Education*, 14(3), 243–250.

Wragg, E. C., Wikeley, F. J., Wragg, C. M. and Haynes, G. S. (1997) *Teacher Appraisal Observed*. London: Routledge.

2

GRADES DON'T COUNT

Building success from the inside out

Emily Barrell

Introduction

For the last few years, being one of only a small minority of providers of adult education in the further education and skills (FES) sector that moved away from the practice of graded lesson observations has meant that we have always stood out at network events as the 'mavericks'. To say that we feel vindicated that Ofsted has since removed the practice of graded observations from its most recent inspection framework (Ofsted 2015) is an understatement. Yet we have always maintained that making the change to an ungraded observation process was the right move for us, but only because we were prepared to fully re-think our quality improvement process and critically reflect on how observation fitted into our organisational culture.

For many organisations, making that ideological shift is the biggest and most difficult step to take. Having staff on board from the most senior to the most junior level within the organisation when embarking on such a significant change is fundamental. Our chosen path was not always an easy option and we would not encourage anyone to take it lightly unless they were committed to the journey of changing a system which for most FES providers is deeply rooted in their basic assumptions of the monitoring and management of teaching and learning. This chapter discusses the reasons as to why we chose to transform our policy, the considerations that accompanied that choice and how it has impacted on our staff and ultimately our learners.

Background

It was only under extreme duress that we first realised that we had to consider radical change. Observation grades across the organisation had plateaued, practice in the classroom seemed to throw up the same recurring issues and our learner success rates were not improving. That was the broad backdrop to embarking on a journey into the unknown and the world of lesson observations without grades. Yet throughout this journey we have found it liberating and the wholesale organisational change that has resulted from it continues to sustain improvement four years later. During this period, we have been able to put into practice our principles of what makes for effective learning, not only with our students but with our teaching staff too. One of the unanticipated benefits of this is that it has opened up new relationships between teaching staff and management, as we have established new and different ways of managing *with* our staff.

In March 2014 we were finally able to remove the 'requires improvement' noose from around our necks as we were judged to be 'good' during our Ofsted inspection. One of the comments in the inspection report struck a particular chord with our staff in relation to how the changes that we had implemented had started to filter into the classroom practice of our teachers:

> The focus across the company on improving teachers' effectiveness in the classroom has had a positive impact on learners' achievement and motivation … Teachers are attentive to learners' needs and often go to great lengths to ensure that learners enjoy their learning, continue with their course if they face obstacles and progress to new opportunities. They succeed in getting the best out of learners.
>
> *Ofsted 2014: 2–3*

For us there is little doubt this improvement was linked to the fundamental re-evaluation we undertook in embracing an ungraded approach to observation. This chapter draws repeated contrasts between our *old ways* of working and the *new*, with the traditional performative observation process being contrasted with a new coaching model of observation. When we speak about the 'traditional' model, we are specifically referring to a model in which observers would observe, often without any notice, for up to 45 minutes and then give 15 minutes of verbal feedback, which would include a grade based on the Ofsted 4-point scale. They would then write up a report and create an action plan for the teacher to follow to improve practice. We were convinced that by observing all our teachers every year, allocating them a grade, feedback and an action plan, this would help to improve the quality of teaching across the organisation. Yet there was no noticeable improvement in grades or teaching as a whole. Reflecting on this, we were determined to explore alternative ways of bringing about meaningful and sustained improvements in teaching and learning across the organisation through the vehicle of lesson observation.

The impetus for change

Change was largely driven by the stagnation in our results. In 2011 we slipped into 'Notice to Improve' for functional skills literacy and maths, with success rates at 65 per cent, achievement 82 per cent and retention 79 per cent. This established a sense of urgency and focus that made change imperative and drove us to examine how effectively we were using our resources. Even then, the concept of the traditional graded observation was so entrenched in our organisational psyche that it made it unimaginable to reposition it as part of a wider problem in our quality improvement efforts.

It was only as we came to recognise the resources we seemed to pour into observations with little effect on improving the quality of teaching and learning that we came to the conclusion that modifying our existing systems was never going to rectify the problem. Quality monitoring had become one of those behemoths which sucked resources in simply as a means of servicing itself rather than furthering the aims of the organisation as a whole.

As an initial review of our policy, we reflected on the underpinning rationale for the way in which observation was being used within the organisation and recognised that whilst it was purportedly being used to serve a multitude of purposes and needs, the extent to which these purposes and needs were being successfully met was questionable:

- to identify trends in teaching groups;
- to contribute data towards the level of quality of the organisation;
- to provide evidence of the quality of the organisation to stakeholders such as Ofsted;
- to compare ourselves against other organisations;
- to explain our retention and achievement rates;
- to inform performance management decisions;
- to create an action plan for teacher improvement;
- to identify training needs at organisation, curriculum and individual teacher level.

We realised that different drivers resulted in a range of differing auditing purposes in observation. What was required by our County Commissioners, for instance, was closely linked to the local picture and the ambitions to link adult education with local business growth. In contrast, the Skills Funding Agency sought success and achievement rates, and the quality assurance requirements of Ofsted were around the requirements of learner engagement, achievement and progression, but were also a driver for national governmental agendas such as national literacy and maths levels, digital literacy and equality and diversity. In trying to find data to evidence meeting these drivers, observation became less and less about the teacher's development and more about data for compliance and measurement. As Stobart (2008) has argued in the context of assessment, managerial processes inevitably seem to outjockey other purposes.

We realised that we were investing an inordinate amount of time and energy in gathering data for a variety of purposes but these data were not necessarily having an impact on changing or improving practice. Instead of finding new ways to measure classroom success and quality, what we needed to do was spend less time gathering data and become more consistent and efficient in how we triangulated our existing data sources and how we used that data to inform our knowledge and thinking about practice. Doing this would enable us to invest more effectively in understanding and supporting that most important resource for any teaching organisation, its teachers.

We realised that our current expenditure on measuring quality was resulting in two fundamental errors. First, in concentrating all of our resources on measuring our teachers' existing skills and knowledge through these costly annual observations, we were neglecting our teachers' continuing professional development (CPD) and thus failing in our duty to help them to grow as professionals and to improve their practice. Second, as a learning centred organisation catering for adults, we understood and espoused ways of working with adult learners which were fundamental to our organisational culture. For example, we had very clear expectations of our teachers as to how they should work to gain learner trust, connect with their previous experiences and their current interests and encourage ownership of their learning. Yet somewhat contradictorily, we failed to practise what we preached with our own teachers when it came to observing their practice. In effect, what we were doing with our teachers was at odds with what we advocated for our learners.

We recognised how far the observation process had become something we did *to* teachers rather than *with* them. It was leading to a lack of professional support for teachers because the process failed to gain their trust, acknowledge their previous experiences or indeed encourage them to take ownership of the action created by management for them. This created a sense of passivity amongst our teachers, as they reacted to a disparity in the way they supported learning and how their own learning was supported or not.

Re-thinking our use of observation

In 2011 we carried out a consultation with managers, observers and teachers to evaluate the organisation's approach to observation. We used forums, interviews, questionnaires and discussions to establish what teacher voice could tell us, we reviewed documents relating to teacher development and the professional development programme and we looked at past observation records in detail to examine what the 'artefacts' of our practice were saying about the reality of our culture. From this, we developed three themed arguments as to why we needed a radical overhaul of the organisation's observation process.

Argument 1: practising what we preach

Our traditional observation process was based on a negative assessment paradigm. By this I mean that it espoused a belief that it was necessary to measure teaching performance against a rather nebulous quintessential model of the perfectly defined learning experience.

As an organisation dedicated to adult lifelong learning, we knew that the way in which our own students learnt did not follow a linear sequential path, which in turn meant that to adopt a linear model of measurement to seek to capture this was inappropriate. While there are multiple theories of adult learning, as an organisation one of the key tenets we impressed upon our teachers was to think of adult learners as complex people with a range of factors influencing their ability and inclination to learn, including historical and social contexts, the micro community within the classroom and the wider context of community, family and work. This was grounded in a social constructivist theory of learning, where learning is co-created and enacted in social contexts (Cobb 1994; Lave and Wenger 1991; McMahon 1997). Accordingly, we wanted our teachers to demonstrate the expertise to respond imaginatively to create a vision for adult learners to move forward in their learning in the classroom.

At the same time as we embarked on this reform, we were also exploring the concepts of *Assessment for Learning* (Black and Wiliam 1998) with our learners. This reinforced the disparity between what we espoused for learners and what we did with our teachers. The evidence from our classroom experiences reinforced our belief that grading learners' work was counterproductive for many in moving their learning forward. Similarly, O'Leary and Brooks (2014) commented that teachers became dependent on the grade given during an observation as an indicator of social standing within the teaching community, with less attention paid to the action points for development. Black and Wiliam (1998) were critical of giving learners' grades for this very reason.

Whilst some senior managers conceptualised the use of grading as having a positive motivational effect on teachers, we found that the reverse was often the case. Grades formed part of performance management cycles and the grade alone would decide what form that performance management took and whether staff were seen as successful or unsuccessful teachers. Managers also reported that teachers were so focused on the grade that they were less likely to hear or engage with formative feedback. As O'Leary and Brooks (2014) found, the summative grade became an obstacle rather than an opportunity for teachers to further their professional learning.

From a quality assurance and monitoring perspective, grades were used by management to measure teachers' performance. Whilst it might have been perceived to serve a purpose for management to be able to say that 75 per cent of observations were graded as 'good' or 'outstanding' in terms of comparing year on year performance of staff internally or externally against other organisations' 'observation grade profiles' (O'Leary 2014), it did nothing to progress individual teacher development or noticeably improve the organisation.

As mentioned previously, the practice we were following in our internal quality assurance systems was completely contradictory to our beliefs about the nature of adult learning. It was therefore clear that we urgently needed a system which would encourage teachers to use observation as tool for continuous professional improvement, with the same values our teachers were expected to promote in our classrooms with our adult learners.

Argument 2: respect, responsibility and agency

By undertaking an organisational review of multiple sets of data from different sources such as staff consultations and working group parties and then cross-referencing these against the gathered data in appraisals, observation reports and the minutes from meetings, we were able to track the development of individual teachers over an extended time, which helped us to consider our organisational progress from the point at which we changed our observation policy.

What was clearly evident in the 2010–11 and 2011–12 years before we changed our observation model was that the same area of focus was often identified as a development need across different observations over time, but there was little evidence of progress. Development points would drop away for a time, but then come back or be listed as a minor point in other actions. Rarely were teachers actively engaged in formulating the action plans drawn up by managers or observers, and even more rarely were they mentioned in any of their correspondence until in direct response to managers' comments. At no point during the process was there was any record of teachers electing an observation focus of their own.

As an example, one teacher who was new to teaching in 2010 had the same development point to improve how targets are used in the classroom for three consecutive years, including the first observation as part of the new coaching non-graded model. In some documentation, it was evident that both the observer and the teacher were frustrated with the development point and its progress. However, after the first non-graded observation it was noticeable that there was a different dynamic between observer and teacher within their joint reflections. The teacher felt empowered to identify her own way of addressing the lack of targets, as she made a number of concrete suggestions for the support she felt she needed. Subsequent appraisal and later observations indicated that target setting had improved dramatically. This teacher eventually went on to become a senior teacher in her field, whose practice was valued so highly that she was asked to take on the role of mentor for other teachers.

Analysis across observations also revealed a greater than average focus by observers on particular themes in any time frame was evident, for instance SMART targets, or the use of ground rules. This observational bias was evident across a range of subject areas and time spans. We suspected that observers were embarking on observations with a pre-established agenda, which drove them to look for certain things in relation to current external and internal priorities. Some teachers suggested that their observers seemed to adopt a generic rather than a specific (personally tailored) focus to observations. Fawcett (1996: 3) argues that we have a propensity to 'see what we are looking for and to look for only what we know about'.

A typical comment was similarly reported by a teacher who remarked in a survey response that 'all they seemed interested in was x but ignored other issues which meant more to me'.

These two particular issues (i.e. observers having a pre-established agenda and teachers not being able to elect the focus of the observation for themselves) gave rise to a biased and one-sided perspective of classroom practice. On the one hand, some observers' views were being influenced by internal and external priorities rather than focusing purely on what they observed in the classroom and the specific needs of individual teachers. On the other hand, some teachers were compliant recipients in the whole process, accepting feedback without making any effort to question how the observation process might best meet their needs. This led to at an imbalance in contributions in the process with observers shaping the focus and resultant actions and teachers taking no ownership of the process at all.

Argument 3: constricting practice and limiting creativity

I've left this argument to the last but in many ways it was the most persuasive argument for us. We had explored our data management systems and recognised the waste of resource and lack of return on our investments in observation. We also found evidence that there was a nullifying impact on innovation with graded observations, which resulted in a decline in the creativity in teachers' practice as they feared taking risks.

Observers' perspectives were that teachers were often playing it safe in the classroom with formulaic delivery leading to a lack of design, imagination and willingness to be flexible during sessions to meet the complex and changing needs of learners. It was noted that we suffered from an over-reliance on worksheets, largely because they were seen as a safe option by many teachers. Teachers' views indicated that a handout was useful to provide quick hits when confronted by observers who expected to see 'evidence' in order to satisfy differing agendas such as target setting, embedding English and maths, and equality and diversity. This corresponds to some later data that was gathered at regional events where teachers attending from a range of providers explicitly discussed how they were wary of showcasing anything that was not standard practice and refused to take risks 'in case the observer did not approve' (EEDN 2014).

Some teachers who were graded 'good' and 'outstanding' at observation explained how they would 'play the game' to achieve the best score at observation. They outlined what was tantamount to an observation checklist which they ticked off to get maximum points in observations, as previous research has highlighted (e.g. O'Leary 2011). Teachers discussed how they would have the 'safe' lesson activities and how they would wrap up one activity when an observer walked in and swap to the tried and tested activity which would tick the most boxes on the observer checklist.

Improvement from the inside out, not the outside in

In the year previous to the introduction of our new observation methodology, we were already going through an organisational restructure. What this enabled us to do was to open up a frank and transparent dialogue with staff about what we believed and valued in our organisation and what our mission statement should be. Although it was difficult to accept some of our teachers' comments regarding the impact of our current observation practices, they were helpful in informing the direction we needed to be moving in to establish and strengthen our organisation's identity.

Central to our success was the ability to shift to an inclusive approach in planning a new observation policy that ensured teachers felt that their leadership in the classroom was not being eroded by management interventions and that equally they had professional responsibility for their learners. It was also important that the teachers felt they had agency to effect change, reflect on problems as partners with the observation team and their line managers and seek solutions in ways which were unrestrained by fear of external censure.

We opened a dialogue with our teachers on what the effective teaching looked like. As managers we were able to contribute our own managerial knowledge of what was required from our auditors and commissioners and equally our teachers were able to contribute their pedagogic knowledge. This helped to ensure that our teaching staff felt part of setting the agenda for observation. The publication of the Institute for Learning report, *Brilliant Teaching and Training in FE and Skills* (IfL 2010) was the final impetus in crystallising our arguments, highlighting as it did many of the same issues we had found ourselves.

Part of our organisational restructure included the introduction of a new appraisal system based on a termly review, which enabled tutors to take responsibility for their learners' progress and enabled managers to have more transparent conversations with staff. The appraisal became the central document for professional improvement. We used it extensively to capture every aspect of a teacher's performance, from feedback and internal quality assurance, to retention, achievement and success rates, to commentary from walk-through and drop-ins, as well as the professional discussion from the new coaching model of observation.

Specific professional development targeted at increasing teacher agency was established. This included encouraging teachers to carry out practitioner research within a peer coaching framework with the benefits of enabling teachers to try out different ways of doing things and removing the censure of potential failure. They had explicit 'permission' to innovate and experiment in a culture of learning together as an organisation, so that learning about *what not to do* was valued as highly as *what to do*. 'Research pods' were formed. i.e. groups of teachers and sometimes other staff interested in exploring a specific topic in depth. Added to this, peer observations, and tailored support from mentors encouraged teaching staff to learn from each other, thus creating a community of peer-based learning. Teachers reported as part of their reflective outcomes that they highly valued the opportunity to take a step back to reflect on their practice with the help of peers and expert teachers and saw this as making an important contribution to moving their classroom practice forward. A specific budget to pay for teachers to take part in specific collaborative, innovative learning opportunities was created.

Our new coaching model of observation

This work supported the introduction of a new coaching model of observation which encouraged teachers to find solutions for themselves in response to observation 'spotlight questions'. Whitmore (2003: 14) identified coaching as 'unlocking the person's potential to maximise their own performance. It is helping them to learn rather than teaching them'. Adopting a coaching model enabled us to address some of the tensions discussed previously, and in doing so increase teacher agency and responsibility for their own development.

We moved away from a tick-box observation document to a radically different structure focusing on learning, teaching and assessment (see Appendix 2.1). The use of this reporting format has enabled an ongoing dialogue between observer and observee, starting before the agreed observation where both discuss what the focus of the observation should be, progressing to the subsequent spotlight topics for reflection directly after the observation and then the later professional discussion based on their written reflections. This gives rise to a development plan, the actions from which are shaped in tandem between observer and observee and are monitored subsequently in the ongoing appraisal. This collaborative reflective dialogue links in with the concepts of developing an individual's ability to reflect as being one of the key concepts of coaching (Barnett and O'Mahony 2006).

No grade is given, no systematic monitoring of documentation and no tick boxes. This enables the teacher to become an equal partner in the observation process and provides them with a greater sense of agency in deciding what their development priorities are. This also means that the observation-cycle no longer sits within a quality assurance remit, but is now located under professional development as primarily for the support of our teachers.

It's important to highlight that the introduction of our new system has taken time and it has not been a quick fix that has yielded positive results instantly. In fact, we deliberated as to whether we should return to the old system of grading simply because it was less problematic and safer. Managers were initially uncomfortable with the removal of grading as so many had come to rely on it as a key reference point. There was a transitional period in which we found managers would not give a grade to the teacher, but would still, in essence, grade by the language they used. It was a common focus at observation moderation meetings where we discussed how to make a judgement without using the discourse of judgement. In reality, it took approximately two years before we achieved consistency across the whole observation team. Whilst we found it challenging to get some of our managers to relinquish their role as 'judges' of classroom practice, training our observation team in coaching techniques and using the appropriate language to support a coaching approach were invaluable in breaking down these engrained mindsets.

We were surprised that some teachers also resisted the lack of grading. To some extent this related to the loss of status without the grade, but there was also an emerging realisation that being responsible for coming up with how to improve meant they had ownership and responsibility to carry it out. They were being challenged to not only be more reflective in identifying their own development but actually being held to account through the appraisal system, whereas before they had been situated more passively. For some it was hard to adapt to this new responsibility.

Reflecting on our journey, we think by investing more resources initially into our teachers during the observation process meant that many were able to develop self-efficacy in identifying and taking forward their professional development for themselves. We shifted resources from quality monitoring into quality improvement activities. This then freed up senior staff to focus on those who were less able or unwilling to develop their teaching practice.

To ensure that a speedy change took place in teaching practice where it was deemed a risk to learner success, we used a system called the 'intensive care plan' which either accelerated improvement or moved onto capability when action plans were not met. This was challenging for the teaching body as a whole to adjust to the idea that they were being held to account to follow through with what they said they would do within the observation dialogue. Our turnover of staff in some areas was quite high (20 per cent) as staff chose to leave rather than take responsibility for classroom improvement in some cases.

Conclusion

At the core of our philosophy is the belief that learning is constructed by the social interactions, expectations and actions which shape the culture of our organisation; this applies equally to our learners and our staff. Our coaching model of observation is just one aspect of how over the past four years we have created a positive, high-performing teaching culture based on the ideals of *respect, responsibility, agency* and *innovation*. This has helped us to finally address the quality of the classroom environment in a sustainable and meaningful way. In 2013–14 we topped learner numbers at 8,000 with a success rate of 93 per cent and in 2014–15 the success rate for our organisation was 95 per cent across the organisation. It would not have been possible to make this change without engaging our teaching staff in self-directed development through the vehicle of our new approach to lesson observation. They have embraced it and as an organisation we are now beginning to reap the rewards!

References

Barnett, B. G. and O'Mahoney, G. R. (2006) 'Developing a Culture of Reflection: Implications for school improvement'. *Reflective Practice*, 7(4), 499–523.

Black, P. and Wiliam, D. (1998) *Inside the Black Box: Raising standards through classroom assessment*. London: School of Education, King's College.

Cobb, P. (1994) 'Where Is the Mind? Constructivist and Sociocultural Perspectives on Mathematical Development'. *Educational Researcher*, 23, 13–20.

EEDN (Easter Educators Development Network) (2014) *Reflections 1 – Impact on Practitioner and Organisation* www.youtube.com/watch?v=B2sw_ka8gyM Date accessed 28 January 2016.

Fawcett, M. (1996) *Learning Through Child Observation*. London: J. Kingsley Publishers.

Institute for Learning (2010) *Brilliant Teaching and Training in FE and Skills: A guide to effective CPD for teachers, trainers and leaders*. London: IfL.

Lave, J. and Wenger, E. (1991) *Situated Learning: Legitimate peripheral participation*. Cambridge, UK: Cambridge University Press.

McMahon, M. (1997, December) 'Social Constructivism and the World Wide Web – A paradigm for learning'. Paper presented at the ASCILITE conference. Perth, Australia.

Office for Standards in Education (Ofsted) (2014) *Further Education and Skills Inspection Report for Suffolk County Council*. Available at: http://reports.ofsted.gov.uk/inspection-reports/find-inspection-report/provider/ELS/54657. Last accessed 12 March 2016.

Office for Standards in Education (Ofsted) (2015) *Common Inspection Framework: Education, skills and early years from September 2015*. 15 June. Available at: www.gov.uk/government/uploads/system/uploads/attachment_data/file/461767/The_common_inspection_framework_education_skills_and_early_years.pdf. Last accessed 16 March 2016.

O'Leary, M. (2011) *The Role of Lesson Observation in Shaping Professional Identity, Learning and Development in Further Education Colleges in the West Midlands*. Unpublished PhD Thesis, University of Warwick, September.

O'Leary, M. (2014) *Classroom Observation: A guide to the Effective Observation of Teaching and Learning*. London: Routledge.

O'Leary, M. and Brooks, V. (2014) 'Raising the Stakes: Classroom observation in the further education sector in England'. *Professional Development in Education*, 40(4), 530–545.

Stobart, G. (2008) *Testing Times: The uses and abuses of assessment*. London: Routledge.

Whitmore, J. (2003) *Coaching for Performance: Growing people, performance and purpose*. London: Nicholas Brealey Publishing.

Appendix 2.1: exemplar observation record

Name of Tutor	Annie Tutor	Course title:	Computers for Beginners
Name of Observer(s)	AN Observer	Curriculum Area:	C&T
Session x of x total	5 of 10	No attending	M: 3 F: 6
Date of Observation:	5 May 2015 10:05–10:35	Date agreed for Prof. Disc:	15 May 2015

Observer and tutor agree key focus of this observation prior to the visit:

Use previous observation, action plan, PDR, focus for tutor research and improvements made:

Annie and I agreed via email (02/05/15) that she would like me to focus the observation on differentiation. I also have suggested that since her last OTL noted that she was going to work on how to use peer evaluation more effectively, I would look for progress on this.

Please tick type of support being offered on the continuum here	Directive Mentoring Coaching ✓ Facilitative Coaching

Examples of learning activity and its impact for the learners:

What and how well are the learners learning? Learner engagement and motivation, differentiation/individualisation on objectives, learner support, Equality, Diversity & Inclusivity (E, D & I) etc.

When I entered the room I noticed that one group of three were sharing a screen at one side of the room. Two learners were working in the centre of the room independently at desks, and two were working together on computers. You were working with two learners together. Everyone was working on a task; no one appeared distracted, or off topic at this point.

As time went by, I took the opportunity to speak to learners. They were almost all able to describe to me what they were doing in answering an email or creating a poster; Most knew what their next step was.

The two working together at a computer were the least sure of that they were doing next, and appeared to be the learners with the lowest skills. **Spotlight question: Can you tell me more about how you structure the learning for Barbara and Neil, and how you support their challenges?**

As you moved around the room working with so many groups, you were not able to spend very long with them. Tom waited for you for about 5 minutes to clarify a question. **Spotlight question: How could you improve the quality of the time you spend with each learner (not quantity)?**

Examples of teaching activity and its impact for the learners:

What the tutor is doing and using? Teaching style, pace, methods, resources, communication, use of ILT, how well does planning support differentiated activities etc.

As noted above, when observation started, you had organised group work already. They stayed in these groupings for the next 20 minutes before you introduced a new topic. **Spotlight question: How do you think group work in your classes has changed in the past six months? What is the impact on learning?**

You appear very calm as you move around. You are clear in your verbal communication and you give detailed explanations. Most learners appear to respond well to this. A few learners were unclear of what to do even after you spent time talking them through the email activity.

The learners had resources which included working on computers (word and outlook) and had two worksheets from which they were sending an email activity or creating a poster. You gave verbal instructions as you moved around the room on what do to. Some learners had personal notes and one learner had a file with handouts from previous weeks. I understand that you had just completed a demonstration using the smartboard before I came in. The smartboard had been switched off.

The learners with personal notes or previous week handouts were referring to them to help them do the activity. Learners who did not have these visible raised their hands more and spent more time waiting. **What do you think is the reason behind this? What does this say about learning?**

Examples of assessment activity and its impact on the learners:

What assessment is taking place? And how Initial assessments, formative assessment and feedback, summative assessments, learner participation in assessment process, evidencing progress, use of ILP, assessment for learning etc.

The learners all appeared to have tasks to complete using the worksheets and you were giving them formative feedback as you moved around and spoke to them. For some learners I could see that they had a learning plan open on screen. However, I noted that not all did so. I also saw that some who did have it open did not have recent feedback in the past two weeks. **Spotlight question: What are the benefits of the learning plan in relation to differentiation?**

Near the end of the observation period, three learners (Jane and Joan and Manuel) completed their work. You suggested that they complete a peer evaluation. They clearly were aware of what this was and knew where to access this sheet. They then held a discussion in which they took turns looking at each other's work and identifying the EBI points. The impact on these learners was clear with good feedback being shared and two of them identifying how to improve their work, which they then went to do. **Please can you share how you have integrated peer feedback into lessons at the next team meeting?**

Spotlights for reflection in the professional discussion:

(Consider how ... Why did you ...? What would have happened if ...? Have you thought about ...? What happened there ...? Tell me about this learner ...?)

Spotlight question: How do you think group work in your classes has changed in the past six months? What is the impact on learning?

Spotlight question: How could you improve the quality of the time you spend with each learner (not quantity)?

Spotlight question: Can you explore why are some learners better at using their notes than others? What does this say about learning? Also, can you explore the challenges which Barbara and Neil experience and how you support them to keep up with the others?

Spotlight question: What are the benefits of the learning plan in relation to differentiation?

Good practice to share: (these should be added by the observer to the good practice database) Please demonstrate how you integrate peer evaluation at the next team meeting.

3

INTRODUCING AND PILOTING A MODEL OF NON-GRADED LESSON OBSERVATION

Chichester College as a case study

Sally Challis-Manning and Sheila Thorpe

Introduction and background

In September 2015, all observations of teaching and learning successfully transferred to a non-graded model at Chichester College. This would not have been possible without a consultative pilot and the development of a cross-college culture that has coaching firmly at its heart. This chapter tells the story of our journey.

In 2010 a new senior management team (SMT) was appointed and with it came a renewed focus on teaching and learning. When the college was inspected by Ofsted in 2008, inspectors identified inconsistency in the lesson observation process, recommending further development to ensure that there was reliable correlation between observers' judgements and the final grade awarded. To address this, we initiated a review of the lesson observation process that eventually led to a training programme for observers centred on using a coaching model. Once this methodology became firmly embedded, the natural next step was then to remove the grade.

Reviewing our observation model

To begin with, a small focus group headed by the Professional Development Manager examined 'where we were' in relation to the quality of teaching, learning and assessment and lesson observation policy and procedures. The group looked at the ethos of lesson observation, how staff viewed lesson observation and the training of observers. It became clear that lesson observation was something that many teachers did not find valuable and, in some cases, feared – for some it was just a 'tick-box' exercise. Many teachers would deliver an unadventurous lesson for their graded observation and did not take advantage of the feedback they received after the observation. O'Leary (2012) highlighted these and other effects on teachers' attitudes to the 'Observation of Teaching and Learning' (OTL). He stated that a lack of 'trust and managerialist cultures where OTL were used as key indicators of professional competence' resulted in teachers feeling 'disempowered as they found themselves at the mercy of a performance system that was presented as scientific and rational but was ultimately inaccessible to reason' (O'Leary 2012: 18).

At Chichester College we realised there was little desire to take a risk in a lesson observation and teachers tended to adhere to the college's rigid planning frameworks. Some teachers indicated that they were anxious about changing from a recognised format. Lesson observation even felt like a very personal intrusion for some, with an expectation of one-way feedback where their opinion did not count. A number of teachers remained coasting at grade 2. For some teachers, there was no desire or motivation to reach a grade 1 as they assumed they would be expected to share good practice with others and take on an additional work-load. Some teachers even utilised the same tried and tested lesson each year when observed, confident of receiving a grade 2.

In some cases, observers rigidly interpreted the college's learning framework. For example, one teacher had their lesson graded as a 2 rather than a 1 as the 'connection of learning' phase was greater than the prescribed ten minutes. This institutional guardedness was a common symptom at the time; our desire to produce the data set needed for inspection and reporting overshadowed the potential advantages of creating a process focused on reflection and coaching to improve teaching practice.

We were convinced that we needed to bring about a significant shift in the cultures of teaching and learning across the college and our teachers' perceptions and attitudes towards observation. A key driver in this was moving the focus onto the quality of teaching rather than the quality of teachers as individuals; this shift was something we began in 2011 to enable our staff to have a shared reflection of successes and developments of the observed teaching session.

Previously, teaching and learning was not commonly discussed in staff meetings or staff rooms. In many cases where excellent practice did occur, it was both intentionally and unintentionally retained by the particular individuals concerned, or within the individual's subject area. This meant that it was rare for excellent practice to be disseminated across the college. Where practice needed to be developed, many teachers felt a sense of fear or shame in disclosing their learning needs. It became clear that the whole process and culture around observing teaching and learning had to be totally revamped to impact and reduce the staff fear and negative feelings. The aim was therefore very much to make lesson observation the most valuable opportunity for one-to-one personalised CPD to develop the skills of the teacher.

The starting point was to look at the observation process and associated documentation, including policies, procedures, the observation handbook, lesson plans, student profiles and schemes of work. We started by asking three fundamental questions:

- Is it explicit?
- Is it relevant?
- Does it have impact?

Introducing the *Licence to Observe*

Prior to 2011, training staff to observe teaching and learning was undertaken in two one-off sessions. There was no additional training or follow up to sustain or further develop skills. Over 80 staff members were registered as observers under this scheme. However, it was clear that a number of trained observers were not necessarily experienced or skilled enough to undertake observations; the reality was that some were observers simply because they were managers. A new training programme, *Licence to Observe*, was therefore developed to address the expectation that all observers would become experts in their role.

The *Licence to Observe* was introduced in early 2011 with the first cohorts being trained through the remainder of the academic year. Any member of staff responsible for observing teaching and learning had to attend five mandatory sessions.

Underpinning the programme was a desire to prioritise the feedback dialogue between observer and observee, as this was considered central to the success of any interaction. Following on from this, a coaching model was adopted to ensure this ethos ran through all the modules. We define coaching as the provision of 'a safe place for clients to identify what is and what is not working, try new behaviours and learn from their new experiences' (NASA, cited in Clutterbuck 2007: 12). We aimed for staff to be empowered through coaching to discover and discuss the learning from their lesson observed. As the programme evolved, we decided to provide further coaching development through an Institute of Leadership and Management (ILM) level 3 Coaching Award, which all observers, managers and senior managers had to complete alongside the *License to Observe*.

License to Observe modules

- **Unit 1: changing the culture of lesson observation and the framework for observing teaching and learning**
  In this unit we explore why we introduced the changes to our observation process, this includes the importance of wholesale support from the college's SMT, effective communication methods and quality processes to support using all available resources to improve teaching, learning and assessment. We also identify and discuss key themes to focus on when observing lessons.

- **Unit 2: observing teaching and learning**
  In this unit we analyse a lesson in its entirety. We include an exemplar observed lesson with comments on the planning, scheme of work, lesson plan and student profiles. This is then followed by observing an edited lesson which includes the opening to the lesson, key learning activities and the close of the lesson.

- **Unit 3: making judgements based on the evidence**
  In this unit we further investigate the recording of evidence and judgements. In particular, we look at the power of language, especially descriptors used for judgements. This is a key area to consider when initiating a non-graded approach to lesson observation as associations are often made between the use of specific language and perceived judgements.

- **Unit 4: feedback using a coaching approach**
  We explore different approaches to feedback or shared dialogue in this unit. We match these approaches to teacher experience. The unit also looks at solution-focused questioning, and goes on to practise skills relating to feeding back on the observed lesson through a series of role-play exercises.

- **Unit 5: setting targets, follow up and supporting underperforming staff**
  In this unit, we look at a suggested format for a robust target practise, and we devise targets for the case study teacher. We also explore ways to support underperforming staff and later ways to develop and support staff in a non-graded framework. When the mandatory sessions were completed, there was an ongoing expectation that all trained staff would take part in three moderation sessions per year and attend any further training. The results of moderations were examined carefully and an ongoing training development plan was drawn up following the results of each session. For example, the observation evidence showed that there was a lack of information regarding the relationship between learning support in the classroom and the teacher. Moderation also highlighted that there was no record of scholarly activity in lessons observed for higher education courses. As a result of these omissions, two new mandatory modules were developed for all observers to attend.

Building a community of peer development and improvement

The impact of the *Licence to Observe* has been demonstrable. Teachers reported that they had increased confidence in their observers and the focus was on what needed developing. Also, the ideas on how to develop fed into new dialogues around teaching and learning. Highlighting successes as well as areas for development led to new strategies for sharing the great teaching practice observed.

All curriculum areas had an associated Professional Learning Coach (PLC) – the equivalent of an advanced practitioner. It was the curriculum areas' responsibility to take information gleaned from lesson observation and create a training programme for the area. The PLCs ran monthly *Spotlight* programmes providing updates on teaching and learning themes which had emerged from the observation data collected. For example, if it emerged that stretch and challenge through questioning techniques was repeatedly being identified, the PLC would run a *Spotlight* on differing questioning techniques and stretch and challenge.

Despite this, there was not a more formal way to share good practice. Again, communication was vital. The Deputy Principal and Assistant Principal of Quality revisited each curriculum area with the new initiative of Teaching and Learning Roadshows, a concept of sharing good practice, 'anytime, anyplace and anywhere'. These sometimes planned, sometimes spontaneous events were then recorded by the PLC. The teaching ideas shared between staff were taken away and practised. These members of staff were then invited to discuss the successes or developments of the new teaching strategy with their PLC. Staff were given an additional day's leave as an incentive to attended four Roadshows, the equivalent of approximately four hours' exchange of ideas.

By using a coaching approach in the post-observation dialogue, it was apparent that teachers were beginning to feel more comfortable about sharing their successes and developments with others. At the same time, some curriculum areas also introduced a set of ungraded developmental observations in addition to the formal graded observations. Teachers were encouraged to take a risk and try something new or invite an observer along to a class where there may be an issue, such as behaviour management for developmental support. The success of these types of observation began to filter into the system through the 'Quality Forum', a weekly meeting of all curriculum heads, deputies and SMT. This prompted further discussion and a desire to promote greater transparency to increase teachers' confidence in the observation process.

At this time, the college also adopted new titles for curriculum heads in order to emphasise the focus on teaching and learning. Curriculum Team Managers became Heads of Learning and Deputy Heads of Learning; Advanced Practitioners were renamed Professional Learning Coaches. Heads of Learning were charged with ensuring that they had a thorough overview of their curriculum area, particularly an understanding of what was being practised in the classroom. It was no longer acceptable for managers who were aware of teaching practice issues, not to have supported the teachers' development prior to their observation taking place, which had sometimes been the case. An open-door policy was adopted where teachers could visit each other's classrooms.

In September 2012, Heads of Learning and observers in the curriculum areas were asked to undertake ten drop-ins (five- to ten-minute observation snapshots) per week and an additional 'learning walk' to get a feel of the positives and development needs of their area. The numbers of drop-ins from 2011–12 rose from 375 to over 1,300 in 2012–13. Heads of Learning were asked to gather feedback relating to the impact of increased drop-ins. The results of this were shared and published in an internal report where, out of 40 statements from curriculum areas, 31 were positive. In one area, teachers began to teach with open-doors to welcome and facilitate any visitor into their class, whereas before the doors had been firmly closed. Teachers commented that it was important to get feedback from drop-ins and the increase in these brief visits also had a knock-on effect in terms of encouraging staff to talk more openly about teaching and learning.

Following further moderation sessions and subsequent action planning, by 2013–14 we were confident that our observers were recording evidence and making judgements consistently. Adopting a coaching approach to teachers' development was impacting upon the quality of teaching and learning in the classrooms. The *Licence to Observe* won a Beacon Award for Professional Development in 2013. This not only demonstrated the sustainability of the associated quality processes but also clearly evidenced a shift in culture and attitude towards lesson observation and, as a result, impacted upon the quality of teaching and learning.

As part of that cultural shift, we became aware that forming judgements and awarding an associated grade conflicted more and more with the culture and ethos underpinning the new approach.

Introduction and structure of the first non-graded pilot

By 2013, staff had developed a high level of confidence and understanding of the observation process and were ready to progress to the next stage of the college's observation development. The initial non-graded pilot was approved following presentations to the SMT and Governing body members, Staff Committee, Trade Unions and after wider discussion with curriculum areas. The Assistant Principal of Quality again carried out face-to-face meetings with every curriculum area team to discuss the pilot. Six curriculum teams who were eager to participate in the project and keen to experiment and contribute to the development of the non-graded model were approached. Alongside the introduction of the non-graded pilot, the Engineering Deputy Head of Learning worked with the Assistant Principal of Quality to introduce a cross-college group to encourage risk taking, known as the 'Innovation Group'.

This initiative quickly grew. It started with all teachers being invited to a meeting where they could share ideas and try something out that they had not dared to do before. Initially, eight teachers met and agreed to try out and feedback their ideas together. At each new innovation meeting, teachers were encouraged to bring along a friend. By the end of the year the group had grown to over 100 teachers, other curriculum areas had also begun to set up their own innovation societies.

The non-graded model introduced a new observation structure based on a developmental cycle. The cycle comprised of two (30-minute) developmental observations and two drop-ins; a drop-in began the cycle. Crucially, each observation would build on the actions from the last. The intended timetable was that a drop-in would occur at the beginning of the academic year, followed by a developmental observation, followed by a further drop-in and finally a developmental observation. This cycle fed into the appraisal process. Figure 3.1 provides an outline of the college's observation cycle.

One accountability obstacle to overcome was to demonstrate an overview of the quality of teaching and learning without grading every lesson observed. It was felt this could be confidently provided through the appraisal process, as there is an overall grade for teaching and learning in the assessment matrix. The grade is allocated holistically and takes into consideration outcomes for learners, learner voice feedback, participation in CPD activities, quality of schemes of work, student profiles, external verifier reports and feedback, course leader management quality, the quality of written feedback and support for student progression. Previously, there had been situations where a teacher had delivered a grade 1 observed lesson, this was recorded on their appraisal, but their overall retention, achievement and success rates and other feedback data seemed at odds with this grade. Under the new holistic framework for assessment of teaching and learning quality, a teacher could be observed and graded a 2 for their lesson, but if they had extremely positive achievement data and students survey comments, we could conclude they should receive a grade 1 for teaching and learning.

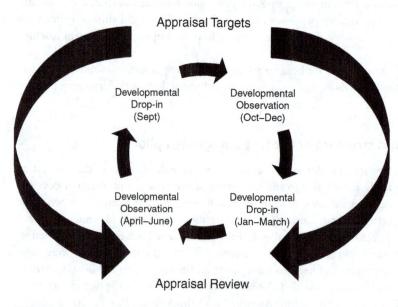

FIGURE 3.1 Observation-Cycle.

'Intensive support' when expectations not met

The pilot groups were identified and the expectations of the pilot's framework were made clear. Teachers were expected to self-reflect and set at least one developmental action for themselves. Teachers were advised that if the observation did not meet expectations, this would trigger 'intensive support'. The triggers for intensive support were:

- no evidence of planning, for example, no scheme of work, no student profile linked or used to individualise learning, including safeguarding and health and safety issues;
- students not engaged;
- insufficient evidence of learning;
- inadequate checking of learning, weak or no assessment methods;
- not following up on previous actions and targets (not engaging in the process).

The pilot was carefully monitored. Each curriculum area taking part allocated a lead observer who was chosen based on their experience of observation. These individuals would be responsible for monitoring that observations were taking place. They would attend and feedback informally at a monthly meeting and formally at a termly focused meeting that explored the progress of the curriculum area. This meeting is chaired by the Assistant Principal of Quality and includes a detailed investigation of key issues.

A key question asked by teachers at the time was how did this intensive support differ from the previous system where teachers were graded as a 3 or 4? In both cases teachers would be referred to the Professional Development Manager and a support plan developed based on the individual needs of the teacher. The key difference has been to do with staff perception and their openness to engage with this intensive support, largely because the teacher does not need to overcome the associated emotional trauma of grade 3 or 4. Poor grades result in a range of emotions from acceptance to anger, denial and distress. Teachers frequently refer to the labelling effects of grading, identifying the individual as a grade 3 teacher, for example, rather than equating this to their teaching practice. This internalisation of teaching quality provides an initial obstacle to progress and development, and we found the emotional response had to be addressed before the work to develop their teaching skills could begin. It is not unheard of for teachers to go off sick due to the anxiety and distress caused by observation feedback as a result of receiving a grade 3 or 4. Such reactions have been well documented elsewhere (e.g. O'Leary 2013). However, by making the process developmental and not associated with a grade, the focus can be shifted from individual performance to pedagogy. In our experience, intensive support has been a wholly successful process.

The non-graded intensive support programme sets in place an agreed mentorship for the teacher. A PLC who has a specific interest in the area to be developed is assigned; importantly this must be someone the teacher can relate to. The pair meet informally to discuss a plan and the PLC then undertakes a purely developmental observation in the first week post-observation to inform the development plan. The teacher is then invited to observe the PLC teaching, discuss what they have seen and then try some agreed strategies that support their development needs. The PLC then reviews the teacher's progress and where appropriate makes recommendations for any further development work. After four weeks of support, the teacher is then re-observed, where evidence of engagement in the process and progress in the identified areas for development becomes the main focus of the observer. Ongoing progress is subsequently monitored at agreed intervals. We are mindful that not all develop-ments can be an instant fix but may take longer to embed in practice and thus require a more longitudinal approach to monitoring.

In those extremely rare cases where a teacher chooses not to engage in the process, alter-native steps to manage performance may be taken, although it is important to stress that to date this has never been an issue in the college. There is a collective understanding that poor teaching cannot be tolerated and that all staff have a duty to continue to do the best they can for their students. However, it is equally the duty of the college to provide support to teach-ers to improve their practice. If teachers find themselves in intensive support again, either because they have not sustained new practice or have new triggers identified, then we would repeat this process once more. Ultimately where there is no desire or hope of development, steps are taken to address this through capability procedures.

Other questions needed to be addressed in order for the pilot to go ahead. Observers in the pilot areas were concerned that the cycle of observations would present an additional work-load for them that may be a challenge to achieve. Time was taken to examine this more closely. Observer staff had already been undertaking a more intensive programme of drop-in observations, some teachers as a result had several observations over an academic year. Observers also began to offer developmental observations and although this was not taken up universally, there was a significant increase in the numbers taking place. Whereas formal graded observations were a minimum of 45 minutes, the new non-graded developmental lesson observation minimum was 30 minutes. Across all existing observation frameworks, the introduction of a set cycle therefore seemed a time-efficient way forward. Some teachers in the pilot felt that they would be observed more than in the past and that this may be a source of stress. In reality, staff fed back that the cycle was helpful, firstly because they were not being judged on a one-off basis and instead they were being offered a series of developmental opportunities, each building upon the last.

Professional dialogue replaces feedback

The importance of communication and the coaching aspect of the feedback were impressed upon the staff observing in the pilot areas. As a result, a new term emerged. We now refer to feedback as a two-way 'professional dialogue', as the term 'feedback' suggests some-thing that is 'done to' rather than being participatory. We advise the observee as to the specific lesson to be observed 48-hours pro-rata before the lesson. At this point we also communicate personally inviting the observee to identify any areas of their teaching that they would like us to comment upon. This may include any particular challenges with the learner groups that they would like help with, or a new teaching strategy or activity that they would appreciate a focus on. After the observed lesson, the observee is asked to reflect and bring positive and developmental points to share at the post-observation discussion meeting.

The offer of developmental advice, in particular around challenging issues, has had a posi-tive effect. Members of staff have commented that they felt that they could share a problem without being afraid that this might downgrade them. The problem is seen in a positive light. Observers have commented that they are pleased to be met with challenges. They are not merely present to validate normal good teaching practice. The end of year 2014

Pilot Survey featured a number of revealing comments which demonstrate this change of emphasis. For example:

> Teachers now openly discuss the good, the bad and the ugly of each lesson, no longer are the bad bits hidden but these are seen as opportunities to develop.

Another elaborates upon this point:

> I feel that the process has truly focused staff on teaching and learning development but more importantly on the outcomes for learners.

This is an important distinction, as the learner experience is referred to rather than the teacher. This helps depersonalise the resulting developmental dialogue. Here are some latest examples of feedback across pilot curriculum areas in the Non-Graded Survey Report:

> I think the most important part is that you feel able to take risks and try things to help you improve as opposed to planning a safe lesson to ensure a good grade. It helps to develop teaching and learning.
>
> The engagement of staff is the most important element of this non-graded process. Staff have to engage with it rather than observation being done to them or ticking a box, this makes it a more intense yet worthwhile experience for all.

At the end of the first year of the pilot, several lessons were learned. These can be summarised briefly in the following bullet points:

- The quality of the coaching dialogue was key to the developmental benefits of the process.
- The pre-observation discourse helped set a really positive framework for development in which to move forward.
- By carefully selecting and getting full buy-in from the initial pilot groups, participating staff were keen to trial this new framework. Soon teachers began to talk to each other, those in the pilot frequently reporting to colleagues in other areas that the professional dialogue they engaged in was both supportive and progressive.
- Teachers also reported that they could try out new ideas or troubleshoot where they had problems without fear. In 2013–14, 88 per cent of teachers surveyed in the pilot felt that they were much more relaxed about being observed.

Expanding the pilot with peer observation and new approaches

In 2014–15, ten more curriculum areas joined the pilot at their request. Those who participated in the first year asked if they could change the format and cycle of the project to better suit their needs. We continued the detailed monitoring but wanted to encourage experimentation. In light of this, we discussed possible modifications with existing areas to try out new cycles of observation. One pilot group was keen to include peer observation, a well-developed practice in that area, to supplement the observation experience and increase the sense of ownership of the observation process and ethos.

Another curriculum area that had been carrying out developmental observations for some time adopted a different approach. They encouraged teachers to identify specific areas of challenge and invite the observer in to comment and help seek solutions. Teachers in this area now have the opportunity to invite observers in for their formal developmental observation to comment on an issue they may be struggling with. The result of this, we would argue, is the evolution of a mature and reflective system that demonstrates a real appreciation of the role of lesson observation in teachers' professional learning. It also highlights how by allowing staff to play an active role in negotiating and shaping their engagement with observation that they are more likely to develop a sense of ownership than if they had a one size fits all model imposed upon them.

The expansion of the non-graded pilot required a revision of the moderation process. The prior tasks undertaken to demonstrate progress in consistency for graded observations were not measurable in the new format. For this reason, we needed to find a new formula to measure impact and inform staff development. The cycle of observations was important for this. For example, we examined anonymised cycle sets of individuals to see how the development themes were identified and responded to, and tracked whether the learning needs were followed through and addressed. We also examined the quality of written evidence in relation to identified successes and developmental points, this helped to identify a number of areas for development. In particular, observers were still expressing judgements which would have the potential to invite staff to grade themselves.

The main findings in our most recent moderation in June 2015 resulted in an electronic observation form which better charts progress between observations. We also ran a new mandatory module for *Licence to Observe* that focused on language to express developments rather than judgements. Notes relating to the lesson observation now focus on what needs to be developed rather than the story of the whole lesson. We trust that if the area of teaching and learning is seen to be of a good standard, there is no need to comment unless to share good practice. Standards are verified through ticking the appropriate box as 'agreed' or 'develop'. Where 'develop' is marked, the detail of what is seen and any ideas to share relating to this are recorded. For example, if the observer sees that 'questioning' for stretch and challenge needs to be developed, they record the teaching behaviour they observe, i.e. 'volunteer questions for all questioning noted throughout the lesson, discuss and develop strategies to target questions to every student'.

From September 2015 we have adopted non-graded lesson observation throughout the college. More members of staff have become interested in observation and we continue to invest in the development of coaching skills. We have developed a *Licence to Coach* programme for all teachers, not only to improve their coaching skills for peer observation, but also to benefit teachers working with students given that the skills and strategies are transferrable. It incorporates theory and a mentoring programme utilising already trained coach staff members to enable the teacher to practise and develop their coaching skills. Teachers are now more interested in the learning they take away from lesson observation. A number have now completed *Licence to Observe* as a development opportunity. We have also developed a module called *Licence to Peer Observe* to highlight and enhance the learning opportunities that can be gleaned from peer observation. This practice is now embedded in our development programme for staff.

The future

Introducing a non-graded observation model has been an eventful journey over the last four years. In 2014 we were graded as Outstanding by Ofsted. Their report stated:

The lesson observation system is mature and highly effective. Judgements on strengths and areas for improvement are accurate and evaluative. Professional learning coaches and quality managers give very good support to teachers in order to further improve the quality of teaching, learning and assessment ... Teachers make very good use of an excellent range of professional development activities specifically aimed at meeting their individual development needs, such as the nationally recognised Licence to Observe.

Ofsted 2014: 12

In 2015 we were awarded the Times Education Supplement (TES) Award for the 'Best Teaching Initiative', which recognised the contribution our coaching approach to development has made to the students' experience in the classroom.

With our commitment to building trust and confidence amongst staff when it comes to developing excellence in teaching and learning, we have achieved positive changes in the organisation. The journey has been not just to communicate the vision, but also to follow through with actions that validate our proposals. The incremental approach to change has been educational and valuable in shaping our non-graded model, through learning from the successes and developments of others who so keenly took part in the pilot. As we continue to develop our model, we look to the future, a future of increased self-regulation and autonomy with hope. We have motivated and reflective staff who appreciate the contribution that they can make to each other and to the learning experience of our students. Our system for observing and developing teaching has had a positive impact. We know that even the label 'outstanding' can be transcended because without a grade there is no limit as to what we can achieve.

References

Clutterbuck, D. (2007) *Coaching the Team at Work*. Boston, MA: Nicholas Brealey International.

Office for Standards in Education (Ofsted) (2014) *Further Education and Skills Inspection Report: Chichester College: General further education college.* (Inspection Number: 429157). Retrieved from http://reports.ofsted.gov.uk/inspection-reports/find-inspection-report/provider/ELS/130843. Last accessed 19 March 2016.

O'Leary. M. (2012) 'Time to Turn Worthless Lesson Observation into a Powerful Tool for Improving Teaching and Learning'. *In Tuition*, (9), 16–18.

O'Leary, M. (2013) *Developing a National Framework for the Effective Use of Lesson Observation in Further Education*. Project report for the University and College Union, November 2013. DOI: 10.13140/RG.2.1.1751.7286. Available at: www.ucu.org.uk/media/6714/Developing-a-national-framework-for-the-effective-use-of-lesson-observation-in-FE-Dr-Matt-OLeary-Nov-13/pdf/ucu_lessonobsproject_nov13.pdf.

PART II

Recent research studies in lesson observation

4

MAXIMISING VOCATIONAL TEACHERS' LEARNING THROUGH DEVELOPMENTAL OBSERVATION

Ann Lahiff

Introduction

This chapter aims to provide an account of case study research which explored the experiences of further education (FE) vocational teachers' observations as they completed in-service initial teacher training (ITT) programmes in England. The research emerged as a result of my own professional experiences as a teacher trainer and, in particular, my interest in the outcomes of teaching observations. My professional reflections over 25 years as both a college and university-based teacher trainer led me to conclude that the process of observation and, particularly, the feedback opportunities it presented, provided one of the most challenging and engaging aspects of initial training for FE teachers. Yet despite the statutory requirement to observe FE teachers-in-training (2007–13), research exploring FE ITT observations has been negligible to date. Case study research into the use and value of ITT observations for vocational teachers was therefore conducted not only to help rectify this situation, but also to ensure that observation practices are more visible in published research. The recommendations that emerged from the research were aimed at developing practice in relation to the initial training of vocational teachers in colleges and also at generating further understanding of the phenomena of observation itself.

The focus for this chapter is an aspect of vocational teachers' observations – the post-observation feedback discussion. It will be argued that it is during the feedback discussion that the so-called developmental aspect of ITT observation takes place. This in itself is not new. Others writing about the ITT of FE teachers more broadly have shown that FE teachers-in-training generally valued ITT observations and saw the feedback that followed observations as helpful in their professional development (Harkin *et al.* 2003; Orr and Simmons 2010). But rarely had the focus been specifically on vocational teachers' experiences of observation as they crossed boundaries from their respective vocational fields into teaching. Furthermore, there were few accounts of the observation experience itself.

The chapter is structured in three parts. First, a background to the research will be provided explaining why it focused on vocational teachers' ITT observations and what was already known about ITT observations. Second, the research approach taken will be explained and the case study sample outlined. The third section presents the findings and offers a discussion of these in relation to understanding vocational teachers' development. The chapter will end with recommendations to maximize vocational teachers' learning through ITT observations.

Why vocational teachers?

For the purpose of this discussion, vocational teachers are defined as those involved in teaching on courses where, following the conclusions of the Commission on Adult Vocational Teaching and Learning (CAVTL) there is a '*clear line of sight to work*' (LSIS 2013: 7). In other words, vocational teachers work with learners to develop the knowledge and skills required for entry into a specific occupational sector. Discussions within the literature on vocational education and training (VET) have established that alongside the development of knowledge and skills, a central aspect of learning on vocational courses is the development of an associated identity described, by some, as a process of becoming (Colley 2003). Given that I have worked with FE teachers-in-training for more than 20 years, I was aware of the complexity in the development of a teacher identity for vocational teachers – their respective 'process of becoming'. This is because vocational teachers have an established vocational expertise and enter teaching with an occupational identity already formed (e.g. Bathmaker and Avis 2005; Orr and Simmons 2010). This has led many to define vocational teachers as being 'dual professionals' (Robson 1998). With this descriptor comes an acknowledgement of a complexity in not only the development of a teacher identity, rarely experienced by other FE teachers of history, physics, maths or English, for example, but also in the development of pedagogy.

Moodie and Wheelahan (2012) argue that this complexity exists because vocational teachers can be seen to be involved in the reformulation of vocational knowledge from work, where it has mainly a productive function, to a teaching/learning function. I have argued elsewhere (Lahiff 2015) that it is this reformulation that is being observed in vocational teachers' teaching observations. For these professional and research-based reasons, the research focused on vocational teachers' experiences of teaching observations and examined the use and value that these experiences afford.

Research on teaching observations

Irrespective of whether ITT for FE has been undertaken on a voluntary or statutory basis, observing teachers in their place of work has always featured in FE ITT programmes since their inception after the Second World War. Prior to the introduction of mandatory observations for FE ITT in 2007, research on FE observations had shown that FE teachers generally valued the observations they experienced in ITT as it assisted their development in the early days of teaching. The research also identified the critical factors underpinning what were seen to be successful ITT teaching observations. These included the establishment of a relationship between the observer and observee and the opportunity to engage in discussion about the observed teaching. Significantly, research by Cockburn (2005) and, most recently, O'Leary (2012, 2013) established that FE teachers clearly differentiated between observations conducted for different purposes. Observations taking place in FE have therefore largely been modelled dualistically – with observations conducted for ITT viewed as part of a developmental discourse as opposed to part of a Quality Assurance (QA) discourse associated with Ofsted grading criteria for inspection. Matt O'Leary has, however, warned of the encroachment of a QA discourse into observations conducted as part of ITT in FE.

While ITT observations had therefore been defined as/understood to be developmental in purpose in contrast to QA observations, two additional issues were of interest to me. These were, first, the rather 'taken-for-granted' nature of the phenomenon of observation and second, the nature of the development envisaged. With respect to the former, I wanted to question how observation *per se* was conducted because this would enhance understanding of ITT observations. With respect to the latter, I wanted to capture the development in action in relation to vocational teachers. This chapter will focus on findings in relation to the second issue. However, a brief overview of the first issue is provided to help set the context for the research.

When the observation process is taken for granted it is assumed that observation 'just happens'. In other words that it is just a matter of watching what takes place. One of the implications of this is that observation is perceived as a passive process. In this kind of understanding of any observation process, such things as the relationship between the observer, the observed and the historical and cultural context in which the observation takes place are deemed less important than adopting the appropriate method of observation. Moreover, the process of observation becomes opaque. However, my research led to the conclusion that any act of observation is actually extraordinarily complex. Far from a passive (and neutral) activity led by an observer, as is often conceived, an examination of processes involved in observation *per se* reveals a more active role for the observer. The observer can be seen to be engaged in a highly selective process when observing, whether they are observing teaching or anything else. This is because in observing action we simply cannot take in everything we see, so implicitly and/or explicitly we use 'filters' to guide our observation. Wragg (1999), in a seminal text on conducting classroom observations in primary schools, drew attention to these conceptual issues when considering the phenomenon of observations of teaching. For Wragg, there is the real possibility that an observer may delude themselves about what is happening, partly because in observing others, we often 'observe what we want to see' (ibid: vii). Similarly, O'Leary's (2014) account of classroom observation as a method for studying teaching and learning demonstrates that, by itself, observation can only provide a 'partial view' (ibid: 68) of teaching and learning and highlights the importance of gathering information from multiple sources before any judgement of practice is made.

Although not the central aspect being discussed in this chapter, my argument is that it is crucial to conceptualise observation as an active, complex, constructed process, framed by context as opposed to a neutral, passive process which ignores context. This means that in researching observations it is important to consider such things as the past experiences observers bring to the observation process and to understand the 'filters' used when observing. Questions such as these necessarily raise important issues regarding how this complex process can be captured in research. The next section therefore provides an overview of the approach taken to the case study research.

Approach taken to research

As has been clarified, observations conducted for FE ITT have traditionally been seen as part of a developmental discourse, with the opportunity for the parties involved to discuss the observed teaching and to consider improvements. These are key aspects of the developmental discourse. However, it has also been established that little attention has been paid in the literature to capturing the processes involved in observations conducted in vocational education. In developing the research strategy, ITT observations for vocational teachers were understood to be framed by a broadly developmental purpose; to occur in workplaces (FE colleges) as examples of situated practice and were conceptualised as a process i.e. as a sequence of events. It was also recognised that teaching observations conducted for ITT have a history – they are the product of cultural practices and historical events that have shaped them with rules and practices guiding practice. For example, with effect from 2007 not only the number of observations to be conducted were regulated for the first time in FE ITT, but also the requirement that workplace mentors should be involved in completing observations.

The starting point for the adoption of a specific methodological framing for this research was the following quote from Miettinen (2000: 63):

> Observation necessarily takes place in a certain activity, context or thought community, using the concepts, instruments and conventions historically developed in that context. They steer the observations, and with them the observer interprets and generalises what is seen and regarded as problematic and important.

This then led to the socio-cultural approach of Cultural Historical Activity Theory (CHAT) framing the research (e.g. Bakhurst 2009). Whilst it is beyond the scope of this chapter to provide a comprehensive overview of the approach, the essence of the approach is captured by the quotation provided above. Specifically, that we should recognise that any type of human activity takes place in a context and that the activity has a cultural, social, historical 'memory'. The focus of inquiry is on the purpose of the activity as it will influence the way in which those involved in the activity approach it and use resources and artefacts designed for the purpose. The activity (in this case, teaching observation) is the prime unit of analysis (Engeström 2001). In relation to ITT observations, adopting CHAT provided a way of modelling and then theorising the complex phenomenon of observation. Specifically, it offered a lens through which to view observation practices in colleges. Crucial to this modelling were the conceptual tools CHAT provided. This meant I could capture observations in action having accepted that they were framed by rules and regulations; took place in specific communities; had specific participants (vocational teachers) and observers (education tutors and vocational mentors), defined as subjects in CHAT; involved specific observation artefacts, such as observation proformas and feedback discussions, and the purpose of the observation was developmental. Figure 4.1 is adapted from the modelling used in the research, with the activity represented by a central triangle, as is common in CHAT.

My intention was not to compare practices but, rather, to develop accounts of what took place in ITT observations and to identify the form(s) that development took. This meant being able to accept that whilst different people were involved in observations at different times and in different settings, they were all, in theory at least, working toward a common goal, i.e. developing the practice of the vocational teacher.

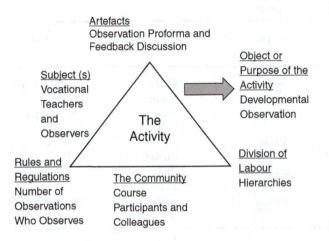

Artefacts
Observation Proforma and
Feedback Discussion

Object or
Purpose of the
Activity
Developmental
Observation

Subject (s)
Vocational
Teachers
and
Observers

The
Activity

Rules and
Regulations
Number of
Observations
Who Observes

The Community
Course
Participants and
Colleagues

Division of
Labour
Hierarchies

FIGURE 4.1 Modelling of ITT teaching observations.

Methodology

Once an appropriate framing had been decided, gaining an understanding of the processes as well as the outcomes of ITT observations meant that in-depth qualitative case studies were most appropriate. My ethical stance towards collecting accounts of observation practices meant that I excluded any prior knowledge of or involvement with the various ITT consortiums I had worked with. This meant that the case study sample built from information about the research that I sent out to a number of ITT consortia which offered part-time, in-service awards in the south-east of England. The sample was, therefore, convenience in type, but because I also wanted to include vocational teachers from different occupational backgrounds and achieve a gender balance, it also had purposive features. The case study sample therefore consisted of six vocational teachers and their two respective ITT observers (education tutors and vocational mentors). During the course of the research, I had to exclude data from one case study partici-pant. This left five vocational areas: catering, health and social care, specialist make-up (hair-dressing for performing arts), plastering and painting and decorating. The vocational teachers were either towards the end of the first year of their ITT or in the second year of the course. All of them had completed at least two ITT observations prior to taking part in the research.

Participants agreed that I could observe their respective practice, which included the ITT observation and the feedback discussion which followed. Field notes and sketches were made to record the observations of teaching and an audio recording of the feedback discussion was made. The research observations were followed by individual in-depth interviews with all participants in the study. The interviews provided information about the participants' previous vocational and/or educational backgrounds (see Table 4.1). Ensuring that participants' biographies were captured enabled me to place the vocational teachers and their observers culturally and historically – a crucial element in adopting a CHAT approach. Interviews also captured participants' accounts of the purpose of ITT observations and gave them the opportunity to discuss the practices that had been observed. Conducted over a period of 18 months, both methods provided rich, qualitative data from which the following discussion is just a small sample.

TABLE 4.1 Summary of research participants

Vocational Area	Vocational Teacher	Education Tutor Vocational Mentor	College
Catering	Johnson	Denis Rachel	West College
Health and Social Care	Maria	Laura Delia	North College
Specialist Make-up (Hairdressing)	Alan	Shirley Miriam	East College
Plastering	Clive	Anna Vince	South College
Painting and Decorating	Simona	Anna Julie	South College

Findings and discussion

Two aspects of the findings are reported in this chapter. Firstly, what was actually being developed during the observation process and secondly, how did the development take-place? When data from the observations and the interviews conducted were analysed, I found that two interacting types of development were evident. I called these types of development *the development of pedagogic expertise* and the *development of pedagogic expertise for vocational practice* (Lahiff 2015). These are explained in the next section.

In relation to the observations where education tutors and vocational teachers were concerned, the theories and concepts which informed respective ITT courses were seen to frame the vocational teachers' development. That is, education tutors approached the observations by focusing on the development of particular approaches to the planning, management and assessment of learning. These can be characterised as more student-centred, active learning approaches to teaching and learning, including the use of group and paired work and clear strategies for differentiating learning and the use of assessment for learning. These approaches to learning have their roots in educational theories from cognitive and social constructivist approaches and commonly underpin ITT courses in England. Vocational teachers and their respective education tutor observers were therefore seen to be working towards the *development of pedagogic expertise* framed by these culturally valued approaches to teaching and learning.

The developmental purpose of observations conducted by vocational mentors is captured by the following quotation from Vince, a vocational mentor observer from the plastering case study:

> If you're going into an observation ... if you're observing anyone, a student, a teacher or whoever, they've all got to be developmental, there's no point in observing someone [otherwise] ... because it doesn't go anywhere.

Where observations involved vocational teachers and their respective vocational mentors, I also found the *development of pedagogic expertise* where parties involved approached the observation by considering accepted theories of learning as described above. However, this approach on its own was not sufficient to capture the vocational aspect of the learning where vocational mentors acted as observers. Instead, the analysis demonstrated that additional elements influenced the type of development envisaged in these cases. In the observations of practice I conducted, and in the accounts of observation practice gleaned from interviews, respective vocational knowledge and the awareness of the purpose of vocational learning underpinned practice. With one exception (the health and social care case study) the vocational was evident due to the emphasis given in the feedback discussion to such things as how vocational teachers took into account the development of vocational students' time-efficient, safe practice when planning and managing learning. The importance of the vocational context in the development of practice was central to the development of practice itself. For these reasons the *development of pedagogic expertise for vocational practice* was seen as a more appropriate descriptor. In the section that follows, some illustrative examples of both of these forms of development are provided.

How did the development take place?

Whether the purpose of the observation was the development of *pedagogic expertise*, or *pedagogic expertise for vocational practice*, the feedback discussion provided the context for development. In all the case studies, vocational teachers relished the opportunity to discuss both the observed teaching and consider how they could put ideas generated into practice. This does not mean to say that ITT observations were anxiety-free for vocational teachers, far from it, but the knowledge that they would talk about the observed session with the observer whose role it was to facilitate their development and with whom they had established a relationship helped ease their anxiety.

The nature of the relationship between the vocational teacher and the observer was certainly a key factor in learning from the experience of observation. In all cases, vocational teachers spoke in earnest about the importance of building a relationship with the observer. With an established relationship, came trust and the realisation that both participants in the observation were actively working towards the same goal, i.e. the vocational teacher's development.

In the examples that follow, the importance and nature of the relationship in these developmental observations are captured. For Maria, the health and social care teacher, the development of trust between observer and observee was something that depended on honesty. As she commented, 'you really need to be honest, not in denial'. Similarly, Clive, the plastering teacher, spoke of honesty and how a positive relationship ensured that there were opportunities to fully engage in the feedback discussion with the observer. In relation to his experience of feedback discussions with education tutor observers, he shed light on the nature of the discussion in the following extract:

> I can question it, there's no problem with that, you can sort of go "well what's all this about then" you know, there's no problem with that. So you can question it and it's honest in my opinion.

The account of the specialist make-up vocational teacher, Alan, endorsed the view that a positive, respectful relationship would bring greater benefits to development. Though as he explained, familiarity did not necessarily breed contempt between observer and observee:

> The observer is not going to fluff around it because she likes you, do you know what I mean? … she's going to tell you how it is.

However, in those instances where the relationship has not been established as firmly as would be liked for developmental observations, one education tutor, Anna, spoke of the damaging effects, not only for the observation experience but for the learning itself. She suggested that in these situations, '[my] students still think it's an Ofsted inspection. They have to get everything right; they have got to show me how they can tell students off and deal with behaviour … There is a mismatch.'

The relationship that had been established therefore provided the foundations for the developmental feedback discussion between observers and vocational teachers. In all cases, the discussion took place face-to-face – either immediately after the observed session or within ten days. The next section moves onto explore the nature of the discussion.

Overall, the research established that the feedback discussion acted as a verbal and developmental space where vocational teachers and observers use and develop the language of pedagogy (Lahiff 2015). In other words, in the analysis of feedback discussions, vocational teachers and their respective observers were, to a greater or lesser extent, actively engaged in developing strategies for practice. An extract from the catering case study feedback discussion is provided, first, to illustrate the nature of engagement and the modelling of feedback practice.

The thirty-minute feedback discussion between the vocational teacher, Johnson and his education tutor, Denis, followed an observation of Johnson in a classroom where he had been teaching students on a short course on food safety. The feedback discussion addressed a complex issue of the frequency, use and length of a number of anecdotal stories that emerged from Johnson's extensive catering experience which were shared with students throughout the lesson.

Denis, who had extensive experience of Teaching English as a Foreign Language (TEFL) prior to becoming an education tutor, thought that these lengthy anecdotes were illustrative of 'incidental language', during which students were seen to be 'just listening'. Nevertheless, to address this in the feedback, Denis first acknowledged the stories as a 'valuable resource' that Johnson could bring to the teaching of food safety in that they brought the topic to life. However, he also asked Johnson to consider ways in which these could be turned to more 'academic advantage in teaching'. He followed this with a number of examples of how the stories could be used as part of a more learner-centred activity, rather than just relying on students' listening passively. Once a couple of examples were given, Johnson joined in and indicated that he had understood what was being proposed:

> Denis: So, you tell the story and then get them to fill the gaps … or make it a case
> study … [or a] problem-solving activity.
> Johnson: And … they could say what happens next!
> Denis: Yes … Yes … Tweaking so it is less listening and more activity.

While it may have been easier to say 'cut these anecdotes down' or to undervalue the contribution of real-life anecdotes to the vocational learner, it is here that Johnson and Denis can be seen to be actively engaged in developing strategies for enhancing practice.

A similar engagement can be seen in the following extract from the plastering case study. In this extract, the observer, Anna, and the vocational teacher, Clive, are discussing the use of peer assessment.

> Anna: I thought that peer assessment was quite well done … it seemed to be quite natural in your session; it's not something out of the ordinary. [You asked a student] … "would you be satisfied as a customer with this?"

> Clive: To be honest with you, that's one of my [approaches]. They need to train themselves to spot errors or problems … And I often say to them "would you pay for it?", that is your [peer assessment] question, "would you pay for it?".

Clive was therefore able to explain to his education tutor observer that his strategy for peer assessment emerged from his vocational context i.e. preparing plastering students for work. The developmental aspect grew out of this exchange in that the discussion then led to a sharing of strategies as to how Clive might move on to develop peer assessment to include the development of strategies to record individual student progression and achievement.

In many instances, it might have been easier for the observer to simply tell the vocational teacher what he/she could do, from their perspective, to enhance the learning of the students. Instead, in all of the case study post-observation feedback discussions observed, there was a form of engagement to either identify the aspects of the session that appeared to work well/less well and/or to draw out the potential strategies for action in future teaching sessions. Furthermore, either consciously or otherwise, the discussion can be seen as modelling processes involved in giving feedback.

As described earlier, in the observations where the purpose was the development of *pedagogic expertise for vocational practice,* the engagement was framed, specifically, by the vocational element. This included an awareness of the need for vocational students to develop time-efficient, safe vocational practice. This framing emphasises the importance of vocationally-specific mentor observers in the development of vocational teachers. Alan, the specialist make-up vocational teacher, clearly demonstrated his existing awareness of the need for his students to develop time-efficient practice in the following extract:

> There's no point in letting [students] take 7 hours or 2 or 3 weeks to make something, because it's impractical, you know. It's like hair styles, when they're putting rollers in, [I'm saying] … "No girls you've got 7 minutes, literally 7 minutes to get a whole head of rollers in; you've got 10 minutes to do a blow dry."

However, although Alan was aware of the need for time-efficient practice, his vocational mentor, Miriam, drew his attention to the need to encourage students to set up their workstations according to whether they were right or left handed in order to enhance speed of practice. She had observed that students were stretching across their workstations which not only limited the development of speed of practice but also compromised student's safe practice. This safe practice reminder extended to the application of health and safety regulations to the checks on the student uniform. As she said: 'big earrings, they all love them, but it is a health and safety risk!'

Similarly, in preparation for the post-observation feedback discussion Rachel, the catering vocational mentor, emphasised the importance of time-efficient practice in catering and why this aspect framed parts of her feedback discussion with Johnson:

> When you go into industry, we haven't got half an hour to go around and collect our ingredients, the chef would be cursing, he'd be swearing at you and he'd go "there's the door, goodbye!"

From Rachel's perspective the vocational teacher therefore needed to be attuned to the learning and teaching compromises necessary when students were at the start as opposed to the later stages of their courses. This meant that feedback discussions needed to reflect the specific challenges of planning teaching and learning in vocational contexts. In the case study example, strategies were shared with Johnson to help his students develop time-bound vocational practice, as illustrated in Rachel's comment below:

> You need a time clock, you need a time clock ticking away. "So you've got 15 minutes, here's the clock", this is how I teach them when I'm teaching it, when they just begin. I put it on the television [in the restaurant] and say "You've got 20 minutes to do this task, at the 20 minutes we stop".

The feedback discussion therefore offered opportunities not only to share strategies for the vocational context, but also to engage in finding solutions to real challenges as experienced by vocational teachers.

Conclusions

In considering the development of vocational teachers through the use of ITT observations, I have argued that, first and foremost, observation has to be conceptualised as an active, complex, constructed process, framed by context. It needs to be accepted that observation is not a neutral, value-free process. The purpose of the observation, I have argued, drives the experience. For observations conducted by education tutors, the purpose was seen to be the *development of pedagogic expertise,* and for observations conducted by vocational mentors, the additional dimension of the development of *pedagogic expertise for vocational practice* was identified. From the case study research conducted, the post-observation feedback discussion was seen to offer a learning space where the development of vocational teachers' pedagogy is situated – framed by the relationships established by participants. This space is particularly important for vocational teachers as they cross boundaries from their vocational contexts and learn to become teachers. To some extent the feedback discussion is a classic example of learning as a social practice, where participants learn as part of social engagement with others (Felstead *et al.* 2009).

Following on from the insight gleaned from this research, there are some very clear implications for practice that are worth summarising:

1. Vocational teachers can and do learn from ITT observations where their purpose is developmental. Observers engaged in ITT observations need to ensure that they resist what might be seen as institutional/policy 'raids' into ITT observation practice.
2. There are no 'quick fixes' regarding the development of vocational teachers' practice. The case studies of vocational teachers on which this research was based were undergoing a two-year part-time programme of study in which they were able to develop relationships with education tutors and vocationally-specific mentors. To maximize learning from ITT observation, vocational teachers need the time and the opportunity to develop their practice with others who mediate their learning.
3. ITT observers whether education tutors or vocational mentors are engaged in a skilled and knowledgeable process. Their expertise includes the ability to draw upon their

respective professional and vocational knowledge to facilitate the development of vocational teachers.

4. Those of us who are involved in and committed to vocational teachers' development should celebrate these workplace learning practices by making them visible in research. It perhaps goes without saying that the development of vocational teachers lies at the heart of attempts to unlock vocational students' learning: we should not therefore undermine its importance or its complexity.

References

Bakhurst, D. (2009) 'Reflections on Activity Theory'. *Educational Review*, 61(2), 197–210.

Bathmaker, A.-M. and Avis, J. (2005) 'Becoming a Lecturer in Further Education in England: The construction of professional identity and the role of communities of practice'. *Journal of Education for Teaching*, 31(1), 47–62.

Cockburn, J. (2005) 'Perspectives and Politics of Classroom Observation'. *Research in Post-Compulsory Education*, 10(3), 373–388.

Colley, H., James, D., Tedder, M. and Diment, K. (2003) 'Learning as Becoming, Vocational Education and Training: Class, gender and the role of vocational habitus'. *Journal of Vocational Education and Training*, 55(4), 471–497.

Engeström, Y. (2001) 'Expansive Learning at Work: Toward an activity theoretical reconceptualisation'. *Journal of Education and Work*, 14(1), 133–156.

Felstead, A., Fuller, A., Jewson, N. and Unwin, L. (2009) *Improving Working for Learning*. London: Routledge.

Harkin, J., Clow, R. and Hillier, Y. (2003) *Recollected in Tranquillity? FE teachers' perceptions of their initial teacher training*. London: Learning and Skills Development Agency.

LSIS (2013) *It's About Work: Excellent adult vocational teaching and learning: the summary report of the Commission on Adult Vocational Teaching and Learning*, LSIS with support from the Department for Business, Innovation and Skills. Available at: http://repository.excellencegateway.org.uk/fedora/objects/eg:5937/datastreams/DOC/content. Last accessed 18 November 2015.

Lahiff, A. (2015) 'Maximizing Vocational Teachers' Learning: The feedback discussion in the observation of teaching for initial teacher training in further education'. *London Review of Education*, 13(1), 3–15.

Miettinen, R. (2000) 'The Concept of Experiential Learning and John Dewey's Theory of Reflective Thought and Action'. *International Journal of Lifelong Education*, 19(1), 54–72.

Moodie, G. and Wheelahan, L. (2012) 'Integration and Fragmentation of Post-Compulsory Teacher Education'. *Journal of Vocational Education and Training*, 64(3), 317–331.

O'Leary, M. (2012) 'Exploring the Role of Lesson Observation in the English Education System: A review of methods, models and meanings'. *Professional Development in Education*, 38(5), 791–810.

O'Leary, M. (2013) 'Surveillance, Performativity and Normalised Practice: The use and impact of graded lesson observations in further education colleges'. *Journal of Further and Higher Education*, 37(5), 694–714.

O'Leary, M. (2014) *Classroom Observation. A guide to the effective observation of teaching and learning*. London: Routledge.

Orr, K. and Simmons, R. (2010) 'Dual Identities: The in-service teacher trainee experience in the English further education sector'. *Journal of Vocational Education and Training*, 62(1), 75–88.

Robson, J. (1998) 'A Profession in Crisis: Status, culture and identity in the further education college'. *Journal of Vocational Education and Training*, 50(4), 585–607.

Wragg, E. C. (1999) *An Introduction to Classroom Observation*, 2nd edition. London: Routledge.

5

THE IMPACT OF LESSON OBSERVATION ON PRACTICE, PROFESSIONALISM AND TEACHER IDENTITY

Lorna Page

Introduction

It wasn't so long ago that arguments abounded about the artistic genius of Tracey Emin's *My Bed* (1998). Could an unmade, soiled, crude-looking bed be truly worthy of a Turner Prize nomination? Many argued that it wasn't art. That to call it art would be to compare it to the greatness of van Gogh or Monet. The point is this though, not to argue what's great art, but to illuminate that what's considered exemplary, magnificent and even mind-blowing art is subjective and that this subjectivity is celebrated, venerated and encouraged. How does this relate to teaching? Well, it's the same principle, or at least it should be. If, as Gage (1978: 15) proposes, that teaching is an art that 'calls for intuition, creativity and improvisation', surely we should be celebrating, awarding and encouraging unique, personalised, diverse teaching practices? We should, but we don't! Instead we have a system that is attempting, through lesson observation, to pigeonhole teaching practices by formula and rules to create uniformed 'good teachers' and 'good teaching practices'.

This chapter's aim is to share segmented findings resulting from a six-year further education (FE) single institution case study. The study sought to expose the much needed voices of FE teachers, their perspectives, experiences and engagement with being observed teaching. Through the unmasking of teachers' voices, a new model for conducting observations was subsequently proposed. This model acknowledges that observation still has a place in the English education system, however it's a model that takes into account teachers' professionalism, experience and development needs.

At the commencement of my research it was assumed that FE teachers experience and engage with myriad forms of observation differently, ergo the meanings teachers give to being observed I supposed were complex and profoundly diverse.

Collectively, any observation, in its simplest form, can be described as the act of watching. Teachers, by the very nature of their work, are 'observed' by their students. Yet as I write this chapter, no definitive definition exists of what constitutes 'lesson observation' in teaching. Indeed, one of the significant problems with observation is the assumption of a one-size-fits-all approach. Such an assumption is wrong as there exists a spectrum of observations, none of which are analogous to one another; each is distinctly independent with differing aims and objectives. Such observations have become part of the wallpaper that embellishes an FE teacher's year. A wallpaper that, on the surface, appears sensible, organised and entirely logical, yet is hiding the cracks of a broken system of teacher surveillance and managerial control. Copious researchers have examined observations as independent processes, though often through the context of schoolteachers, the main thinkers being: Cullingford (1999); Montgomery (1999); Wragg (1999); Gosling (2002) and Shortland (2004). Within the FE sector it's arguably the studies of O'Leary (2006, 2011, 2013, 2014) whose are the most comprehensive to date.

Observation and teacher professionalism

Teachers within my study were interviewed to ascertain which forms of observation they recognised and had experienced. Their responses expounded my previous assumption that teachers encounter many forms of observations e.g. quality assurance, teacher training, peer, mentor, Ofsted, interviews, appraisal and 'intervention' observations. It was possible to ascertain that some teachers in my study, by virtue of circumstance, experienced up to 19 observations over a two-year period.

Being observed is not a new concept to the British education system, its roots can be traced back to 1839 where 'different methods of school inspection, based on observation, have been in place' (Grubb 2000: 696). Over time, observation like education, has journeyed through flip-flop processes of tinkering and re-touching through to complete transformation. Whilst governments and policy makers may collectively have understood the requirement for such processes, it needed to be known whether the teachers, who, let us not forget remain at the heart of observations, knew why they were being observed. Why then did the teachers in my study believe they were observed? The most common responses were: 'To check you're doing your job properly; To check targets are being met; To test you on what you can remember'.

Although these, and subsequent references, are mere samples of responses, there was a startling brevity of variation echoed by their colleagues. Teachers felt that they were being observed as a monitoring or surveillance. What was so obviously missing from the teachers' accounts was that observation can be used as an instrument and platform for professional development, an opportunity to obtain feedback, to learn, to reflect and to grow as a professional. If such responses to observation were not at the forefront of teachers' minds, it was becoming clear that observation was viewed with a distinct uniformity, as a mechanism of managerial control.

It may be argued that this is a common-sense view by teachers. Teachers do, after all, operate in a climate that has seen an increase in student monitoring, measuring and testing. But the point is this, teachers are professionals and being a professional involves the linking of three issues: knowledge, responsibility and autonomy (Furlong et al. 2000). If being observed is removing teachers' autonomy to practice according to the needs as *they* see it, then arguably, are they being allowed to operate as 'professionals'? It was a question that required further exploration. To do this, I needed to understand the meanings teachers gave to being a professional. What did they perceive a 'professional teacher' to be? After some reflective pauses and moments of hesitation, the teachers in my study responded confidently in their answers: 'Does everything by the book'; 'Gets results'; 'Does paperwork and stuff professionally'.

Such responses led me to ask how these teachers saw themselves. Did they, for example, regard themselves as 'professionals'?

'I'll class myself as a professional once I get a good graded degree'.
'I'm a professional tradesman'.
'Not until I've my teaching licence'.

It was noteworthy that those who taught vocational subjects struggled more with the concept of being a 'professional teacher' than those who taught academic subjects:

I often struggle with the idea 'cos being a welder by trade, for a long time I considered myself a welder that taught ... it's a big step from working in the trade to coming into FE. It took me quite a while ... to go from being a welder that taught to teaching welding.

How teachers described themselves became a further area of interest, particularly since Gleeson *et al.* (2005: 447) stated that understanding teacher professionalism in FE 'is complicated by the proliferation of job titles'. Indeed, whilst here in this chapter I am referring to 'teachers', the interviewees in my study were officially employed as 'lecturers'. I was interested in exploring the terms my interviewees attributed to themselves. For example, did they see themselves as teachers, lecturers, or even other nomenclature? Did it matter? The results revealed that interviewees viewed their professional identities through multiple lenses:

- Academic
- Lecturer
- Teacher
- Trades-person
- Educator
- Instructor
- Independent Skills Tutor
- Facilitator
- Tutor.

Why teachers might be reluctant to characterise themselves as a 'lecturer', despite the term being explicitly used on their contracts of employment and in their job title, intrigued and perplexed me: 'My job says that I am an academic lecturer, but I don't lecture in the way a HE tutor may lecture' reported one teacher. 'Because I teach students at lower level entry qualifications and do not deliver lectures' declared another. It became abundantly clear that few teachers viewed themselves as 'lecturers' unless they were teaching undergraduate programmes. Was this a contributing factor to them not perceiving themselves as professional teachers? It certainly appeared that teachers were creating identities which they felt more comfortable, familiar and agreeable with. What does all this have to do with observation you may ask? My response is straightforward, if teachers do not see themselves as teachers, or lecturers, does this affect their perception and engagement with the observation process? At this early juncture of my study it certainly appeared that vocational teachers were less troubled by observations than academic teachers. This may have been because their industry background had prepared them for being observed. Following on from this, I sought to capture teachers' opinions on being observed and subsequently graded, typically in the context of quality assurance and teacher training observations.

Grading

The grading of teachers, whether by numbers, letters or competency tick-boxes, is perhaps the most contentious of debates around lesson observation. As one teacher put it, 'I think it's the only profession ... who have to be put through this very, what I'd call, undignified process'.

But, what is it about grading that causes such contention? My research revealed discernible differences in opinion. Irma, who started teaching in 2000 and was what might be called an experienced observee said, 'Grading can make you feel insecure. It can make you question your own judgement. And it becomes very, very negative'. Whilst Lynn, who'd been teaching a similar length to Irma said, 'it can knock your confidence ... it reflects on that person, their grade ... It's very negative. It's just a waste of time people think. It's not valued'. Their views shared similarities to Cockburn's (2005) research, reporting that experienced teachers often associated being observed with 'early training and novice performance'. Consider then the views of Casey, a teacher who was undertaking initial teacher training at the time of my research: 'A number is quite critical, especially when you get a bad number', such echoing suggests that for experienced teachers, being observed does recreate negative feelings associated with their early career.

Some teachers, though against being observed, still liked being graded. This was particularly the case for those teachers who were graded favourably when observed and would often see the grade as a personal identifier, a badge to create what Ball (2003: 218) refers to as the 'triumphant self'. Teachers referred to their grading as giving them 'Something to mark against'. As Matt said, 'It gives you confidence that what you're doing is right ... it gives me a target to aim for'. Matt had been teaching for three years and had recently completed his final teacher training observation. On such observations, Matt said he would like to see them graded 'Because there are eight of them. Over the two years you'd see development'. Clearly Matt was using the number as a gauge, not only to affirm that he was doing things 'right' (at least as he perceived it), but that the gradings also showed him personal 'development' and improvement.

At the time of conducting my research, Matt had just received his first grade one (the highest grade), often juxtaposed with the adjective 'outstanding'. He was asked how he might feel if he were not graded a one next time: 'I'd be disappointed without a shadow of a doubt ... I'd think I'm obviously not doing something right'. In giving novice teachers grade ones, it can be argued that it communicates low expectations of instructional performance and leaves them no-where to develop. Matt, because of his grades, believed through just three years that he'd already reached his performance heights. For Matt, gradings had become synonymous with accuracy, precision and a sense of 'passing', views consistent with Marriott (2001). These points also affirm O'Leary's research (2011), that teachers use gradings as a far greater authority on their teaching than can really be the case, since they do not consider wider issues such as a teacher's experience and qualifications, nor indeed the complexity of the classrooms and contexts in which they are working.

If the views of Archie are taken into account, then grading scales also appear to have a detrimental effect: 'You set yourself standards and once you get a grade one you can't get any higher. The only way is down'. Archie had been teaching the longest of all interviewees. He continued with: 'I'd think the day I get a grade two I would be totally devastated, but you know it's going to happen sometime'. Evidently for Archie, receiving a 'good' grade two was not good enough, but he'd resigned himself to the fact that 'It's going to happen'. Was Archie a perfectionist? Or was he expressing something more entrenched? Later Archie referred to teachers being afraid of observation gradings because it's: 'The culture of this college. I think in some ways there's a fear culture ... but no-one ever does anything about it'. Archie's comments chime with Mather and Seifert's (2014: 105) findings who stated that 'lecturers were all well aware that failure to comply would trigger further management action'. Archie recalled a time he'd watched a programme about Ofsted inspections and a teacher being filmed:

> There was a school on TV ... there was a teacher who I remember who was really bolshie. He was arguing with the inspector saying "I haven't got a formal lesson plan; I don't need one. I get 100 percent pass rate in the exam what else do you want"? He was absolutely bolshie with the inspector and I thought that's brilliant why aren't I that guy? Why aren't I brave enough to do that?"

Archie saying 'Why aren't I that guy?' illustrates how subtle the coercion is to conform to lesson observations at managerial level. Archie sees his inability to challenge observation as a weakness in him rather than a systemic weakness. The impact of the grading structure and being observed for Archie was precisely as Wragg (1999: 103) suggested, that 'outstanding' observations, 'Can be such that even gifted teachers may pale at the thought of trying to achieve them'. It came as a surprise then that even though Archie was fearful, he still wanted to be graded:

> If I get good [observation] grades that provides me with a defence does it not? One could argue "Well you've seen me teach, so it's not me. You know I'm an excellent teacher". I believe in the concept of defence.

In effect, what Archie was saying was that he perceived the grading system as a form of personal insurance, security or 'defence' against any potential attack or questioning of his professional competence and ability as a teacher. If Archie could maintain a grade 1 profile, then as far as he was concerned, student failure or underachievement could not be attributed to his teaching. This was both revealing and depressing insomuch as it situated his conceptualization of the observation experience in a climate of fear and defensiveness, yet equally sought to separate the symbiotic relationship between teaching and learning.

What Archie and the other teachers failed to identify was the aspects of managerial control grading provokes. Foucault (1977) labelled one of the distinctive features of modern disciplinary control as 'normalizing judgement'. It sees individuals judged by their acts and ranked against others. In this case, a teacher cannot simply 'teach', but must attain a certain standard. A standard that is derived from an obsession with classifying, ordering and comparing. 'Normalizing judgement' is an extremely subtle, unassuming form of control, since whatever grading a teacher achieves it will always be bound with issues of 'abnormality' and what is perceived as 'acceptable'. Lynn correctly pointed out that, 'there aren't many professions that somebody slaps a number on you and tells you you're only as good as 1, 2, 3 or 4. I think that's what a lot of people find difficult'. Her comments echo what has long since been a well-known mantra popularised by the 1960s television programme *The Prisoner*, 'I am not a number'. Yet despite feeling uneasy about such practice, Lynn was at a loss as to how things might be done differently: 'I don't know what they can do in its place. It's the one thing that I have always felt is wrong, to grade somebody and to tell them that they can only be satisfactory'.

It is worth pointing out here that in 2012 Ofsted announced that the term 'satisfactory' was to be replaced with 'needs improvement'. This point was not lost on Eva:

> I think [grading] is really bad. Before, if you got a grade three, you felt fine about that; you would prefer better, but it was ok to get a three. Now it's not ok to get a three, it's like getting a grade four now, isn't it? Really, you're aiming for a two now … If somebody gets a three or four, all of a sudden they've no confidence. They don't want to go to lessons. They think they are failing their students.

Eva's comments suggested that a grade 3 or 4 were both deemed to be failing; both were perceived by teachers as underperforming grades, or in Foucault's (1977) concept of 'normalizing judgement', the difference between being a 'normal' or 'abnormal' teacher.

Watching and being watched

Whilst the subject of grading could extend far beyond these few paragraphs, the brevity of this chapter means I must now turn to another aspect of my research: the issue of watching. As introduced at the beginning of this chapter, classroom teachers are watched daily, similarly, teachers watch students. Watching, and being watched, is a natural and accepted part of a teacher's role. It can be argued that this acceptance is underpinned by differing power sources. One such source is the power of authority i.e. the authority teachers have over students. Despite being watched by students, a teacher's behaviour is broadly the same for each lesson. A teacher does not ordinarily change their behaviour just because students are watching them on say a Tuesday rather than a Wednesday; however, when it comes to being 'watched' in formal lesson observations, evidence suggests that teachers' behaviour does change.

It is well documented that the knowledge of being observed can bring about changes in behaviour. Such reactivity to being watched is sometimes referred to as the 'Hawthorne Effect'. The foundations of the Hawthorne Effect lie in the theory that when people, in their natural surroundings are aware of being observed, their behaviour alters. Since Roethlisberger and Dickson's original experiments at the Hawthorne manufacturing plant in 1927, the 'effect' has undergone much debate, most recently to argue whether it does in fact exist (Levitt and List 2011). An assumption of my study was that the Hawthorne Effect does exist and refers to the 'unintended effects that result from [being observed]' (Komblum 2012: 32). Furthering this thought, consideration was given as to whether teachers in my study were aware of any behavioural changes in themselves whilst being observed. Moreover, whether they consequently and purposefully altered their practices because of this. It was a comment by Robert that prompted such further exploration, '[Observation] is not a very good check as it's just staged mostly'. This idea of 'staging' a lesson intrigued me; surely teachers would not create lessons just for the purposes of being observed? Evidence from my interviews however confirmed this:

> Like everyone else I pull a lesson out of the hat that I wouldn't normally teach. We all have our own what we call 'sexy lesson', the one that ticks the boxes.

Others said:

> I tend to never sit down when I'm being observed, I move around. I don't know why … maybe physiologically it's expected … it's almost like being on a stage.
>
> It's a bit staged … You plan your lesson around an observation. I know there's certain people who do the same lesson every year whether they're teaching that subject or not.
>
> I don't know if I should be saying this. I think you change your session slightly for an observation than what you'd do normally'.
>
> There's some people that just have their observation lesson in place regardless of whether it is a spring, summer or autumn term, that lesson will be rolled out.

These teachers' accounts confirm that teachers do produce artificially staged, orchestrated lessons for the purposes of being observed. Their actions infer what others such as O'Leary (2014: 62) have found, that teachers view and react to observation as a 'mechanism of surveillance in the workplace'. Such surveillance parallels the ideas of Foucault who, in his notable work *Discipline and Punish* (1977) describes surveillance as a means of punishment and control.

Surveillance in colleges is not a new concept. Nestled in the corner of a corridor a camera can often be seen, its black rotating eye, protected by a dome of dusky plastic, silently surveys all that passes. Although it's becoming more prevalent, moving these cameras into college classrooms is not as yet commonplace. Instead, surveillance cameras are replaced by principals, managers, even governors. So, if it can be agreed that lesson observation is a mechanism of workplace surveillance, thought needs to be given as to who is conducting the surveillance if not the students or digital camera. What qualifies an observer to make a formalised judgement on a teacher? Should an observer have training? Hold certain knowledge based qualifications? Be a qualified and currently practicing teacher? Such questions circle the wrangling and bickering that surround the validity of lesson observations as a means of measuring teacher effectiveness.

As the interviews progressed, it became apparent that teachers did not have a clear picture of the skills, experience and training of their observers, though there was an assumption, as in O'Leary's study (2006), that observers were trained as one teacher commented, 'I'm sure they do don't they? I'm sure they have training. They have checklists of what they're looking for. Yes … definitely'.

To date, there are no formalised qualifications observers should hold. However, the work of Hatzipanagos and Lygo-Baker (2006: 6) found that teachers 'appeared to be concerned that observers might not have the right qualifications to assess teaching ability … [and that] those undertaking observation should have some qualification or training in Education'. Surprisingly, my interview data did not reflect these findings, indeed the opposite. Many teachers had not considered what prerequisite qualifications and training observers should have to observe them. But, why should they? When a doctor observes a patient there's an acceptance, an assumption by the patient that they're qualified and trained to do one's job. Similarly, my teachers assumed that observers would have 'appropriate qualifications' to undertake their role, as Dennis' response indicates: 'Obviously the full teaching qualification as that's what they're checking the quality of'. Matt likewise referred to teaching qualifications: 'I would have thought they take on some additional training, but most of their training is obviously from teaching'. Urma said:

> I'd hope that they have all achieved a grade one in their career to be able to judge me ... if you're not of that calibre then you shouldn't be doing it ... [They should] have taught for probably a minimum of five years before they have the privilege of observing.

It's interesting that Urma described observing as a 'privilege' indicating notions of regard for observers.

The 4Rs model

The teachers' voices in my study affirmed that teachers perceive, experience and engage with lesson observation in profoundly complex ways. It should be reiterated that only a snapshot of voices has been presented here. However, the richness of the full study allowed for a new way of thinking and for me to formulate a unique model for managing, conducting and understanding lesson observations to emerge, what I coined as the '4Rs model'.

The model charts teachers' observation career journeys through a series of transitional stages. The current 'one-size-fits-all' approach to lesson observation has been voiced by teachers as fractured and not fit for purpose. It's blanketed by negativity and over time has resulted in a system that has brought a weakening of teachers' perceptions of self-identity; discouragements from self-growth and frustrated responses to being part of a community where they feel silenced and more often from which they feel disengaged. Teachers' current compliance with observation is misconstrued by those in power as rational behaviour towards a system they support and see relevant.

My 4Rs model presented in Figure 5.1 fosters a more positive experience of being observed, a more committed engagement from teachers and a more developmentally, supportive, learning focused approach. Each 'R' in the model represents a stage in a teacher's response to being observed: *Readiness, Receptive, Reactive* and *Reluctant Realist*.

Stage 1 represents the *Readiness Stage*. Here FE teachers are at the pre-teacher training phase of their career, though some may have partial teaching qualifications. Teachers here are concerned with whether they are 'doing things right'. They seek clarification of their novice practices and are ready to learn, particularly from more experienced, qualified teachers whom they should have opportunities to peer observe. Being observed is exceedingly stressful for Stage 1 teachers so an observation should not exceed 30 minutes, nor should it be graded since it communicates unrealistic expectations. Instead, observations should focus on the teaching basics such as did the teacher take a register? Are students safe in the classroom? Teachers in this stage may describe themselves as 'accidental teachers' often coming to FE from a career in industry. Their eagerness to learn needs to recognise that they are at a

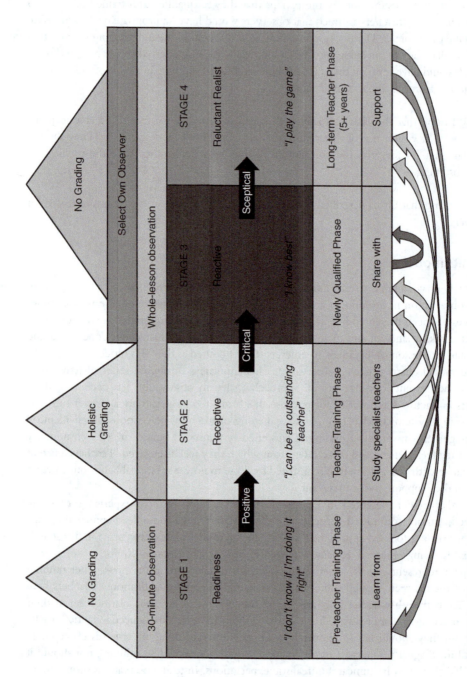

FIGURE 5.1 The 4Rs model.

cross-over in their professional identity as a teacher and therefore observations should serve as a supportive opportunity to lay the foundations of what it means to be a professional teacher in the FE sector.

Stage 2 of the model, the *Receptive Stage*, is used as teachers enrol onto full teacher training programmes. Here it's probable that teachers will engage with more observations than at any other time in their career. Teachers are in this 'receptive' phase so long as the aims and objectives of differing observations are clearly articulated. They're eager to learn and swiftly develop feelings of self-actualisation: 'I can be an outstanding teacher'. My research showed that some teachers in this stage liked to be graded as they use it as a marker of their continued improvement, though it has to be acknowledge that wider evidence can contradict this (e.g. O'Leary 2013). A further recommendation is that whole lessons are observed as trainee teachers like to showcase their entire lesson. Like their Stage 1 colleagues, Stage 2 teachers are eager to learn from specialist experienced teachers and should have the opportunity to peer observe them.

Stage 3: *The Reactive Stage* is reached once a teacher has achieved their full teaching qualification. Post-teacher training sees the start of teachers 'reacting' to the conditions being placed on them through observation. Stage 3 teachers begin to manipulate the different observation systems' requirements, though remain compliant, on an external level to all demands placed on them. They display emotions that reinforce the idea that teachers know what good teaching is, so to be told otherwise produces strong emotions.

As Stage 3 teachers transition into Stage 4 they become exceedingly sceptical towards observation. Teachers are aware that being observed creates behavioural factors, which in turn inhibit their instincts to act as professionals as they see them. They recognise that the sophisticated nature of managerial power structures leaves limited room for agency. Stage 3 teachers require room to experiment with their new found professional status and the feelings associated with being qualified to do one's job. Having achieved their teaching qualification, they are beginning to feel part of a professional teaching community as they see it. Therefore, Stage 3 teachers should have opportunities to peer observe other Stage 3 teachers, to build on shared commonalities and responsibilities that they may otherwise lose. It was found that Stage 3 teachers do not appear overly concerned with developing their practice through peer observation, possibly because they feel that since they are already qualified, they 'know best'. Failure to peer observe teachers outside their teaching trade or academic discipline can fuel a 'them and us' culture, those that teach vocational trades and those that teach academic subjects. Therefore, peer observation has to be presented as a tool for fostering peer relationships and building a wider supportive community of practice of teacher learning.

Stage 3 teachers disagree with current systems of being graded. A commonly cited objection to such practice is the notion of being 'badged' or 'labelled'. Again, teachers in Stage 3 feel that because they are qualified to teach, their qualification should stand as a measure of their effectiveness. My study found that grading Stage 3, and Stage 4, teachers predominantly communicates issues of low trust and feelings of having to 'perform'.

Like their Stage 2 colleagues, when Stage 3 teachers are formally observed, they would prefer the whole lesson to be observed. Moreover, it's important for these teachers that their observer focuses not only on them, but takes an active interest in their students too. It's crucial to Stage 3 teachers that, should they be graded, they can choose their observer. Stage 3 teachers believe this approach would strengthen the validity of observations, providing observer choice fosters a sense of professional peer colleague respect, as respect for observers is often missing at this stage. For Stage 3 teachers, observers need to be current practitioners that are knowledgeable, in particular, about aspects of professional developments in education. Observers must be able to give specific feedback since the quality of feedback is a fundamental factor in Stage 3 teachers' acceptance and engagement with being observed. Further still, it supports their association with observation being a contributory tool for professional development.

Stage 4: *The Reluctant Realist* is the final characteristic stage for an FE teacher. It is typically reached three years after qualifying. At this stage of their career, teachers are reluctant to engage with observation since they've seen little or no tangible reward to engage. However, they are 'realists' in terms of their compliance with the systems recognising wider negative implications should they not comply, particularly in relation to the possibility of losing their job. As teachers' move from Stages 3 to 4 they become increasingly sceptical towards observation. They feel that their only autonomy comes in the shape of how much they choose to share with their observer and what aspects of their teaching they wish to embellish, denude or disguise. Outwardly, Stage 4 teachers appear to operate in Foucault's (1977) terms as 'docile-bodies', subservient to the micro-management power systems that control them being observed. In real terms, their experience allows them sufficient knowledge of observations to, in their words, 'play the game'. Although Stage 4 teachers do not want to be observed, it is known that teachers in this stage often possess what they call 'observation lessons'. Lessons that they fall back on when they are being observed, or as O'Leary (2014: 34) calls them 'rehearsed' or 'showcase lesson[s]'.

Stage 4 teachers no longer perceive observation as an opportunity for them to develop professionally. Part of this comes from, like their Stage 3 colleagues, a desire to choose their own observer. My study illustrated that all too often long-term teachers felt observers were overly critical and negatively judgemental towards their teaching. Being able to choose their observer would be seen as a positive step for Stage 4 teachers in any acceptance of being observed. Furthermore, they are particularly eager to select a subject specialist which in turn they hope would encourage more meaningful feedback and a relationship built on mutual respect. Like their Stage 3 colleagues, Stage 4 teachers generally don't want to be graded, it makes them feel inferior and weakens their perceived professional identity. Stage 4 teachers would prefer to engage in a professional dialogue about their practice with a colleague they respect and trust; however, sufficient time must be allocated to foster meaningful discussion rather than a one-way subjective critique of their practice.

Stage 4 teachers desire recognition for their long-term practice, education and achievements, though are undecided about what form this should take. They feel that they are beyond the novice Stage 1 of their career and it's their professional right to be treated accordingly. Again, they see no tangible reward for being observed or graded and will only ever 'play the game'. It was found that Stage 4 teachers firmly organise themselves into distinct communities of practice, determined by their teaching specialism and longevity of service. This was found to be a contributing factor to their often purposeful avoidance of peer observation. Such avoidance means that they do not foster valuable, mentoring style relationships with other lower stage members that would enable them 'to learn from each other' (Wenger, 2006).

Stage 4 teachers describe themselves as 'professionals' due to their longevity in service, though fail to see relationships between being a professional and the subsequent earned right to act with autonomy void of subjective observational judgements. Teachers feel confident in their abilities, and status as a teacher to make judgements about their teaching and not to be under continuous observation scrutiny for the purposes of measuring their 'effectiveness'. Outwardly, it appears that Stage 4 teachers remain compliant to observation requirements, but this is because they currently see no other way forward.

Conclusion

The 4Rs model suggests that it is time to put to bed all defective, tiresome, one-size-fits-all forms of lesson observation and move our thinking on. Teaching is about experiences. To make sense and learn from experience requires one to retell, reshape and readjust it in one's mind. Furthermore, to experience teaching requires sharing teaching. Sharing with other teachers in a culture that supports and fosters curious minds. A culture that celebrates and nurtures success rather than spews toxic criticisms. The 4Rs model proposed here is not the solution, nor does it claim to be, however, it is a step forward. A step forward in a new direction that is firmly grounded in FE teachers' voices. It is time to transform observation from being a burr on the creative landscape, an irritant that causes distress, anxiety and disillusion. Observing teachers is not akin to observing nature. In observing teachers, we are dealing with human emotions, human feelings, human beings. Observation must move from being a system of self-preservation to a system of self-actualisation underpinned by the realisation that teachers are trusted professionals.

References

Ball, S. (2003) 'The Teacher's Soul and the Terrors of Performativity'. *Journal of Education Policy*, 18(2), 215–228.

Cockburn, J. (2005) 'Perspectives and Politics of Classroom Observation'. *Research in Post-Compulsory Education*, 10(3), 373–388.

Cullingford, C. (ed.) (1999) *An Inspector Calls: Ofsted and its effect on school standards.* London: Kogan Page Limited.

Foucault, M. (1977) *Discipline and Punish: The birth of the prison.* London: Penguin.

Furlong, J., Barton, L., Miles, S., Whiting, C. and Whitty, G. (2000) *Teacher Education In Transition: Re-forming professionalism?* Buckingham: Open University Press.

Gage, N. L. (1978) *The Scientific Basis of the Art of Teaching.* New York: Teachers College Press.

Gleeson, D., Davies, J. and Wheeler, E. (2005) 'On the Making and Taking of Professionalism in the Further Education (FE) Workforce'. *British Journal of Sociology of Education*, 26(4), 445–460.

Gosling, D. (2002) *Models of Peer Observation of Teaching.* York: LTSN Generic Centre Learning and Teaching Support Network: The Higher Education Academy.

Grubb, W. N. (2000) 'Opening Classrooms and Improving Teaching: Lessons from school inspectors in England'. *Teachers College Record*, 102(4), 696–723.

Hatzipanagos, S. and Lygo-Baker, S. (2006) 'Teaching Observations: Promoting development through critical reflection'. *Journal of Further and Higher Education*, 30(4), 421–431.

Komblum, W. (2012) *Sociology in a Changing World.* Belmont: Wadsworth.

Levitt, S. and List, J. (2011) 'Was There Really a Hawthorne Effect at the Hawthorne Plant? An analysis of the original illumination experiments'. *American Economic Journal: Applied Economics*, 3(1), 224–238.

Marriott, G. (2001) *Observing Teachers at Work.* Oxford: Heinemann Educational Publishers.

Mather, K. and Seifert, R. (2014) 'The Close Supervision of Further Education Lecturers: "You have been weighed, measured and found wanting"'. *Work, Employment and Society*, 28(1), 95–111.

Montgomery, D. (1999) *Positive Teacher Appraisal through Classroom Observation.* London: David Fulton Publishers Ltd.

O'Leary, M. (2006) 'Can Inspectors Really Improve the Quality of Teaching In the PCE Sector? Classroom observations under the microscope'. *Research in Post-Compulsory Education*, 11(2), 191–198.

O'Leary, M. (2011) *The Role of Lesson Observation in Shaping Professional Identity, Learning and Development in Further Education Colleges in the West Midlands*. PhD. University of Warwick: Institute of Education.

O'Leary, M. (2013) *Developing a National Framework for the Effective Use of Lesson Observation in Further Education*. Project report for the University and College Union, November 2013. DOI: 10.13140/RG.2.1.1751.7286. Available at: www.ucu.org.uk/media/6714/Developing-a-national-framework-for-the-effective-use-of-lesson-observation-in-FE-Dr-Matt-OLeary-Nov-13/pdf/ucu_lessonobsproject_nov13.pdf.

O'Leary, M. (2014) *Classroom Observation: A guide to the effective observation of teaching and learning*. London: Routledge.

Shortland, S. (2004) 'Peer Observation: A tool for staff development or compliance?' *Journal of Further and Higher Education*, 28(2), 219–228.

Wenger, E. (2006) *Communities of Practice: A brief introduction*. Available from www.ewenger.com. Last accessed 21 January 2013.

Wragg, E. C. (1999) *An Introduction to Classroom Observation*. 2nd edition. London: Routledge.

6

EXAMINING LESSON OBSERVATION FEEDBACK

Victoria Wright

Introduction

I am a Senior Lecturer in Post-Compulsory Education (PCE) at the University of Wolverhampton. In this chapter, I share some of my research in to my experiences of being a tutor observer on the Post-Graduate Certificate in Post-Compulsory Education course. First, I contextualize my research by explaining the nature of that course and my role within it. I then outline key milestones in my career in order to introduce my strong personal motivation for exploring my research focus. That focus is lesson observation feedback on the teacher education course (PGCE in PCE).

I share some of my past experiences of giving observation feedback, in a quality assurance role (grading lessons in further education colleges as part of an internal quality team) and in teacher education. This is in line with autoethnography where autobiography and ethnography form the core approaches (Ellis *et al.* 2011). Autoethnography is defined as an approach to research and writing that seeks to describe and systematically analyse (*graphy*) personal experience (*auto*) in order to understand cultural experience (*ethno*) (Holman-Jones 2005). I am a participant in the culture I describe and I consciously share some of my experiences ('auto') that resonate with and describe the culture ('ethno') of the research i.e. lesson observation feedback in further education and on a higher education course.

In this chapter, I share some of my autobiography including my initial training as a quality observer, a synthesised account of giving graded observation feedback, and a dramatised narrative relating to preparing for an inspection. In order to problematise some of the power dynamics and complexity of giving observation feedback, I also draw on cultural historical activity theory, on Copland's research in to English Language Teacher Education triadic feedback (where peers feedback alongside the assessor), and on specific data sets (student focus groups, my tutor observation feedback and peer observation feedback where students gave feedback to each other). In the conclusion, I share some suggestions for both observers and observees in negotiating and managing observation feedback.

Contextualising the PGCE in PCE course

The post-graduate course (the PGCE in PCE or Post-Graduate Certificate in Post-Compulsory Education course) is one year and full time. It leads to a teacher education qualification for students (primarily) wanting to work in the Lifelong learning sector, UK. The Lifelong learning sector comprises a range of provision i.e. work-based learning, further education (FE) colleges, sixth form colleges, adult and community education settings and prisons.

After the students have completed the course, and once they get a teaching post, they can then apply for Qualified Teaching and Learning Status. The status QTLS (Qualified Teaching and Learning Status) is much more recent than QTS (the school teacher Qualified Teacher Status). It was part of historical developments linked to aspirations such as greater flexibility for college lecturers to cross over in to schools posts and greater parity of pay and esteem across the compulsory and post-compulsory education sectors. When I completed my teacher education course, I, like my PGCE in PCE students, did a course specifically for post-compulsory education rather than school teaching. At that time (about 15 or so years ago), there was no such thing as QTLS. Once you finished the course, you were fully qualified. It was also only in 2012 that 'the professional status of Qualified Teacher Learning and Skills (QTLS) became recognised as equal to Qualified Teacher Status (QTS) for teaching in schools' (Institute for Learning 2012: 7).

My role as tutor observer on the PGCE in PCE

A central feature of the course is the teaching experience the students complete in a Lifelong learning setting. Students are supported by a mentor in the institution i.e. a subject specialist lecturer in the provider in which they are placed. They are also supported through the course itself (at the university) and very particularly through their personal tutor.

Each year I am a personal tutor and therefore have particular responsibility for one group of students within the cohort. That role involves a number of priorities. I teach module content which I also assess. I visit the students on their teaching placements (in the institutions in which they are placed) and I record lesson observations of them. Lesson observations by myself as university tutor and by their subject specialist mentors are either passed or failed (with a limited number of opportunities to retake a failed observation). This is a very important part of the students' overall success. Personal tutors also have a pastoral role. Students have diverse previous and current experiences: they might have just completed a degree or master's degree at university, they might have already had substantial work and/or teaching experience, they might have children and/or other particular personal commitments. The role of personal tutor is therefore relatively complex including the work of module tutor, personal/pastoral tutor, assessor and observer.

In the research shared here, I focus on my work as an observer of a group of students for whom I am also personal tutor. Something I was keen to consider was how my previous experiences of observing lessons and also of having been observed myself might be influencing the ways in which I conducted observations of my student group. In the following section, I therefore include some key milestones in my career.

My professional journey

After I completed my PGCE (for post-compulsory education), I worked in various FE colleges before joining the university. I taught mainly on English programmes and then later in teacher education. It was while I was an English lecturer that I took on a temporary role working as part of a college's quality assurance team. The role was within my own department and included conducting graded (echoing Ofsted) lesson observations of fellow lecturers (see, for example, O'Leary 2013). Shortly after that temporary quality role, I moved into teacher education and literacy/English teacher education. I was then observing lessons of (typically) experienced lecturers as part of their successful completion of their teacher education qualification.

My next post was in a different FE college and was a dual role. It was a teacher educator post that also included a department specific quality assurance role. Similar to my previous experience, it included conducting graded lesson observations within the department and across college. In my time as observer, I have therefore assessed experienced staff and student teachers, some of whom were already employed in the role of teacher.

When I was interviewed for my current job at the university, I was asked what I would like to research. Having been a college lecturer since I finished my teacher education qualification, no one had asked me that before. Any previous interviewers wanted to know how I managed and motivated the learners, what the extent of my subject knowledge was and what different courses I had taught on. In later interviews, they wanted to know what my impact was so they asked me about performance data. If you are a teacher you will know exactly what I mean. How many learners did I retain? How many of them achieved? What did they achieve? What responsibilities had I taken on? What was my own observation record?

When asked what I wanted to research, I could only answer hesitantly. At that time, I couldn't anticipate any of the details of my then future research. I only knew that I wanted to look at lesson observation feedback. I had become increasingly uncomfortable with the different roles I had played in that dialogue. I had observed as part of colleges' quality assurance processes and as part of delivering on teacher education programmes. As a member of teaching staff, I was also of course observed myself. I was struggling increasingly, and I felt morally, with the way in which observation feedback was given to me and the way in which I also gave observation feedback to others.

Including my own experiences was important as I wanted to see how my past expectations and practices as an observer informed my current role as tutor observer. I would echo Denzin's (2006: 334) view that in writing retrospectively: 'I insert myself into the past and create the conditions for rewriting and hence re-experiencing it'. For instance, I remembered my first experience of being trained for a new quality role (whilst continuing to be a subject lecturer):

> I came to the role of the observer aware of a recent past experience of being observed and being told how difficult it was to get a grade 1. I also remember having an uneasy feeling that if I gave a grade 1, it would be very noticeable to other observers and would really have to be justified. How would I justify the grade without revealing a personal bias? And when observing in my own department, how would I be able to identify colleagues in this way? I was thus very hesitant to award it. I knew a grade 1 had to be something out of the ordinary, something different, perhaps it even amounted to a feeling I had that everything was going well. I trusted that I would know it when I saw it. As if it would be a eureka moment.

Writing that reminded me of the subjectivity of giving grades and the tensions I had experienced. When I started my research, I was concerned that I was applying a particular structure

I had drawn on in graded lesson observation feedback. Concerns I had included: making a graded judgement on an isolated lesson, recognising that I didn't always know the lecturers I observed and acknowledging that while I wanted to make it more dialogic, I had already confirmed the grade and written up the report. One example is included below:

> I start to critique the lesson practice and already I'm thinking remember that praise sandwich. Start positive, put the crunchy difficult stuff in the middle. I retreat not only in to the language but also in to the structure. Clichéd phrases: 'maximising opportunities' (as in you didn't and you need to), 'supporting all learners to achieve' (where was your differentiation?), 'using a range of methods' (it was dull) etcetera. It's becoming a school report where subtext is key. I write it as if it's for someone else, an auditor, an Ofsted Inspector, a Quality manager. Checking back. Yes, I've filled out all of the boxes. Yes, I saw them for an hour. Yes, I've written in full sentences. Yes, the action points are identified and they are bullet pointed and yes they are SMART – well from one perspective anyway.

Issues of power in observation feedback practices

While part of my research is introspective as it focuses on my practice as a tutor observer, it also looks outwards to the political context of which lesson observation and observation feedback are a part. I wanted to explore issues of power between the observer, the observee and the context in which the observation took place. I had often felt 'parachuted in' in my previous roles as quality observer in colleges. I didn't always know the teachers I observed, I hadn't met their students or taught in their subject areas. Re-writing some of my past experiences contextualised observation feedback as messy and complex. One of my ongoing reflections was around the extent to which and the ways in which I work within 'relations of power' (Foucault 2003a: 34) i.e. the context my PGCE PCE student is in, their expectations, the class they're teaching, their mentor's expectations, the political context we work within, the stakeholders.

As you read this chapter, you will realise that I do not present a model of how to give observation feedback more effectively. I seek instead to share some of the complexity of that dialogue with fellow observers and teachers. As Foucault (2003b: 172) says: 'As soon as people begin to have trouble thinking things the way they have been thought, transformation becomes at the same time very urgent, very difficult, and entirely possible'. I was interested in the different influences, not just of the assessment criteria I was using, but also of my own experiences of being a teacher, of being observed, of being the observer and my sense of Ofsted/external inspection expectations. In the extract below, I share some of my sense of the impact of an inspection on a teacher's practice.

Announcement of a college inspection

> The announcement makes us move more quickly. Even the carpet in the Principal's corridor can't dull the thud, thud, run of our footsteps. There are loud discussions in open spaces and whispered ones by the photocopiers and the kettles. There are boxes of files in offices and under desks. There are shared areas growing on our computers. (Even the pot plants have been dusted).

The students know. We've drilled them. Remember what we did with you in the first few weeks? How we made you feel welcome and found out all about you? Remember all the policies we told you about? And who to go to for help? And what a range of experiences you have had with us since! Now will you remember when you're asked?

In class we're practising over-zealous reinforcement. Oh no, you're horribly late! It's one minute past by my watch. Ooh that's fabulous Ryan! I think that should go on the wall. Now everyone, let's stop a minute, gather our thoughts, check those outcomes. See them there, displayed on the board? And on the wall? And on your handout sheet? So, what is it we're enjoying learning about today? Everybody take a turn. No, it doesn't matter if you start to repeat.

I was also interested in how the observation feedback dialogue provided an insight into ideas of what constitutes an 'effective' teacher (implied in the extract above). I acknowledged the goal of observation feedback to be variously: to give feedback and agree actions, to improve the teaching of the student teacher, and to support them becoming effective teachers. In my research I became increasingly critical of my dominance as observer. I will now share selected excerpts from empirical data sets to exemplify.

Giving observation feedback

Having conducted quality assurance graded and explicitly developmental teacher education observations, I wanted to see the mediation of power in my feedback dialogues and to improve my practice. In looking at my own feedback, I paid particular attention to my dominance as observer, to the balance between the sharing of my knowledge and experience and the opportunities given to students to express their reflections. Looking at a tutor observation feedback report from 2012–13, I identified high order questions i.e. 'You said about differentiated questioning to what extent do you think you actually achieved it?' I saw that I was asking some closed questions that I became critical of, such as 'Would that have been worthwhile to do that with them?' In another tutor observation feedback report from 2012–13, I again saw that at times I asked very focused questions with no or little pause for the student's response. I had asked the student if the way in which they had grouped their students had worked. I wanted their opinion on whether or not all students had discussed with each other. I followed this point up by asking 'How could you make sure they did talk? How could you support all of the groups actually … but how could you support all of them in participating more actively as individuals? What could you do?' Looking at such instances made me more mindful of times when I might have stopped the student sharing their reflections. My analysis echoed Copland's (2008a: 8) suggestion that:

> The Questioning Phase is perhaps the most peripatetic of the phases. It is only performed by trainers and can interrupt self-evaluation and peer feedback as well as being embedded in trainer feedback and the Summary Phase.

Copland (ibid) has written extensively on observation feedback in the context of English Language Teacher Education. She explores the idea that the feedback dialogue is a distinct genre with 'conventionalised expectations that members of a social group or network use to

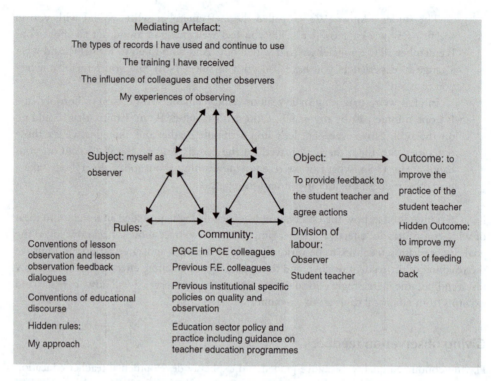

FIGURE 6.1 Observation feedback activity triangle.

shape and construe the communicative activity they are engaged in'. I drew on Engeström's description and emerging application of activity theory (1987, Central Activity system, Figure 2.7, chapter 2, online) as a theoretical lens through which to explore the tutor observation feedback dialogue (on the PGCE PCE) as a genre: Figure 6.1. The Figure is explained through a key and description.

Key to Figure 6.1

Subject: the focus is on myself as tutor observer.

Mediating Artefact: as described I have observed in different contexts and used different institutional paperwork. At times I have shadowed or moderated other observers. I have also been observed as a teacher. I could add the following: the university assessment criteria, my own personal sense of what constitutes an effective teacher and my language choices. Copland (2008b: 9) notes that:

> Language is the key resource in the feedback event. Trainers in particular use their language resources to represent their positions and ensure that the feedback event proceeds smoothly and that trainees learn from the experience.

Rules: I highlighted this as I started to think about my particular sets of expectations and knowledge of observation feedback conventions.

Community: I drew broadly in order to indicate the influence of the various communities to which I belong.

Division of labour: in this depiction, I recognised that while there are two roles in observation feedback, I am an experienced observer and I have accumulated particular expectations and approaches.

Object: at its simplest, the dialogue provides feedback and triggers action points for the student to work on for their next observation.

Outcomes: the main focus is to improve the practice of the student teacher. I could also add that in teacher education we work to facilitate the students own reflective practices. For myself, I recorded a 'Hidden Outcome' to look at my feedback in order to improve it.

I held two focus groups with volunteers from my tutor groups in 2011–12 and 2012–13 in order to gain some insight in to the student teachers' own perspectives of observation and feedback practices. In each case, I asked the following questions:

- What is the purpose of lesson observations?
- What are we (tutor/mentor/peer) looking for when we observe?
- What is the purpose of the feedback dialogue?
- What is the role of the observer in the feedback dialogue?
- What is the role of the observee in the feedback dialogue?
- How are the actions identified?

One of the students (PGCE cohort 2011–12) was particularly clear in identifying what observers look for:

> The delivery, the presentation, the knowledge displayed by the tutor that you're observing you probably want to look at how successful, how appropriate, how activities are being implemented and carried out, how you are making a connection with students, are they being engaged with the learning a whole range of things.

This was a strong student, in Semester Two, who was carefully indicating some of the complexities of the observation process.

All of the students (Semester Two, 2011–12) had had a number of lesson observations by this point. When asked about the purpose of the feedback dialogue, the first student to respond stated: 'basically it pulls out the points that you need to work on'. They saw the dialogue as explicitly dyadic saying that 'it does allow two points of view to be incorporated which is good'. The next student drew attention to the fact that 'a good mentor will always ask you, what you thought first before actually planting thoughts'.

Listening to the focus group, I was interested that the students explicitly commented: 'if they ask you first and you give your feedback it's not such a like blow then', 'you can actually get your original [...] true opinion of what or how it went'. The discussion developed to identify the role of the observer as telling you something you might have missed. There was also mention of negotiation on action points with the observer seen as helping to identify important points.

In another focus group (Semester One, 2012–13) and before a few students had been formally observed, the feedback dialogue was represented as identifying what went wrong and giving key points to work on. It wasn't explicitly linked to acknowledging their strengths though it appeared to be regarded in a positive light. That group placed considerable emphasis on the emotional dimension of observation feedback. One student commented: 'a dialogue has more emotional feelings than a written observation'. Another student added to this: 'you get the tone of the voice and the body language … like they're trying to understand what you're trying to say, you can tell whether they agree or not and so you can use that'. There was a sense that they could clarify their decisions. Another student reflected: 'the value of it is the fact that someone's taken their time out to sit with you and tell you, you feel more appreciative'.

Across the focus group data, the observer was identified as leaving feedback, giving advice and providing a more experienced perspective. When I looked at my tutor observation feedback, I became critical of the extent to which the feedback was in fact dyadic. I had hoped to see a more 'dialogic' and 'co-constructed' approach (Copland and Mann 2010, in Cirocki *et al.* 2010: 21) i.e. a dialogue in which power was more sensitively mediated. However, I lead as the observer and saw that I asked a lot of questions. I have already identified hyper questioning i.e. asking too many questions too quickly. I positioned myself as more experienced by using jargon and giving detailed and explicit advice. I was critical at times of the balance I achieved between talking about the strengths of the lesson and indicating the next steps. In one dialogue, I reflected: 'seems as if I say a strength which also has an area of development in it' (echoing Montgomery 2002: 55). As a class teacher, I use praise to acknowledge strengths. In the observation feedback dialogues however, I was sometimes late to identify strengths. That surprised me. I was also uncomfortable at times in seeing the extent to which some of those strengths might be quickly subsumed by the next steps.

In another dialogue in 2012–13, I had prompted the student to 'think about the follow up questions so you ask them a question you get an answer, think about the strength of that answer, think about how you can push them that little bit further'. In my memo I queried whether I was setting myself up as the perfect teacher. Wragg (1994: 64) advises the observer to be mindful of two likely tendencies – to present themselves as an ideal 'imagin(ing) themselves teaching flawlessly the class they are observing, forgetting their own errors and infelicities' and 'compensat(ing) for their own deficiencies, that is to feel they must correct particularly strongly any aspect in which they are themselves weak'.

In my research, I also compared my tutor observation feedback to peer observation feedback where students gave feedback to each other. I had collected two dialogues in 2010–11 as part of a pilot project. That early analysis informed the questions I asked in the focus groups. I returned to those dialogues after having analysed my tutor observation feedback dialogues. I compared both those two peer dialogues and a third, collected in 2012–13, with my ways of giving observation feedback. The three sets of pairs (peers) had willingly volunteered to record their feedback and paired themselves up. I was struck by a number of differences. There were very few questions, and certainly no questions used to elicit reflections. The peer observation dialogues did at times reflect modelling (Peer Observations 1 and 3) and offering suggestions. Observers were more likely to focus on strengths and to keep to the order of items in the written lesson observation form. The observer was still more dominant (inevitably leading the dialogue) but peers were clearly actively learning from each other by readily sharing their practice. One pair started to compare notes on their ways of dealing with latecomers for instance and another pair referred to ways of working with a support worker in the class. There was shared 'teacher'/ 'teacher education' vocabulary and expectations, such as I might employ in my feedback.

I saw the following as significantly different: their use of questioning which at times was a point of reassurance for the observer i.e. 'are you happy with the things I've said?', the lack of eliciting strategies, and the translation of the dialogue into a 'learning conversation' (by which I mean the sharing of related experience). Interestingly, two observers lead the nego-tiation of actions, something I noted that I did in all of the observation feedback dialogues I sampled. In all three dialogues, there remained a natural hesitancy about directly critiquing practice. In each case, their positive relationship with each other came through. This was something that I also thought was reflected in the way in which their dialogues moved beyond the scope of the assessment criteria to more directly share their own concerns (e.g. about lateness, and about working with a support worker). I saw a difference between their reflection with their peer and their reflection with me. I was pleased to see that they sought to share practice. It seemed a natural characteristic of the peer lesson observation feedback. It is perhaps captured by Copland's term 'dialogic' (2008a) where students are more active and equal participants.

In looking ongoing at my tutor observation feedback dialogues, I gave myself areas for development. One of those was to minimise the use of closed questions and to reflect on the use of follow-up questions. A key point was to continue to monitor the extent to which the student had a chance to reflect for themselves. This was something that I high-lighted in Figure 6.1. Although the division of labour shows that there are two roles in the dialogue, I was critical of the level to which I opened up that dialogue to the students. Something I would like to consider in the future is the extent to which and the ways in which I might modify my feedback i.e. opening up more spaces for the student's reflec-tions as I continue to observe them over the time of the course. This is something I explain in the conclusion.

Conclusion

At the heart of my research was a strong personal motivation to see my role in the observation feedback dialogue more clearly and to think through the power dynamics and broader con-text of that feedback more carefully. In selecting past experiences, I saw that I was identifying my own shift from being a quality assurance observer conducting graded lesson observations to becoming a teacher educator observer conducting strictly developmental observations. Rather than giving a judgement on one lesson at that time, I was now building a relationship with a student teacher and monitoring and working with them throughout their time on the course. I recognised that I have a powerful role, something that was revealed in the connec-tions students made (in the focus groups) between observation feedback and their reflective practice and action planning. The research reiterates the importance of looking at observa-tion feedback in the context in which it occurs. Student teachers work within a variety of expectations: their own, their mentors' and other colleagues', the placement setting they are working within, and the university's own requirements (its assessment criteria for the course). Rather than reducing observation feedback to one model, as observers and teachers, we have to critically engage with our practices ongoing.

In looking at my practice, I echoed Copland's (2008a) identification of a 'genre', though her context is English Language Teacher Education triadic feedback. My teacher education feedback dialogues start by reviewing action points from previous observations and end by agreeing to the action points for next time. Observation is a common method of making judgements on teaching and learning. As a teacher educator, I am mindful of supporting students in becoming flexible class teachers and also in participating in internal and external quality assurance processes. It is important that student teachers learn to situate themselves actively in that discourse. For myself as teacher educator, I will continue to monitor the level to which I facilitate the students' own reflections. As Martin (1995: 8–12) suggests, as the students 'mature' over the time of the course, so I as observer need to adapt my approach. There is a balance to strike between advising (or telling) and eliciting their reflections.

I do not present a model of how to give observation feedback. I hope instead to have illustrated Foucault's (2001: 236) view: 'what we need to know are relations: the subject's relations with everything around him'. In looking at my practice, I have seen those 'relations' (ibid) more clearly. By relations, I refer to the context in which the observation takes place. I would include the relationship between student teacher and observer as captured subjectively here in a poem:

> My relationship with my students
> Humanistic, personal, intuitive,
> surprisingly emotional.
>
> I'm ahead of you
> but I'm also alongside you,
> working with you,
> standing by you.
>
> A way marker,
> I mark your progress.
> You have come this far.
> (I indicate how far with my hands).
>
> I am also the gatekeeper.
> I will stop you if I have to.
> Those dreaded words–
> this observation is a fail.
>
> I'm also your champion.
> I carry your flag.
> I say who you are,
> And who you might become?

The research reinforced the need for me (and other teacher educators) to remember what stage the student is at and thereby move to more 'dialogic' (Copland and Mann, 2010, in Cirocki *et al.* 2010: 21) talk. As teacher educator, I am now much more conscious of allowing the student the opportunity to voice their views on the lesson. That includes thinking about when and how I ask questions, how and to what extent I advise, how actions are agreed, and; underpinning all of those points, reflecting on their perceived needs including the stage they are at in their development. I hope to have shown how important it is not to present isolated (context free) models or checklists of future observation and feedback practices. In sharing some of my experiences I also hope to prompt your exploration of the ways in which your past experiences inform your current practices.

References

Cirocki, A., Park, G. and Widodo, H. (2010) *Observation of Teaching: Bridging theory and practice through research on teaching.* München, Germany: LINCOM Europa, 175–194.

Copland, F. (2008a) *Feedback in Pre-Service English Language Teacher Training: Discourses of process and power.* Unpublished PhD thesis, University of Birmingham.

Copland, F. (2008b) 'Deconstructing the Discourse: Understanding the feedback event'. In Garton, S. and Richards, K. (eds.) *Professional Encounters in TESOL,* London: Palgrave, 1–11.

Copland, F. and Mann, S. (2010) 'Dialogic Talk in the Post-Observation Conference: An investment for reflection'. In Cirocki, A., Park, G. and Widodo, H. (eds.) *Observation of Teaching: Bridging theory and practice through research on teaching.* München, Germany: LINCOM Europa, 175–194.

Copland, F., Ma, G. and Mann, S. (2009) 'Reflecting in and on Post-Observation Feedback in Initial Teacher Training on Certificate Courses'. *ELTED,* 12, 14–23.

Denzin, N. (2006) 'Pedagogy, Performance and Autoethnography'. *Text and Performance Quarterly,* 26(4), 333–338.

Ellis, C., Adams, T. and Bochner, A. (2011) 'Autoethnography: An overview. Available (online) at *Forum Qualitative Social Research,* 12(1): www.qualitative-research.net/index.php/fqs/article/view/1589/3095. Last accessed 21 June 2014.

Engeström, Y. (1987) *Learning By Expanding. An activity-theoretical approach to developmental research.* Available from: http://lchc.ucsd.edu/MCA/Paper/Engestrom/expanding/toc.htm. Last accessed 8 October 2013.

Eribon, D. (1992) *Michel Foucault.* London: Faber and Faber.

Foucault, M. (2003a) 'The Ethics of the Concern of the Self as a Practice of Freedom'. In Rabinow, P. and Rose, N. (eds.) *The Essential Foucault: Selections from the essential works of Foucault, 1954–1984.* New York: The New Press, 25–43.

Foucault, M. (2003b) 'So Is It Important to Think?' In Rabinow, P. and Rose, N. (eds.) *The Essential Foucault: Selections from the essential works of Foucault, 1954–1984.* New York: The New Press, 170–174.

Holman-Jones, S. (2005) 'Autoethnography: Making the personal political'. In Denzin, N. K. and Lincoln, Y. S. (eds.) *The Sage Handbook of Qualitative Research.* Thousand Oaks, CA: Sage, 763–790.

Institute for Learning (2012) Impact Review. Available from: www.ifl.ac.uk/media/96690/2013_06_25_Impact_review_2012.pdf. Accessed 21 June 2014.

Martin, T. (1995) 'Giving feedback after a lesson observation'. *Mentoring and tutoring,* 3(2), 8–12.

Montgomery, D. (2002) *Helping Teachers Develop through Classroom Observation.* 2nd ed. London: David Fulton Publishers.

O'Leary, M. (2013) 'Surveillance, Performativity and Normalised Practice: The use and impact of graded lesson observations in further education colleges'. *Journal of Further and Higher Education,* 37(5), 694–714.

Wragg, E. (1994) *An Introduction to Classroom Observation.* London: Routledge.

PART III

Peer observation, coaching and mentoring

7

THE ROLE OF COACHING APPROACHES IN OBSERVING TEACHING AND LEARNING IN FURTHER EDUCATION

Joanne Miles

Introduction

Coaching has many faces in the further education (FE) sector in England, with its features and purposes varying across contexts. Coaching skills can be part of the manager's toolkit for encouraging individuals and teams to reflect on their practice and identify specific action points to take forward. These skills are harnessed in team meetings and also in one-to-one interactions such as appraisal and line management meetings. Coaching questions and models are often used by Advanced Practitioners to foster reflective dialogue with colleagues about aspects of their classroom practice, lesson planning and use of technology for learning. Increasingly, coaching approaches are used in pre- and post-observation conversations, led by Teaching and Learning Coaches (TLCs). In many colleges, the TLCs receive training to build their coaching skills in order to play a specific role within the lesson observation process. This may involve meeting the teacher for a coaching conversation before the lesson to identify learners' needs, review the lesson plan and identify several areas of focus for the observation. This ensures that part of the professional dialogue after the lesson covers areas of practice that the teacher has a particular interest in as part of their developmental journey. Coaching skills are also used in the professional dialogue stage and subsequent action planning review meetings, to enable the teacher to take ownership of their developmental steps.

In some settings, observers (the formal observation team, generally comprising of managers) receive training to develop coaching skills for use in professional dialogue and action planning after the observed lesson. These skills help the observers to facilitate deeper reflection on learning in both that lesson and the wider learning context. Coaching approaches can also help to foster greater ownership of action points by the teacher as they arrive at their own actions through a collaborative dialogue as opposed to receiving an action plan imposed by their observer.

This chapter will put forward the case for why it is important to embed coaching into the observation process and outline ways to address some of the challenges involved. The chapter will conclude with some practical suggestions for embedding coaching approaches within observation cycles and provide contextualised examples to assist in that process.

Conceptualising, coaching and mentoring in further education

No single, unified definition and understanding of coaching and mentoring seems to be applied to FE at present and equally it is an under-researched area of practice. As noted in a recent study carried out in the sector by Hobson *et al.* (2015: 1):

> Within FE, as in education more widely, there is a 'lack of clarity' over what mentoring is or ought to involve (Tedder and Lawy 2009) and varying understandings and enactments of mentoring are evident (Maxwell 2014). In addition, some activity that is labelled 'coaching' within FE has significant overlaps with mentoring in terms of aims and processes.
>
> *Hobson* et al. *2015*

Whilst much research has been carried out on school-based mentoring, a relatively small amount of research exists in the FE sector (Oti 2012; Swain and Conlan 2012; Maxwell 2014). Coach and mentor are used in the vocabulary of many colleges but the City and Guilds report on the role of coaching in vocational education and training (2012) highlights the different ways in which the terms are understood and used:

> In different contexts, the term 'coaching' and the associated term 'mentoring' are used to capture a range of concepts. Some definitions of coaching emphasise the importance of equipping the person receiving coaching with the ability to increasingly direct their own learning. For example, in CUREE's national Framework for Mentoring and Coaching, produced for the development of teachers, coaching is seen as a non-judgemental process where emotional support is provided and the focus is on equipping the coachee to make their own decisions. Mentoring, on the other hand, is seen as a goal-directed process linked with career progression.
>
> *City and Guilds 2012: 9*

The point of departure between coaching and mentoring seems to be around the issue of how much advice and direction to give within the conversation. In some contexts, observers/TLCs are moving along the spectrum from coaching towards mentoring, by providing suggestions and outlining steps that the teacher can take to implement certain methods or activities in their practice. The mentoring conversation here is much more directive and involves the sharing of expertise and advice in pursuit of a developmental goal, as opposed to a conversation built primarily on questioning to foster reflection and elicit the teacher's own path towards change.

This move towards providing suggestions or classroom resources as part of the coaching conversation is a point of debate, with a range of views about its potential to enhance or inhibit teachers' reflective skills and professional development. Some feel that providing solutions using a mentoring approach limits the depth of reflective thinking by the teacher, encourages reliance on the coach and reduces creative independence in lesson planning. This view receives some support in the report entitled *Developing Great Teaching*, in which a range of professional development interventions were reviewed:

> All the reviews involved in this meta-analysis offered a number of clear statements about forms of Continuing Professional Development and Learning that do NOT lead

to positive outcomes for participants or students. A didactic model in which facilitators simply tell teachers what to do, or give them materials without giving them opportunities to develop skills and inquire into their impact on pupil learning is not effective.

Cordingley et al. *2015: 8*

Within a coaching approach, the focus is on acting as a thinking partner for the teacher, helping them to extend and develop their reflection and planning. It is not meant to be about imposing a set of currently fashionable methods for the classroom or assuming that the approaches the coach uses will work well for that teacher in their context. It is about a long-term developmental journey for that teacher as opposed to a quick fix of some specific points from one lesson.

However, some coaches comment that there are situations when a questioning-based approach alone will not necessarily yield great development:

I think the only potentially negative aspect of using a coaching approach to improvement is if the teacher, despite their best efforts, cannot see any potential solutions to problems for themselves. This means that the observer is forced to adapt their approach from using only coaching strategies to using a more mentor-based approach. This doesn't necessarily mean that the observer has to suggest what they perceive as the ideal solution to the teacher's problem; they might instead suggest two or three potential solutions that the teacher might want to consider. This way, the autonomy of the teacher is maintained as they are still taking responsibility for the decisions they reach. Likewise, with the action planning process, the observer might outline some areas to develop based on their observations but the teacher should maintain the ultimate responsibility for the plan.

Dave, Teacher and Coach, Eastwind College

Many coaches are aware of this spectrum of approaches, from coaching through questioning to mentoring with suggestions and navigate it within each conversation they have. Awareness of the teacher's level of experience, attitude to observation and current context all help the coach to adjust their approach to meet that teacher's needs. Time is well spent establishing those facts before and during the initial coaching conversations when the coachee is new to the coach.

When a teacher is new to the profession or role, the coach may decide to highlight some useful research to read or offer some alternative classroom approaches to consider without imposing their own preferred approach. This content acts as input to subsequent conversations involving more questions than suggestions from the coach, as the interactions move along the spectrum from mentoring into coaching.

Many coaches are also aware of the benefits of using an approach founded on asking questions and listening actively and attentively to the responses without necessarily making specific suggestions. This approach can create a space for reflection, analysis and even the challenging of assumptions about learning and learners. Experienced teachers with well-developed reflective skills can respond particularly well to this style of coaching, enjoying the intellectual rigour of articulating beliefs about learning and evaluating their own practice.

Attitude, mindset and the emotional baggage brought into the coaching conversation from previous experiences of observation can all have a great impact on the teacher's capacity to engage with coaching at the outset. If the teacher is used to sitting through feedback from an observer, with little platform for discussion or ownership of the action plan, they may not view the coaching conversation as a safe, reflective space. They come to the coaching meeting ready to be *talked at* by the observer who they perceive as occupying a position of senior authority and thus are less likely to expect a collaborative dialogue to occur. These prior experiences can lead to the kind of response outlined below:

> Some teachers make very little effort to reflect. Moreover, they would rather the observer tell them what they should be doing than consider ways to improve their own teaching. Nevertheless, I still think for these teachers a coaching approach is more effective as if they are going to make any change to their practice, it is more likely to come from this coaching approach.
>
> *Yvette, Teacher Trainer, Easter Egg College*

A helpful starting point for any institution can be to build awareness of what a coaching conversation is like through discussions with staff, briefings, publicity, video clips of coaching conversations and testimonials from people who have been coached. This awareness raising is particularly important if a college is moving towards a more developmental coaching approach from a less interactive model of observation feedback. Communication of this sort helps to alter expectations and indicates that coaching can be collaborative, interactive and teacher-centred. This can help build the trusting relationship that underpins any effective coaching conversation. The initial contact that the coach makes with the coachee can therefore be significant in setting the tone and engaging the member of staff. Many coaches talk about the need to clarify their role, their approach as a coach and the different ways that they can support the teacher, in those early interactions via email and face-to-face conversation.

The inherent challenges of coaching within a wider quality process mean that coaches can feel pressure to provide solutions instead of taking the time to elicit them, as highlighted by the following comment:

> It can be a challenge as the perception is that helping coachees find their own solutions by using coaching conversations and questioning techniques takes too long. It is also difficult to stop yourself giving suggestions and solutions. However, by persisting and feeling confident in using this coaching language, the benefits are far greater.
>
> *Jessica, Head of Teaching, Learning and Development, Waterspout College*

As Jessica comments here, observers/TLCs need to develop confidence and skills in coaching and focus on the longer term benefits of investing time and effort in them with staff. Training in listening and questioning skills, as well as a range of coaching conversation models, can enable them to bring a variety of skills and approaches into their work. Time and space for them to practise these skills in a safe environment among themselves is a key part of this skills building process, so network meetings need to be built into the college calendar for observers and TLCs.

Despite these shifting definitions of coach and mentor, there are some approaches that are often deployed by both observers and TLCs in their conversations about lessons:

- The coach uses active listening skills to follow the teacher's thread of thinking and interpret body language and tone.
- The coach uses evidence of what happened in the lesson as a platform for analysis and reflection.
- The coach uses questioning skills to foster deeper reflection by the teacher.
- The coach supports the teacher in defining, refining and planning the action steps to take after the coaching session.
- The coach is focused on having respectful, professional dialogue that creates a useful thinking space for that teacher.

These coaching conversations happen before the observed lesson in some settings but most commonly take place afterwards, during the professional dialogue and action planning. In many colleges, there has been a positive reframing of the feedback conversation as the professional dialogue or the professional learning conversation. This change seems to reflect the current sector-wide focus on the importance of developing reflective practitioners, who can think deeply about their practice, as noted by Dymoke and Harrison (2008: 8):

> John Loughran (2002) describes reflective practice as 'a lens into the world of practice' (p. 33), recognizing that it offers a chance for questioning of often taken-for-granted assumptions. In other words, it provides a chance to see one's own practice through the eyes of others. It is through both questioning and investigating that reflection has the potential to lead to a developing understanding of professional practice. Brookfield (1995) talks about our 'assumption hunting' (p. 218) as we learn about and experiment with, different approaches to our teaching practices.

There seems to be a clear fit between coaching approaches and this purpose of fostering deep reflection and potent action plans. The active listening and insightful questions from the coach can enhance the depth of thinking by the teacher, enabling them to analyse choices they made in planning and lesson delivery and how those impacted on the learning experience. Coaches encourage teachers to consider how specific learners responded to particular stages of the lesson and how that links to the wider learning context for that learner. Coaches ask teachers to think about choices they made in the lesson staging and classroom resources and elicit alternatives that could have enhanced learning further. The questions encourage a forensic look at that lesson but do not stop there, moving beyond the snapshot approach to lesson observation. Coaches use questioning to encourage reflection on underpinning assumptions about learning, how best to facilitate it and how that could be developed in future. Appendix 7.1 includes some examples of coaching questions for use in professional dialogues.

The coaching conversation is a balance of reflection and action planning, encouraging the teacher to identify concrete, achievable steps to move forward with specific areas for development. Two key skills here are helping the teacher prioritise their areas to work on and selecting those with most impact for learners. Action steps need to be specific and concrete, as well as set in a realistic time frame. For many coaches, this means that there is a need for follow-up meetings or other activities such as short observations or collaborative lesson planning, to ensure that the teacher is supported within that process. For coaches

TABLE 7.1 Self-assessment task on coaching skills for observations

Individually identify three areas for exploration or development within your practice. Share those with a colleague and identify some useful action steps.

Coaching Skill	Areas for exploration or development?
1. Planning relevant questions to prompt reflection during the professional dialogue.	
2. Clustering points ready for the professional dialogue meeting, to focus on underlying strengths and areas for discussion/development.	
3. Drafting questions to encourage discussion of underpinning assumptions and beliefs about learning.	
4. Shaping questions so they draw on the teacher's experience and expertise.	
5. Asking follow-up questions that deepen the reflection/learning.	
6. Listening actively to the content and tone of the teacher's points.	
7. Watching energy levels and body language for additional information.	
8. Creating space so the teacher can think through the lesson without interruption.	
9. Raising areas for development with sensitivity, to encourage ownership.	
10. Asking questions that challenge assumptions, in constructive ways.	
11. Using evidence from the lesson as a platform for a question.	
12. Signposting useful resources or people for the teacher to draw on.	
13. Providing suggestions where appropriate, without imposing them.	
14. Helping the teacher to define specific, small action steps for themselves.	
15. Following up the action plan and reviewing impact with the teacher or others.	

who would like to reflect on their current skills, Table 7.1 provides a self-assessment checklist of coaching skills.

In summary, coaching is conceptualised and implemented in a wide range of ways in FE but the underpinning aim is related. City and Guilds, one of the key awarding bodies in the sector, encapsulates this in the following quote:

> There is a spectrum of approaches that coaches use, with the underlying aim of helping the coachee to improve their performance. Coaching appears to include both situations where coaches assert their judgement of the performance standards, and situations where coaches facilitate the development of coachees' ability to make these judgements for themselves. Sometimes one or the other will be more dominant, depending on the context, but in all cases the goal is that the coachee ultimately owns the new 'performance' or learning.
>
> *City and Guilds 2012: 10*

The benefits of coaching in lesson observations

When colleges move to a professional dialogue model, with coaching approaches embedded within the observation cycle, observers and observees report a range of benefits. They often comment on how different the conversation is, in terms of the mindset and participation of both observer and observee, as the focus is on reflective dialogue and moves beyond mere feedback. They comment on how these approaches foster greater teacher ownership and engagement with development planning and subsequent action, as the following extract illustrates:

> This year we are trying a whole college developmental approach to lesson observation, with every teacher involved having a 'teaching & learning conversation' to discuss their priorities before being observed, a short informal observation and then another conversation to plan future development. We are concentrating on highlighting the positive aspects of every lesson seen and then using a series of coaching questions to help the teacher identify key areas to work on and tease out ways of improving them. This month I have seen 13 teachers and every one of them has commented how much more positive this experience has been compared to the graded approach they have been used to. It is proving so productive – teachers are volunteering to sign up for further coaching, asking to peer observe and happy to recommend the process to their colleagues.
>
> *Saskia, Head of Teacher Education and Development, Less Emails College*

As outlined above, the use of coaching approaches is often embedded within an ungraded observation model, focused firmly on development, as Maisie and Loretta's comments below reinforce:

> One of the observation team has just completed feedback on 3 observations in the new ungraded model with a coaching approach and has said that it has completely changed the whole process – with a much more discursive approach and the observee working much harder in the feedback to identify how to improve.
>
> *Maisie, Director, Saucepan College*

> I like the process more than the old graded observations because it's more about you as a practitioner and your skills, rather than what an observer thinks about just one lesson. There is more time to reflect on other methods of delivering when things go differently than expected.
>
> *Loretta, teacher, Saucepan College*

If we are keen to make our lesson observations a driver of improvement as opposed to a tool limited to questionable quality assurance, the use of coaching approaches can be a powerful part of that process. There is an obvious synergy with ungraded models of observation, unconstrained by all the negative and reductive focus on grades, so clearly highlighted in a recent national study on lesson observations (O'Leary 2013).

Observers/TLCs often comment on the way that coaching approaches foster a more equal and collaborative relationship within the observation process. This has potential to mitigate some of the negative effects inherent in a hierarchical discussion with an observer who often has the power to judge your practice within a quality cycle. As O'Leary (2014: 114) argues:

> Conceptualizing observation as a tool for reciprocal learning has the potential to break down some of the traditional hierarchies and power imbalances associated with the

observer–observee relationship, particularly if it is not linked to summative assessment for high-stakes purposes, i.e. graded lesson observation.

As Jessica's comments below reinforce, coaching approaches help to put the teacher's voice at the centre of the dialogue, where it needs to be:

> It immediately ensures I (the observer/coach) listen and that they (the observee) are listened to. Also the coachee/observee gets a voice straightaway. I can tell a lot from what they say about how aware they are of strengths and areas for improvement. It automatically sets the scene for a two-way process and encourages co-ownership of developmental action points.
>
> *Jessica, Head of Teaching, Learning and Development, Waterspout College*

For the observer/TLC, the professional dialogue is a chance for two practitioners to discuss learners and learning together as opposed to an opportunity to impose feedback on a colleague. The use of questions allows the observer/TLC to see how the teacher conceptualises learning and views their class, and they can therefore target their questions to probe deeper in a personalised way. There are parallels here with the ways that we often elicit knowledge and experiences from learners in the classroom as opposed to talk at them.

For observers/TLCs, there are also benefits to creating more space for the observee to share their thoughts, as it gives us a more informed, insightful platform from which to elicit action points. For both parties in the coaching conversation, preparation and effort is involved, with a clear and constructive aim in mind – refining the focus on what to do next to enhance learning:

> Developmental ungraded observations using coaching approaches are hard work, but like a gym work out or a run, you feel great afterwards. I think they are rewarding if you have put as much into the feedback as the teacher has in delivering the session. It helps me to prepare key coaching questions relating to the observation in advance for the professional conversation after the lesson. The observee said that she thought the new observations were clever (as in canny!) Her reasoning was that they enable teachers to take an active rather than a passive role and therefore create responsibility for self-development.
>
> *Rashida, Head of Teaching and Learning, Longlegs College*

For observers/TLCs new to coaching within observation cycles, the practice of preparing questions prior to the professional dialogue can be beneficial. It helps to pick out aspects of the lesson that were thought provoking for the observer, problematic for learners or particularly effective for them. The questions devised can be used to challenge assumptions, elicit reflections and ideas for improvement from the teacher, ensuring they are active in the conversation and selecting developmental steps for themselves. Here are some exemplar questions that can be used:

- How does that lesson link to previous and subsequent sessions? How can you make that clear to learners?
- How did you decide the sequence of activities in the lesson?

- Were there any learners struggling in the lesson and what would show you that?
- How can you provide effective follow-up activities to consolidate or extend the learning from that lesson?

The place of coaching in observation cycles

In recent years it has been encouraging to note the growing emphasis on coaching skills within key roles in the FE sector. Observers and TLCs are all part of this picture, developing and deploying coaching skills within their respective remits. These skills are being used within graded and ungraded observations, on mentoring programmes for new teachers and on teacher training courses. Most recently, peer coaching skills for teachers are being developed in some settings as well, enhancing classroom visits with a peer and other CPD activities.

In terms of lesson observations, coaching approaches can be seen within these everyday activities in colleges around the country:

Pre-observation dialogue between observer/TLC and observee

Focused on learners' needs; links between previous lessons and the observed one; challenges with that group, underpinning assumptions about structuring the learning session etc. This conversation can indicate areas of focus for the observer and help the teacher to refine their plan before teaching the lesson. Sadly, a lack of time and the perception of lesson observation as a performance to be judged can prevent colleges from using this step as part of their process. This step can be made possible through email, SKYPE or video conferencing, if the will and commitment are there to do it.

Professional dialogue/feedback meeting after the lesson

A deep, reflective dialogue about learning in that lesson and a broader focus on that teacher's thinking and practice. Questions can focus on topics such as exploring assumptions about learners' behaviour, resources for flipped learning, methods of embedding English into the Scheme of Work or the impact of the way the teacher questioned students. The TLC/observer does not limit themselves to the confines of the feedback form; the lesson and the learners in it form a springboard for a wider discussion and professional learning.

Action/development planning sessions after the observed lesson

In some colleges, these happen within the professional dialogue meeting; in others, they are completed later by another party such as a manager or a TLC who did not observe the lesson. Coaching approaches are useful here to ensure that concrete action steps are elicited *from* the teacher and refined so they are clear and helpful. As an observer/manager/coach mentions in the following extract:

> I think the greatest benefit to using coaching questions in the post-observation feedback has been reducing development issues to small, manageable steps – the most

productive questions so far have been "What is one thing you can change (or add or do) in planning (the first activity, questioning, reviewing, giving instructions)?" and "How will you do that?"

Saskia, Head of Teacher Education and Development, Less Emails College

Review meetings to follow up development plans

Some TLCs and observers are using coaching questions in subsequent meetings to follow up on actions set in the initial conversation. It can be helpful here to email questions to the teacher beforehand to give time for reflection before the meeting. Questions tend to focus on the impact on learners and the teacher from the developmental activities. Coachees are asked to reflect on what has worked well, their evidence for this and where there are areas to enhance further or glitches to work through. In some settings, the observer needs to agree with the teacher who is best placed to provide this follow-up support, so there are challenges in communications and closing the loop on actions. It is often noted in colleges that this is a pitfall, deserving some attention and effort if they are to maximise the benefits of their observation process.

The challenges of coaching within observation cycles for TLCs

In the FE sector there is an ever-growing focus on 'managing performance' and in many colleges, the TLCs find themselves in an uncomfortable position within this process. If a teacher has been identified as requiring support after the formal lesson observation, a TLC is often allocated and certain challenges are immediately apparent, especially if a poor lesson grade is involved.

Coaches are given a 'caseload' of coachees and the coachees often have little choice in who that coach might be or whether coaching is the most suitable approach. This can reduce the likelihood of the teacher really taking ownership of the developmental process; it can foster a resigned, compliance-focused feel to the coaching interactions. It can be difficult for both parties when coachees are 'sent' to the coach and are not willing participants in that relationship.

Coaches are frequently in a dilemma about where to place their attention during developmental dialogues with teachers. As part of the performance management process, they are aware of the pressure of being seen to convert areas for development into areas of strength as a sign of improvement in the subsequent lesson observation. They want to support the teacher, but they also want to have the time and scope to encourage reflection and rich, authentic development. This can lead to an uneasy compromise, driven by practical constraints and external pressures as opposed to the wider developmental needs of the teacher.

Many coaches comment that they feel that they can only scratch the surface with coachees in the time allocated to this support. Many colleges have a fixed entitlement of several hours, dedicated to teachers who are perceived to be under performing. How long does it take to develop thinking and practical skills to enhance an aspect of someone's teaching in a sustainable way? Once teachers are signed off in the quality process, how are changes in thinking and practice to receive consolidation? Why present coaching as a deficit-focused activity, when strong teachers could benefit from it too?

Some suggestions on how to overcome these challenges

1. Encourage a richer, more sophisticated discussion at the outset about what the best form of development might be for each teacher. A discussion between teacher, manager, observer and coach can be fruitful. It may be that peer observation with structured reflection is a better option than coaching as the teacher would benefit from seeing certain approaches in action, e.g. for managing behaviour, maximising student talk or setting up group work activities. It could be that the coaching needs to focus on underpinning approaches to planning, so that joint planning and review will help. The manager/observer may be the best placed person to work on the development points in some cases, particularly if they involve embedding departmental practices and procedures such as managing punctuality or supporting at risk students.

2. Wherever possible, invite the teacher to choose a coach, based on their skills and background. An element of ownership and choice can really help in anchoring this process on the right footing. It helps to have a profile of the coaches so that their curriculum specialism and experience are available for review. If personalities don't gel together, create a space for raising the issue and look at finding a new coach.

3. Early in the coaching relationship, see if the coachee is happy for the coach to watch them teach and review some of their plans for learning. From this, the coach can get their own feel for that teacher and start to discuss with them which areas to work on. This can ensure that other aspects of learning not highlighted in the snapshot observed lesson get attention and also helps the teacher engage with the process more actively. Some coaches start work on the area the teacher wants to develop and then move onto the observation feedback points later on, once a relationship and some trust has been built.

4. Look at who/what else can support the teacher outside the coaching sessions. Sometimes there is a well-placed colleague who can provide mentoring or share resources; sometimes peer observation triangles add extra richness; sometimes there is in-house CPD available that complements the coaching; staff intranet areas and Twitter provide a wealth of food for thought and experimentation too.

5. As a coaching team look at support across time and what your college can offer:

    *   Once a teacher has finished their initial coaching sessions, what follow-up activities are offered?
    *   Do action learning sets and communities of practice exist to encourage further development?
    *   How do you look at their progress after coaching, across time?
    *   How can you offer a rich variety of CPD opportunities so that coaching isn't reduced to a quick fix within performance management constraints?
    *   How can coaching support and develop strong performers in the classroom as well?

Embedding coaching approaches within observations

When colleges are embedding coaching within observations, there are several aspects to consider:

1. How and when will coaching approaches fit into the observation cycle?
2. Who will need to receive training in coaching and action planning skills?

3. How can these coaching approaches enhance the wider CPD cycle?
4. How will the impact of coaching conversations be tracked and evidenced?
5. How can observers and TLCs collaborate to maximise the effectiveness of coaching interventions over time?

It can be helpful to foster an ongoing dialogue between observers and TLCs about their journey with coaching. The use of reflection tools and developmental activities can facilitate this process and Appendices 7.1 and 7.2 contain several contextualised examples designed with this in mind.

Staff surveys, individual feedback, testimonial quotes, video clips from teachers and focus group consultations can play a vital role in the dialogue with teachers about the impact of coaching. Capturing this feedback regularly and through a range of channels helps the quality team to develop the observation cycle collaboratively with the wider staff.

If we use coaching approaches in these ways, we can begin to bring to life a more constructive and developmental model of observation in our colleges. This would be a positive response to some of the recommendations from the recent national study on lesson observations (O'Leary 2013: 90):

- **Prioritising improvements in teaching**: Practitioners need more support with how to improve their teaching and less emphasis on measuring their performance. Thus any future use of observation should seek to prioritise the professional development needs of staff rather than the production of statistical data to serve performance management systems.
- **Observee empowerment**: There is a need to empower observees with the opportunity to play an active role in the focus of their observation and the ability to decide and prioritise key areas for development in collaboration with their observers. Thus action plans following on from observations need to be negotiated and mutually agreed between the observer and observee.

Conclusion

Coaching approaches have much to offer FE and the education sector as a whole, as it grapples with devising more developmental models of observation. These skills and approaches support deeper reflection on practice and encourage incisive action planning, which together engage teachers in driving their own developmental journey.

References

Brookfield, S. D. (1995) *Becoming a Critically Reflective Teacher*. San Francisco, CA: Jossey-Bass.

City and Guilds Centre for Skills Development (2012) *The Role of Coaching in Vocational Education and Training*. Available at: www.skillsdevelopment.org/PDF/Insights-the-role-of-coaching-in-vocational-education.pdf. Last accessed 20 March 2016.

Cordingley, P., Higgins, S., Greany, T., Buckler, N., Coles-Jordan, D., Crisp, B., Saunders, L. and Coe, R. (2015) *Developing Great Teaching: Lessons from the international reviews into effective professional development*. London: Teacher Development Trust.

Dymoke, S. and Harrison, J. (2008) *Reflective Teaching and Learning*. London: SAGE Publications Ltd.

Hobson, A., Maxwell, B., Stevens, A., Doyle, K. and Malderez, A. (2015) *Mentoring and Coaching for Teachers in the Further Education and Skills Sector in England.* Project Report. London, Gatsby Charitable Foundation. Available at: www.gatsby.org.uk/uploads/education/reports/pdf/mentoring-full-report.pdf. Last accessed 20 March 2016.

Loughran, J. (2002) 'Effective Reflective Practice. In search of meaning about teaching'. *Journal of Teacher Education,* 53(1), 33–43.

Maxwell, B. (2014) 'Improving Workplace Learning of Lifelong Learning Sector Trainee Teachers in the UK'. *Journal of Further and Higher Education,* 38(3), 377–399.

O'Leary, M. (2013) *Developing a National Framework for the Effective Use of Lesson Observation in Further Education.* Project report for the University and College Union, November 2013. DOI: 10.13140/RG.2.1.1751.7286. Available at: www.ucu.org.uk/media/6714/Developing-a-national-framework-for-the-effective-use-of-lesson-observation-in-FE-Dr-Matt-OLeary-Nov13/pdf/ucu_lessonobsproject_nov13.pdf.

O'Leary, M. (2014) *Classroom Observation: A guide to the effective observation of teaching and learning.* London: Routledge.

Oti, J. (2012) 'Mentoring and Coaching in Further Education'. In Fletcher, S. and Mullen, C. (eds.) *The SAGE Handbook of Mentoring and Coaching in Education,* 59–73, London: SAGE.

Swain, J. and Conlan, J. (2012) *Mentoring for STEM teachers in the lifelong learning sector.* Report to the Gatsby Foundation. Available at: www.yumpu.com/en/document/view/23470289/download-institute-of-education- university-of-london. Last accessed 15 February 2014.

Tedder, M. and Lawy, R. (2009) 'The Pursuit of "Excellence": Mentoring in further education initial teacher training in England'. *Journal of Vocational Education and Training,* 61(4), 413–429.

Appendix 7.1

Some reflective coaching questions for professional dialogues

1. What strengths do you have as a facilitator of learning? How did those strengths impact the learners in that lesson?
2. Think about a strong learner in that group. Was there any evidence that they felt stretched in that lesson? What options are there for stretching them further, if appropriate?
3. Who do you think struggled the most in that lesson/activity and how could you tell? What would have supported them further?
4. Can you tell me more about the staging of the lesson and the reasons behind it? How did it make links with previous learning for the students? What is the best follow-up?
5. Equality and diversity/English and maths can be challenging things to highlight in lessons. Where were there natural opportunities to do this? How could you have enhanced that further for certain individuals?
6. If we'd filmed that lesson, which parts looked active; which parts were quieter? How effective do you think the balance was for different learners and what showed you that?

Appendix 7.2

Development activities for observers/TLCs

1. Film or tape yourself conducting a professional dialogue and then review it, with the teacher's permission, of course.
2. Dual observations with another observer/TLC, to compare feedback points and discuss style and tone after the professional dialogue.

3. Buddy system – pair up with another observer/TLC and use them as an informal sounding board to develop your skills.
4. Network meetings – observers/TLCs meet to share issues, processes and skills. This could be in-house or linked to another college to get a wider perspective on observations.
5. Reflective log or journal about your experiences.
6. Make links through Twitter with others interested in lesson observations and coaching and then share approaches.
7. Look out for external events in the wider sector related to coaching and observation skills.

8

EMBEDDING COACHING AND MENTORING IN PEER OBSERVATION

Jane Martin

Introduction

This chapter focuses on a case study based in a college of further education (FE) and explores the impact of a peer review strategy into which the principles of coaching have been embedded and which is supported by a framework of Professional Learning Communities (PLCs). It explores the concept of observation and peer observation, discussing the characteristics of different approaches and identifying the advantages and disadvantages and impact on professional development. Analysis of coaching as a key strategic initiative and the consequent impact on organisational culture and approaches to professional development clarifies the rationale for the scheme. A brief reflection on the historical perspective of observation within the college contextualises the case study and is substantiated by consideration of the contribution made by PLCs and coaching frameworks to effective implementation of peer review. The chapter concludes by reflecting on the impact of the peer review process and proposes ways in which to shape future developments.

Perspective on observation and professional development

Observation as a tool by which to monitor, measure and improve performance and to collect evidence on the efficacy of practice by the Office for Standards in Education (Ofsted) is prevalent across the FE sector. There is little doubt, and significant evidence (e.g. O'Leary 2013a), of the strongly held views that this provokes amongst teachers in the sector. The focus of disquiet tends towards aspects of grading, superficiality ('box-ticking') and the potential for subsequent disciplinary action as part of a performance review process. Cockburn (2005: 376) reported on a 'typology of resistance' that encompassed concerns about the artificiality of observed lessons, giving credence to the belief in a model for effective teaching and learning. Further concerns emerged from O'Leary's (2011) research on the validity of observations, either on the basis that observers were unfamiliar with the subject area or had scant recent teaching experience. Observers are generally drawn from management teams, and may also include Advanced Practitioners, Advanced Learning Coaches and members of the Initial Teacher Education (ITE) team. The potential power imbalance (Wragg 1999) in this relationship has the capacity to undermine further practitioner autonomy and ownership and diminish significantly any potential the process has for enhancing professional practice.

The issues surrounding grading of observations are contentious. However skilfully feedback is delivered or professional dialogue encouraged, the developmental impact of such transactions is frequently compromised by grading. It is acknowledged that whilst observation of teaching and learning can play an important part in professional development (O'Leary 2013a), concern and anxiety on the part of the observee may dilute its effect.

O'Leary and Brooks (2014: 530) argue that classroom observation 'has been increasingly appropriated as a policy tool that seeks to combine its original formative purpose with a new focus on accountability'. This 'high-stakes' assessment of the professional development of teachers has repercussions, both nationally and internationally, yet has little in common with the ownership and autonomy that is characteristic of peer observation schemes. O'Leary (2014: 120) describes this approach as a:

> Collaborative and reciprocal model of observation whereby peers observe each other as a means of enhancing their pedagogic practice through reflective dialogue, with a view to feeding forward into their CPD and ultimately leading to improvements in the quality of teaching and learning.

The notion of collaboration is reflected in Tilstone's (2012: 59) concept of '*partnership observation*' and inherent in Joyce and Shower's model of peer coaching to enhance the quality of student learning through innovation in teaching and learning. It resonates too with Bell's (2008: 736) definition of peer observation as a:

> Collaborative, developmental activity in which professionals offer mutual support by observing each other teach; explaining and discussing what was observed; sharing ideas about teaching; gathering student feedback on teaching effectiveness; reflecting on understandings, feelings, actions and feedback and trying out new ideas.

Fundamental to these definitions is the notion of quality improvement to initiate change in practice, rather than a measurement of quality performance, 'an essential process for reviewing ideas and "catching mistakes" informed by a constructive "culture of criticism" (Cole, cited by Blackmore 2005: 221).

Reflecting on the conceptualisation of peer observation of teaching (POT), Peel (2005: 490) recognised that the most significant benefit had been an enhanced understanding of herself as a learner, a journey that supported the emergence of 'a relatively mature critical learner and more confident teacher in an ongoing dynamic of change'. The importance of considered and critical reflection as a key element in effective peer observation is a recurrent feature of literature reviews. Of particular value is the approach proposed by Brookfield (1995) who offers the concept of four lenses through which practitioners can reflect on their practice and gain advantage through alternative perspectives, and outlines ways in which peer discussion can offer 'critical mirrors' to illuminate assumptions, beliefs, philosophies and practice.

Effective peer observation encourages reflection on teaching practice, facilitates collaborative consideration of developmental needs and supports the implementation of innovative and constructive responses. Hammersley-Fletcher and Orsmond (2005) argue that this model of best practice is reliant on the quality of processes and on the practices of those observing and those being observed. Their research identified concerns around confidentiality and anxieties about giving feedback and the possible impact of perceived criticism. It is essential that critical feedback is presented constructively to allay these fears and create a framework to foster continuing, confident and well-informed development.

The nature of relationships within peer observation is vital to the success and sustainability of the scheme (Hammersley-Fletcher and Orsmond 2005; O'Leary 2014; Tilstone: 2012). A relationship based on mutual respect, accountability, trust and honesty is one that supports a depth of commitment to the growth and development of the other, but will also be invaluable to the individual and, ultimately, to the process, organisation, professional body and the learners. For the observer, though, there may be a reluctance to adopt the role, based on feelings of inadequacy linked to perceived lack of knowledge, experience and credibility. Hammersley-Fletcher and Orsmond's (2005) research also raises issues of vulnerability on the part of the observer, some reporting feelings of anxiety about giving feedback and constraints linked to criticality of suggestions. Observees too experienced apprehension about potentially negative feedback and the impact that this may have on relationships between colleagues. However, these aspects may be mitigated by the understanding that 'insiders' possess of the student profile, supporting structures and organisational ethos (Tilstone 2012). The concept of equality within the partnership is further enhanced if the process is one in which both parties are willing to accept joint responsibility for the potential and quality of learning.

The gradual move from professional development to professional learning involves: focusing on students, attending to requisite knowledge and skills, engaging in systematic inquiry into the effectiveness of practice, being explicit about underpinning theories of professionalism and engaging everyone in the system in learning (Timperley 2011: 4).

This encapsulates the rationale for a fundamental change of direction in approaches to staff development at the college. The ambition has been to improve the quality of the student experience through enhanced teacher practice and professionalism, using collaborative strategies to facilitate experimentation and innovation.

Peer review in practice: a college case study

Background

Over the past 20 years, the college has operated a model in which graded observations have taken place, either of individual staff on an annual basis or as part of 'mini-inspections' of curriculum areas. This approach shares similar characteristics to those described in the first of Gosling's three models of third-party observation, 'The Evaluation Model' i.e. observation of a teacher by a 'superior', often within the management hierarchy, as part of the management process (McMahon *et al.* 2007). It forms part of the quality assurance and performance review process within the college, contributing to a profile of individual teachers, curriculum areas and the teaching body as a whole.

The second of the three types of third-party observation, 'The Development Model', differs from the first by the emphasis it places on the role of feedback on teaching expertise and subsequent agreed action plans. However, McMahon *et al.* (2007) argue that there is little to discern this from the evaluation model, adding that the pivotal aspect of any third-party observation is the use made of information resulting from an observation. The developmental model is reflected in the observations of trainees by personal tutors on the Post-Graduate

Certificate of Education programme at the college. Feedback to the trainee is informed by reference to the Professional Standards for the further education and skills (FES) sector, issued by the Education and Training Foundation in 2014, and graded on guidelines provided by the partner Higher Education Institution (HEI). Whilst observers have reported feeling a conflict arising from an emphasis on development through critical dialogue and the need to award a grade, trainees appear to accept the duality of purpose. Even in this context, however, there is a discernible focus by trainees on the grade awarded which occasionally gives rise to a competitive element amongst peers. The developmental approach is also characteristic of informal observations held as part of one-to-one coaching interventions, arising either from 'self-referral' of staff or in response to areas for development identified in graded observation reports.

The third category suggested by Gosling is 'The Peer Review Model', a formative process in which peers engage in discussion, observation of practice and constructive, non-judgemental feedback. This resonates with Bell's (2008) 'Development and Training Model' which emphasises the importance of reflection over the process of observation. Equality and mutual respect are significant aspects of this model and are factors that informed the development of the college's approach to peer observation. The initial peer observation scheme required teachers to identify a peer within their curriculum area and arrange mutual observations of teaching practice. Observation notes were summarised and used as the basis for planning professional development activity.

Whilst the response from practitioners was generally positive, the outcomes were variable. Mutual respect and equality of partnerships was evident but reflective dialogue, consideration of student feedback, discussion, dissemination and evaluation of impact were less prominent. A cross-college review carried out in March 2012 noted:

> Peer observations are currently on-going, however, the team feel that they are often just a way of 'ticking a box' and there has been a perception of 'observation overload', when combined with Ofsted and internal graded observations.

The quality of feedback or professional dialogue was questionable and the vital element of mutual reflection (McMahon *et al.* 2007) was not a common feature in the observations. The following comments, also noted in the cross-college review, captured the views of staff who had adopted a very proactive approach to professional collaboration with colleagues as part of the college's Sharing Fair forum, but questioned the process and impact of peer observation:

> Peer observation can be inconsistent in terms of benefit, depending on the selected peer and subject area. Sometimes the feedback received gives some good ideas and suggestions which can be transferred to one's own practice, but at other times, very little or no constructive criticism is gained from the process.

For other curriculum teams, the experience proved to be more positive. In this case, staff had started to use a coaching model that uses a sequence of questions following four distinct headings of the GROW model: (1) Goal setting; (2) Reality checking; (3) Obstacles, Options and alternative strategies; (4) What is to be done, When, and by Whom, together with a consideration of the Will to achieve it. Whitmore (2009) argues that for the GROW model to be truly effective, it is important that practitioners exercise a sense of awareness and responsibility and harness the power of skilful questioning; used in this way the model is able to support a collaborative approach to professional dialogue, rather than one-way feedback:

> The team is piloting the idea of working in triads, with at least one person from outside their curriculum area. Two members of the team have been regularly shadowing each other, followed by feedback. They have found this two-way sharing of strategies very beneficial and have done this more regularly as there has been no paperwork to complete. They feel that the pairings have to be right in order for there to be real benefit from peer observation.

The compromise associated with linking peer observation to any form of performance management was evident in the report, an aspect that reflects Gosling's assertion that the fundamental difference between this and other approaches to observation is the issue of confidentiality and ownership of information emerging from the process.

Feedback indicated that the close collegiality of the process had, in some cases, compromised the constructively critical aspect of the process, giving rise in some instances to 'self-congratulatory and therefore inaccurate' assessment (Blackmore 2005: 223). If best practice 'is a process that encourages reflection on teaching practice, identifies developmental needs, and fosters debate and dissemination around best practice' (Hammersley-Fletcher and Orsmond 2005: 213), further thought and evaluation were required to create the conditions in which such activities could flourish.

As a consequence, a new observation strategy was initiated as part of the Teaching and Learning Quality Assurance Framework with a mandate to focus on improving professional practice and the experience for the students. Summative (graded) observation remained a feature of the new strategy but more significantly, a framework for formative observation was introduced that incorporated coaching and mentoring into peer discussions. This five-stage model provided opportunities for peer coaching to take place at an initial meeting prior to an informal, formative observation; this was followed by a further meeting with an option to repeat the cycle with agreement from both observer and observee. The observations were carried out by a team of 25 'formative observers', all of whom attended training sessions outlining the nature and purpose of coaching.

In spite of a credible rationale, the effectiveness of this scheme was mitigated; limited remission was awarded to observers and some were responsible for significant numbers of observations. Whilst different communication channels were used to introduce the scheme, it was evident that confusion about the nature and purpose of the process persisted. In common with other peer observation schemes, it 'appeared to operate on the margins of activity' (O'Leary and Brooks 2014: 535) and have little sustained impact on the quality of teaching and learning.

Establishing a coaching culture

During this period, the concept of coaching and mentoring as a key element of professional development emerged in the college, a trend congruent with many other organisations in the UK (Tulpa in Passmore: 2010), and there was a sense that as it gained momentum it also gained credence. Initially, responses were tentative but evidence accumulated, reflecting the extent to which the organisation had embraced and embedded the concept of coaching and mentoring in strategic initiatives. Advanced Practitioners developed coaching and mentoring skills through training and accreditation, the changing focus of the role reflected in revised job descriptions and titles, Advanced Learning Coaches (ALC) and a small team of Learning Coaches (LC) were appointed to cross-college roles.

Grant (in Passmore 2010: 94) offers the following definition of coaching:

> A collaborative, solution-focused, results-oriented and systematic process, in which the coach facilitates the enhancement of performance, life experience, self-directed learning and personal growth of individuals and organisations.

At the heart of this process lies a relationship of equals based on mutual honesty and trust, and a belief in the potential for individual growth supported by a commitment to the process. All are characteristics of effective peer observation schemes.

Using incisive questions to stimulate awareness, clarify understanding and prompt action is an integral part of effective teaching and learning. When used as part of a coaching conversation, together with an intuitive depth of listening and empathic use of silence, it can help to overcome 'debilitating assumptions', and create time 'to think of things inconceivable before' with powerful effect (Kline 1999: 18). The importance of listening is reinforced by Hattie (2012: 73), not only because it demonstrates mutual respect but it 'also allows for sharing genuine depth of thinking and processing in our questioning, and permitting the dialogue so necessary if we are to engage students successfully in learning'. As this is true of students, so it is for peers.

Coaching as an integral part of a peer observation process helps to establish and confirm the essential equality of partnership and is inclusive of the respect and rapport necessary for constructive, supportive and challenging collaboration. The definition emphasises the forward-looking, 'growth mindset' nature of coaching as an intervention. It offers a non-judgemental space in which to examine key issues within current practice and draw on the expertise of teachers, acknowledges that teaching is 'highly individualised and contextualised', and that in 'the better models the focus is more one of discovery and illumination whereby the nuances of practice which occurred at a particular point in time are brought in to the open and explored and deliberated in a collegiate way' (O'Leary 2013a: 89).

Professional learning communities

The prevalence of coaching within the organisation was a contributory factor to the reconsideration of professional development policy. Concern over the limited impact of training interventions, whether due to a mismatch between provision and need, a focus on individual, rather than situated learning linked to practice, or the conceptualisation of practitioners as passive recipients (Yildrim, in Kimble *et al.* 2008), culminated in a constructive process to evaluate the existing model. Co-incidental research noted the similarities between organisational strategy and intent and the characteristics of Communities of Practice identified by Wenger (Smith 2003, 2009): a shared domain of interest; a community in which members build relationships that foster mutual learning opportunities through collaborative and supportive activity, and the development of a shared practice.

A proposal to create curriculum-based PLCs, each co-ordinated by an LC, was implemented across the college. Initially focusing on specific areas for development identified through observation, these practice-based, collaborative teams met on a regular basis to discuss current approaches to teaching and learning, reflect on their effectiveness and support innovative responses. The shift that this approach afforded from isolated activity to situated learning, developed from experience and social interaction, proved successful for several curriculum teams though the profile was not uniform across the college. A study carried out to evaluate the impact both on staff and students (July 2014), provided compelling evidence to suggest that the strategy had been a key influence in the improved profile of teaching and learning, a conclusion reflected in the report published by Ofsted following inspection in June 2014.

A peer review strategy

The growth of coaching, together with the emergence of PLC, made a significant contribution to an enhanced sense of professionalism, impetus for change and momentum for growth. This new landscape created the conditions conducive to a fresh approach to peer observation. Research into HEIs and FE colleges operating similar schemes contributed to a peer review strategy that recognised the professional status of staff and their commitment to the achievement of consistently outstanding performance; it also recognised the significant benefits of a revised peer observation strategy that promoted increased teacher confidence, greater collegiality, debate and dissemination of best practice. Under the new system, each member of the teaching staff was encouraged to form professional partnerships with two colleagues: one from within area and one from a different team. A conscious decision was taken to move from 'peer observation' to 'peer review' in order to widen the focus from classroom observation and also to remove a term associated for some with feelings of anxiety, disempowerment and disillusionment.

The process is co-ordinated by LCs on a curriculum basis; this enables them to discuss individual needs and preferences with practitioners and work with their colleagues in the LC team to facilitate cross-college partnerships. Practitioners use the Professional Standards as a point of reference and note their observations and reflections on a simple template. These are summarised by the LC and forwarded to the Professional Development Manager in order to evaluate the strengths and areas for development within each team. The PLCs provided the network through which communication was facilitated by the LCs, and additional resources were produced to support the process, including the use of augmented reality that provided links to the Professional Standards, and to video clips of coaching conversations, and peer feedback on the impact of engaging in peer review.

The role of coaching in the peer review scheme is pivotal and was informed by the work of Joyce and Showers (2002). Research into the effective transfer of training on staff development and its effect on student learning was scarce but indicated a negligible impact. However, when coaching was incorporated into the sequence, there was a dramatic improvement in terms of sustained change in practice and impact on student achievement. The proactive role required of the organisation to foster experimentation, collaboration and development is also an important factor.

Critical reflection on past experiences of peer observation based on practitioner feedback and research prompted several other key changes. Equality of partnership is fostered through peer-to-peer relationships; choice of partner and focus of review enhance a sense of autonomy and ownership; responsibility is shared through coaching conversations pre- and post-review, and PLCs provide a forum for dissemination, feedback and, perhaps, accountability.

Reflections on the impact of peer review

After a short initial period, the peer review process was reviewed to determine practitioner response and impact. Staff from different curriculum areas were asked to comment on their experience of the process. The benefits of collaboration, particularly cross-college, were highlighted in several responses:

> I think the peer review process has been really very beneficial for me because it has taken the fear of observation away. It's put the power more to the tutor so we can actually make it part of our development and an extension of the conversations that we have been having and it has benefitted us because we have seen the good practice teachers are doing in other areas of the college whereas previously we haven't.

The importance of a professional coaching dialogue was noted by another respondent:

> In terms of being able to talk about what you are going to do before and after ... that was great because you get input from different areas, input from different people's perceptions. It's very much a team effort. Where it was linked to GROW, we looked at generating ideas, reviewing them and looking at how they actually translate into practice and how they went afterwards.

And the element of peer support and encouragement was reflected in the following comment:

> I think the great thing is that you can discuss what has gone on, and how this maybe can be improved or developed with a member of staff who also wants to see that your practice has developed and these students achieve what they need to achieve.

A 'best practice' framework for peer review (Blackmore 2005) provides several points of reference to consider the effectiveness of the current process. Training for participants prior to engaging in the review process was led by LCs, and PLCs provided a forum in which practitioners could explore the process and practise coaching skills. The current pairings support team and cross-college partnerships, the latter proving particularly rewarding in terms of creating valuable interaction within the organisational community. The sense of ownership and autonomy is evident as practitioners have expressed their preference to work with a peer on a particular aspect of professional practice. A mid-year review has highlighted some encouraging progress; the Creative Arts and Media team report 'a positive impact in developing the culture of the department, teachers seem far more open to sharing good practice and are happy to discuss issues and concerns in the community'. The Hair and Therapies team identified a 'positive insight into varied questioning techniques, group work activities, classroom management and different teaching styles'. The Construction team have found that working with colleagues in the English and Maths department has been beneficial in helping to embed literacy and numeracy in their lessons. Such is the impact on levels of confidence that some staff have suggested a move to an open-door policy where peers are welcomed into the classroom at any time. Staff interpretation of the strategy has frequently resulted in the observer being coached by the person observed, an aspect that reinforces the flexibility of the process and focus on collaborative learning. Whilst some partnerships have continued to a second year, periodic change will be encouraged.

The peer review process has been deliberately separated from performance review although emerging strands are linked to alternative interventions within the wider professional development strategy. Professional growth is fostered within PLCs, which offer opportunities to reflect on current practice and formulate new approaches, thus enabling the follow up activity advocated as an aspect of best practice. The open and trusting nature of relationships is evident in participant feedback, though the quality of critical reflection is less assured. The cross-college partnerships have mitigated the potential for superficiality; a trend supported by a sense of accountability to the wider professional community, evidencing what has been achieved and the impact that this has had on learning for both parties. This illustrates the value added by critical friends who bring specific, and different, expertise, experience and insights (Tilstone 2012). It appears that the focus engendered through the coaching dialogue has also played a significant part in encouraging participants to adopt a supportive yet challenging approach towards peer learning, prompting self-awareness and creating a depth of partnership.

Proposals for development

The direction of future developments will be informed by regular review of the scheme based on feedback from practitioners both on the process and the impact it is having on the quality of teaching and learning. The changing culture of the college is reflected in altered philosophy and practice. The sense of community is growing through collaboration, professionalism through autonomy and confidence through ownership. However, this is not evident across all areas, a situation that arises perhaps from the fact that not all practitioners recognise the 'underlying dynamic of equality and mutuality of learning' (Bennett and Barp cited by O'Leary 2014: 71) that is integral to effective peer review.

Evaluation of the impact of peer review is a priority. Cowie and Wallace (2000) argue that engagement in evaluative activity can increase confidence in the implementation of innovative practice, measurement of impact on all stakeholders, critical reflection and consequent changes in practice. The mid-year review has illustrated the benefits to those involved, even in these early stages, and provided an indication of development needs which currently focus on enhancing coaching skills and practice. However, a more thorough review will be undertaken at the end of the academic year which will be informed by the views of practitioners from all areas, members of the management team, together with consideration of changes in organisational ethos and the nature of professional partnership and collaboration. The importance of student feedback in triangulating the evaluative process has been recognised and will be included as a key element in the evaluative process. Developmentally, the process will be enhanced by achieving greater clarity around anticipated outcomes and impact, a baseline to impact approach, (Porritt in Crowley 2014) and a shared understanding of how this will be achieved.

Joyce and Showers (2002) identify five ways in which coaching contributes to the transfer of training: a greater propensity to practise new strategies, and more appropriate use of these, longer term retention of associated knowledge and skills, a willingness to explain new approaches to teaching and learning to their students and a clearer understanding of the purpose and use of innovative practices. These are reflected to a degree in the impact of coaching to date, but also emphasise the need to support practitioners in the development of coaching skills and enhanced knowledge and understanding of effective pedagogy. The interdependent relationship between peer review, coaching and PLCs is becoming more apparent and the process becomes common practice.

It is through this network that the process can be further refined. For example, the use of non-judgemental language within coaching conversations encourages independent thought, helps to focus entirely on the individual and often generates inventive and idiosyncratic thought by keeping the coachee's words intact and asking questions that contain fewer pre-suppositions; for example, a question such as 'What are you thinking?' becomes 'Is there anything else about x?' (Arnold 2009). This resonates with the view that the observer should seek to provide as objective a view of the session as possible, reflecting with the observee as a mirror to inform changes to future practice (Hammersley-Fletcher and Orsmond 2005). It also helps to reduce any tendency towards evaluative or judgemental feedback, thus fostering equality of relationship within professional partnerships based on mutual respect and trust (O'Leary 2014).

Critical reflection is frequently improved through peer collaboration and when situated within a learning context. Thus, the opportunity to develop this crucial aspect of peer review is facilitated both by the coaching process and the opportunity to discuss in a wider forum through PLCs. However, use of a framework such as Brookfield's (1995) 'four lenses' would enhance the quality of reflection through consideration of student feedback and reference to wider research as well as self-reflection and peer perspective. Furthermore, Peel (2005) discusses the potential for transformatory learning that can be gained through the progressive process engendered by the layering of reflective activities.

The current situation for some curriculum teams suggests that fusing peer review and professional collaboration towards a lesson study approach may have a 'demonstrable impact on the quality of teaching and on pupil progress and attainment' and be the 'popular, powerful and replicable process for innovating, developing and transferring pedagogic practices' (Dudley, cited by O'Leary 2012: 796). It may also strengthen professional relationships and team cohesion that have been affected by a period of significant change and upheaval, or possibly as a strategy to stimulate further growth of a high performing team. The lesson study cycle (Lewis et al., cited by O'Leary 2014) provides a four-stage framework which engages teams in considering long-term goals for students' learning and development informed by study of the curriculum, collaborative planning, research through observation and data collection and shared reflective activity. This approach prioritises improvements in teaching and learning and helps to maintain the focus on the quality of student experience. Perhaps PLCs will become 'communities of discovery'? (Coffield and Williamson 2011).

The significance of management commitment to the development of coaching, PLCs and peer review has been a vital component in this case study. Apart from considerable financial investment, the impact of encouragement and endorsement cannot be overestimated. In many ways this model, and its continuing revision and development, has endeavoured to create a 'genuine spirit of enquiry and research. To explore what's happening in that messy business of learning, and to be a starting point for professional discussion and debate' (O'Leary 2013a: 89).

References

Arnold, J. (2009) *Coaching Skills for Leaders in the Workplace*. Oxford: How to Books Ltd.

Bell, A. and Mladenovic, R. (2008) 'The Benefits of Peer Observation of Teaching for Tutor Development'. *Higher Education*, 55(6), 735–752.

Blackmore, J. (2005) 'A Critical Evaluation of Peer Review via Teaching Observation with Higher Education'. *International Journal of Educational Management*, 19(3), 218–232.

Brookfield, S. (1995) *Becoming a Critically Reflective Teacher*. San Francisco, CA: Jossey-Bass Inc.

Cockburn, J. (2005) 'Perspectives and Politics of Classroom Observation'. *Research in Post Compulsory Education*, 10(3), 373–388.

Coffield, F. and Williamson, B. (2011) *From Exam Factories to Communities of Discovery*. London: Institute of Education, University of London.

Cowie, H. and Wallace, P. (2000) *Peer Support in Action*. London: SAGE Publications Ltd.

Crowley, S. (ed.) (2014) *Challenging Professional Learning*. London: Routledge.

Hammersley-Fletcher, L. and Orsmond, P. (2005) Reflecting on Reflective Practices within Peer Observation'. *Studies in Higher Education*, 30(2), 213–224.

Hattie, J. (2012) *Visible Learning for Teachers*. London: Routledge.

Joyce, B. and Showers, B. (2002) *Student Achievement Through Staff Development*. 3rd ed. Alexandria, Virginia: Association for Supervision and Curriculum Development.

Kimble, C., Hildreth, P. and Bourdon, I. (eds.) (2008) *Communities of Practice: creating learning environments for educators Vol 1*. Charlotte, NC: Information Age Publishing, Inc.

Kline, N. (1999) *Time to Think*. London: Ward Lock Cassell Illustrated.

McMahon, T., Barrett, T. and O'Neill, G. (2007) 'Using Observation of Teaching to Improve Quality: Finding your way through the muddle of competing conceptions, confusion of practice and mutually exclusive intentions'. *Teaching in Higher Education*, 12(4), 499–511.

O'Leary, M. (2011) *The Role of Lesson Observation in Shaping Professional Identity, Learning and Development in Further Education Colleges in The West Midlands*. Unpublished PhD thesis. University of Warwick, Institute of Education, UK.

O'Leary, M. (2012) 'Exploring the Role of Lesson Observation in the English Education System: A review of methods, models and meanings'. *Professional Development in Education*, 38(5), 791–810.

O'Leary, M. (2013a) *Developing a National Framework for the Effective Use of Lesson Observation in Further Education*. Project report for the University and College Union, November 2013. DOI: 10.13140/RG.2.1.1751.7286. Available at: www.ucu.org.uk/media/6714/Developing-a-national-framework-for-the-effective-use-of-lesson-observation-in-FE-Dr-Matt-OLeary-Nov-13/pdf/ucu_lessonobsproject_nov13.pdf.

O'Leary, M. (2013b) 'Surveillance, Performativity and Normalised Practice: The use and impact of graded lesson observations in further education colleges'. *Journal of Further and Higher Education*, 37(5), 694–714.

O'Leary, M. (2014) *Classroom Observation: A guide to the effective observation of teaching and learning*. London: Routledge.

O'Leary, M. and Brooks, V. (2014) 'Raising the Stakes: Classroom observation in the further education sector in England'. *Professional Development in Education*, 40(4), 530–545.

Passmore, J. (ed.) (2010) *Excellence in Coaching*. 2nd ed. London: Kogan Page Limited.

Peel, D. (2005) 'Peer Observation as a Transformatory Tool?' *Teaching in Higher Education*, 10(4), 489–504.

Smith, M. K. (2003, 2009) 'Jean Lave, Etienne Wenger and Communities of Practice'. In *The Encyclopedia of Informal Education*: www.infed.org/biblio/communities_of_practice.htm. Last accessed 9 December 2015.

Tilstone, C. (2012) *Observing Teaching and Learning*. 2nd ed. London: Routledge.

Timperley, H. (2011) *Realizing the Power of Professional Learning*. Berkshire: Open University Press.

Whitmore, J. (2009) *Coaching for Performance*. 4th ed. London: Nicholas Brealey Publishing.

Wragg, E. C. (1999) *An Introduction to Classroom Observation*. 2nd ed. London: Routledge.

9

PEER OBSERVATION AS A SPRINGBOARD FOR TEACHER LEARNING

Matt O'Leary and Dean Price

Introduction

Few areas of practice have provoked such heated opinion and emotion amongst teachers in recent years as that of lesson observation. Just the very mention of the word 'observation' can cause panic and trepidation in some quarters. This is largely linked to how its use as a reductive form of high-stakes assessment has dominated the way in which most teachers have come to experience observation in the workplace. As dominant and contentious as performance management models have become, they are by no means the only models in use. It would be all too easy to dismiss observation as little more than a mechanism of managerial control based on recent history, but there is growing evidence of it being used much more collaboratively and formatively across the further education (FE) sector. This chapter explores such uses, focusing specifically on peer-based models of observation.

Peer-based models of observation are becoming increasingly more commonplace across the sector. To date, these have tended to operate under the radar of audit-driven activity in FE providers with little evidence of the data generated from them being formally acknowledged or feeding into performance activity related to teaching and learning. Yet this does not mean that they are less valuable or have less impact on improving the quality of teaching and learning than those that purportedly seek to measure performance in a formal, itemised way. In fact, there is growing evidence to suggest that peer-based models of observation are more conducive to bringing about the kind of meaningful and sustained improvements in teacher learning that are likely to have a greater impact on improving learning outcomes for students in the long run. So, what do these peer-based models look like? How do they differ to their dominant, performance management counterparts? And how do they work in practice? This chapter seeks to answer these questions by discussing some of the core elements of peer observation, sharing recent research evidence from the sector and hearing about the introduction of peer observation in a case study college.

What is peer observation?

Peer observation is generally understood to refer to a collaborative, often reciprocal, model of observation where peers get together to observe each other's practice. The observation is not regarded as an end in itself but as a springboard for sharing ideas and stimulating reflective dialogue. The general idea is this will then feed forward into their ongoing professional development and ultimately lead to improvements in the quality of their teaching and the students' learning experience. Tilstone (1998) uses the term 'partnership observation' instead of peer observation and argues that the object of such partnerships is to offer 'another pair of friendly eyes' in order to improve the teaching and learning taking place (Tilstone: 59). She maintains that any successful partnership should be underpinned by notions of 'trust, commitment, common understanding and the identification of individual needs' (ibid: 60).

One of the distinguishing characteristics of many peer-based models of observation compared to performance management models is the notion of reciprocal learning and the expectation that those involved will mutually support each other rather than simply assess each other's classroom performance. For this to work effectively, however, it requires more than a commitment to reciprocity. There are also implications for the way in which power is managed and the extent to which there is equal agency amongst those involved. Regardless of someone's hierarchical position and status within the institution, the success of a peer observation scheme often rests on the establishment of key principles of trust and collegiality.

There is no doubt that power relations are an important consideration in any model of peer observation, but ultimately the clarity of the core values and purposes underpinning its use should help to serve as a central reference point. Thus, for example, if the notion of reciprocal learning is seen as a key priority, then this has fundamental consequences for the roles of observer and observee. As has been argued elsewhere:

> Conceptualising observation as a tool for reciprocal learning has the potential to break down some of the traditional hierarchies and power imbalances associated with the observer–observee relationship, particularly if it is not linked to summative assessment for high-stakes' purposes i.e. graded lesson observation.
>
> *O'Leary 2014: 114*

The purpose of many peer observation schemes is largely meant to be formative. Such schemes are intended to be supportive rather than evaluative; they seek to foster a culture of collaboration and collegiality. In contrast to performative models where observers take on the role of assessors, teachers are encouraged to see themselves as 'co-researchers'.

In Table 9.1, O'Leary (2014: 122) summarises some of the key purposes and outcomes of peer observation.

What are some of the strengths and limitations of peer observation?

Like any other mechanism, peer observation has its strengths, weaknesses, opportunities and threats for individuals and institutions alike. Research carried out among GP teachers, for example, revealed opposition to schemes that used peer observation to address the twin aims of teacher development and quality assurance. Such schemes were considered 'unlikely to succeed if seen to be conveying quality assurance in the guise of tutor support' (Adshead *et al.* 2006: 72). As with any other model of observation, the transparency of the aims and objectives of a peer observation scheme is fundamental to avoid it being viewed suspiciously by teachers.

TABLE 9.1 Key purposes and outcomes of models of peer observation

Purposes	Outcomes
• To stimulate professional dialogue and critical reflection on practice	• The creation of a network or community of critically reflective practitioners
• To create reciprocal opportunities for the exchange of ideas and/or good practice among colleagues	• The development of a culture of collaboration and sharing of ideas and resources among practitioners
• To develop teachers' knowledge base and skills set	• A team of teachers with updated knowledge and skills
• To act as a key learning tool in the development of NQTs	• Well-prepared and competent NQTs
• To act as a support mechanism for teachers who are in need of guidance on specific aspects of practice.	• Improvement in the classroom competence of practitioners.

Any analysis of policy and its practical implementation needs to consider the underpinning purpose(s) of the policy in question. All too often there can be incongruences between the purported aim(s) of the written policy and how it is implemented and experienced in practice. Key questions for any institution to consider when designing a peer observation policy are: What is/are the perceived purpose(s) of the scheme? How will the scheme be implemented? What are the needs of staff to ensure the successful implementation of the scheme?

In a small-scale qualitative study involving 18 interviews with lecturers from two academic schools of a post-1992 English university, Hammersley-Fletcher and Orsmond (2005) explored their experiences as participants in a peer observation scheme. Their findings revealed uncertainty regarding the expectations of their roles as both observer and observee. Some lecturers felt uncomfortable about providing critical feedback for their peers. The uncertainty and unease expressed by lecturers showed how a shared understanding of what was meant by the term 'critical feedback' was missing. It also exposed their lack of experience in providing constructive feedback.

In Hammersley-Fletcher and Orsmond's study the success of the peer relationship between observer and observee was seen to be dependent on the notions of trust and confidentiality. These were considered fundamental to facilitating honest reflection. Gosling (2002: 2) talks about the need for staff to be seen as 'genuine peers in which there is real mutuality and respect for each of the participants as equal'. He suggests that the process can be undermined if the observer is senior in hierarchy to the observee, although his claim is unsubstantiated. His concerns seem to be based on the premise that such a relationship is likely to result in more senior members of staff taking charge, hence threatening the equality of the interaction.

Peel (2005) reflects on her personal experiences as a new lecturer and examines the arguments for and against peer observation. She maintains that it can be a useful means of facilitating reflection as long as it incorporates reflection on wider issues of the teaching and learning process and not just that of the observed lesson. She remarks that it was as a result of engaging in critical reflective thinking triggered by the feedback element that led to her successful continuing professional development (CPD) rather than discussion centring on the observation itself. Thus, peer observation is being used as a 'lens' to stimulate critical reflection (Brookfield 1995) and the peer observer takes on the role of 'critical friend'.

Within the context of peer observation, a critical friend is regarded as a respected and trusted colleague whose relationship with their peers is such that they are comfortable in asking searching and challenging questions to stretch and push their understanding and applied practice. Crucial to the legitimacy of the critical friend is their willingness to invest time in understanding the context in which their peers are working, what they are trying to achieve and how successful their current approach to achieving their outcomes is. The role of a critical friend is not that of a trouble shooter assessing the effectiveness of their practice or finding solutions to specific solutions, but to ask questions that will encourage their peers to reflect critically on their practice.

In discussing the findings from their small-scale study involving university lecturers participating in a peer observation scheme in Ireland, McMahon *et al.* (2007: 505) concluded that their research participants 'were in no doubt that having control over the five key dimensions of choice of observer, focus of observation, form and method of feedback, resultant data flow and the next steps encouraged them to focus on improvement of practice rather than demonstration of existing good practice'. We would extend this argument further and say that when practitioners are actively involved in the decision making about the protocols and procedures of a scheme, they are more likely to engage with it meaningfully and this inevitably impacts on its sustainability and the value attached to it.

So, for example, let us consider the issue of choice. Allowing practitioners to choose who they wish to peer observe with is an important consideration. Will they work in pairs or can this be extended to triads or even foursomes? Will peer groupings be intra or inter departmental? For example, might engineering and construction teachers have something to learn from their peers in the hair and beauty department? Will there be a particular focus to the observation? If so, who will decide? Will this vary according to the experience of those involved? If a specific development need is identified, then staff may be encouraged to approach colleagues who are regarded as skilled practitioners in that area.

One of the biggest challenges to undertaking peer observation is the issue of time. It can prove very difficult for teachers to coordinate timetables to identify times to peer observe, especially part-time teachers. Ways around this might include negotiating cover work with line managers as well as videoing lessons and sharing the clips amongst peers.

A common criticism levelled at peer observation is that it can easily descend into a friendly, uncritical chat about classroom practice with neither the observer nor the observee benefitting from the experience. The injection of formal processes and procedures into any model of peer observation is no guarantee of increasing the meaningfulness of the activity. There is a strong case for arguing that the greater the degree of formal processes introduced, the more onerous involvement can become for all concerned. However, the application of a systematic approach to the peer observation process can arguably result in a greater degree of success and increased sustainability. As Buskist *et al.* (2014: 50) maintain in their discussion of peer review, 'successful peer review is the product of planned and intentional discussion of pedagogy with the teacher and detailed analysis of the teacher's pedagogical practices and how those practices impact student learning'. Yet that is not to discount the value of those spontaneous and unplanned discussions that take place between colleagues on a daily basis. There is clearly a balance to be had here in adopting a systematic approach, whilst allowing room for flexibility and spontaneity.

What do FE practitioners think about peer observation?

In a recent national study exploring the use and impact of lesson observation on the profes-sional lives of staff working in FE, one of the few aspects of observation practice that was looked on favourably was peer-based models of observation (O'Leary 2013). It is interesting to note the language used by practitioners in some of the comments featured in Table 9.2 to describe/refer to peer observation and how this reflected a significant difference in their attitudes towards this model of observation compared to performative models. They talked about it being 'less stressful' and feeling 'safe enough to be observed and to observe', as the emphasis was on 'sharing best practice' and 'learning from observing others' rather than having someone make subjective judgements about their teaching.

One of the reasons why peer-based models of observation seemed to appeal so much to practitioners was the removal of the high-stakes assessment element, often identified as the main trigger for creating 'fear' and 'stress'.

In addition, peer observation for assessment purposes was regarded as less contrived and thus a more authentic experience. This last point could have significant repercussions for future uses of observation as a form of assessment as it would suggest that the low-stakes nature

TABLE 9.2 Practitioners' views about peer observation

Value of peer observation

I believe in observations between respected and supportive peers, who know the teaching area, who know the issues amongst the students and who would provide constructive and supportive feedback to encourage improvement (*Sarah, curriculum coordinator*)

I'm not against unannounced lesson observations if they remain ungraded. It's clear in most departments in my workplace that peer observation is the most effective at improving performance and showing a better understanding of context (*Elizabeth, Head of Department*)

In a collegiate atmosphere ungraded peer observation is the way forward, where honesty is fostered because there is no implicit threat to the process. It's about sharing best practice and thus improving standards, rather than raising the threat of a poor grade. Teachers do not perform at their best in such circumstances, thus graded or unannounced observation cannot give a true picture of that teacher's capabilities (*Suzanne, lecturer*)

I think that observations have their place in our teaching practice, but it is stressful, we have a lot of work to do and this does not make it easier. Peer assessments on the other hand is more useful and you learn from because you are not under the same amount of stress (*921*)

Would welcome peer assessment/honest feedback from peers who have no axe to grind. I find my colleagues' input the most instructive I have had to date and would welcome more opportunities to be involved in this. I learn so much from observing others, and if I agree to cover for a colleague, whenever possible, I observe the class prior to taking over. Not only for a seamless continuity, but also because I have previously learnt so much in this capacity about both the groups and students I am taking on but also, my own teaching and how things can work differently, or better, if approached from a different angle (*1013*)

Wouldn't it be amazing to work somewhere with a culture of peer observation where we all felt safe enough to be observed and to observe. How much better might our teaching be if that was our workplace culture rather than the one of fear of a low grade as at present (*1114*)

I'd like the opportunity to observe and be observed by peers to allow us to swap good practice and support each other. For example, a group I teach but struggle with (*1169*)

of peer observations means that they are more conducive to capturing reliable snapshots of practice than high-stakes graded observations. Still, there are question marks surrounding whether or not assessment and judgement per se should have a place in peer observations at all. Given the complexity of teaching and learning, the multitude of variables involved and the lack of consensus as to what constitutes 'good teaching', it begs the question if anyone is qualified to make an informed and reliable judgement about peers' teaching? There is also the argument that removing evaluative judgement from the observation process facilitates more genuine collaboration between peers, as highlighted by others in this book.

The benefits of peer observation and its potential to act as a springboard for substantive professional dialogue are neatly captured in the extracts from interviews with Barry and Vera, two experienced observers below:

> The best I think we can achieve is to uncover more about good practice than we currently do by providing more opportunities for teachers to see each other at work in their classrooms and to talk to one another about their practice, the experiences they have had and the theories and values that underpin their work.
>
> *Barry, observer*

> The most effective staff development happens when teachers talk to and work with other teachers, not managers or observers, but peers. Those of us who observe know how much we gain and learn from watching others teach, and I really do think that the best model is one where the power balance is equal and both partners in the process share common aims.
>
> *Vera, observer*

Peer observation in practice: a case study of Hilltop College

Background

Over the previous decade there has been a gradual increase in the use of peer observation in specific departments across Hilltop College. Although increasingly encouraged amongst staff, it has always been a voluntary process that has varied tremendously in its application and impact from being positively embraced by some, to begrudgingly undertaken by others. It was no coincidence that many of the college's consistently high performing teaching areas had been using a developmental peer observation process for many years and were familiar with its evolving structure and application before it was adopted as a college-wide initiative.

Individual subject area peer observation models were highly varied in how they were used to promote best practice at Hilltop College. All of the models used were reasonably effective, though some were more structured and guarded then others. The utopian nirvana of peer observations is often outlined as something that resembles an 'open-door' policy where a pair/trio of staff zig-zag across teaching corridors professionally buzzing and high-fiving as they share their new pearls of good practice. We realised that we had a long way to go and that the current system had plateaued in its use across the college. There were certainly some areas where an open-door culture existed. Other areas had a more formalised system where the teacher had some warning of when colleagues would observe them and were often provided with a focus of the observation. In contrast, many other areas simply refused to engage with peer observation.

It was therefore decided that a more formalised structure might be helpful in improving and standardising the current model so that all staff would be involved and that there was a clear focus and purpose to these visits. However, the informality of the current system was also seen as a strength, and for teaching staff to move towards embracing this new model, it had to be short on time but high on quality, highly coordinated and, perhaps most crucially, an individually beneficial model that focused entirely on the specific professional development needs of each member of teaching staff.

Importantly, the old model was not disbanded as it was important for those subject areas that had a long history of peer observation to continue with this practice, as they were making excellent progress towards a highly effective, self-developing model of sharing good practice. Interestingly, these organic models of peer observation were moving steadily away from the highly prescriptive and often detached examples of the college's formalised annual lesson observation process and were beginning to reflect the more apposite day-to-day teaching of what many staff consider to be their 'real teaching'.

Rationale for the introduction of peer observation

The new model was introduced as a means of getting all college teaching staff to be involved in the peer observation process. Many of the college's underperforming areas (evidenced by a suite of poor lesson observation grades, student data and perception surveys etc.) showed that these areas were not voluntarily involved in any activity focused on the sharing of good professional practice. Although suggestions for sharing good practice may have been identified on past lesson observation action plans, these were often paid lip service to and it was not unusual to find little or no evidence of them being acted upon.

In keeping with the ever-changing nature of the FE landscape, and with the college moving towards an ungraded observation model, it saw the heightened need for a more standardised and staff-driven peer observation process. Although there has been an increased focus on weekly, individually-tailored staff development sessions, the college's observation grade profile, which, albeit contentiously, has been the barometer for the quality of teaching and learning, revealed a plateauing effect. A more staff-centred peer observation process which would address everyone's individual needs was therefore devised and implemented.

For the purposes of the pilot of the cross-college peer observation scheme, the decision was taken to target those staff who had received a 'good' in their formal lesson observation in that academic year. The reason for this was that there was a growing number of teachers who were assessed as 'good' across all subject areas, yet, the percentage of those teachers assessed as 'outstanding' seemed to be diminishing. It was therefore agreed at a senior level that a more focused peer observation model might serve as an antidote to part of the problem regarding the plateauing of performance.

How does the peer observation process work at Hilltop College?

The entire peer observation process is centrally coordinated by a member of the college's Standards and Performance team. The teaching and learning strengths of every outstanding teacher are taken from their previous lesson observation action plan and stored in a database. When a member of staff is observed and judged to be 'good', their developmental points and suggested actions (e.g. peer observation, attendance at staff development sessions) are listed in an action plan which accompanies their written feedback. These developmental points are then carefully cross-matched to members of staff for whom there is evidence of having these points as a strength in their own teaching. This then provides a targeted focus to the peer observation.

The teacher and peer observer are sent an email confirming the focus, time and location of the observation. Observers are requested to stay for a minimum of 30 minutes, although they can stay longer if the observee agrees. There is paperwork attached to this activity but it is not a compulsory component of this process. The paperwork is brief and is largely meant to act as a stimulus for professional reflection and development. The paperwork consists of three simple questions:

- What teaching and learning skills/activities did you enjoy?
- How could you apply these skills/activities to your own teaching?
- Do you have any other comments to make?

Whenever possible, staff are sent in pairs to aid the crucial post-peer observation professional discussion. This is encouraged to be informal to enhance professional discussion without too many constraints such as paperwork or structure, which can restrict the process and over-shadow the more important reflective professional dialogue.

After the observation has taken place, the observee is emailed by a member of the Standards and Performance team to ensure that their peer observer attended the lesson and is asked to provide some brief feedback on the process. As the observee and observer are not from the same subject area, non-attendance is usually very quickly relayed to the relevant member of staff who is responsible for tracking attendance, but to date has proven to be rare.

What do practitioners think of the college's peer observation model?

The positives of this new cross-college peer observation scheme are that there is now a more structured approach that engages the vast majority of college staff. As it is linked to the action plan to emerge from practitioners' formal lesson observations, there is a clear audit trail, but one that is underpinned by the professional development needs of staff rather than those of performance management systems. In reality, most practitioners seem to enjoy the whole observation process and not just the pre-selected observational focus. Staff can now see closer relevance between their CPD and the action plan from their formal observations. In the past, this action plan has often been seen as more of a tick-box exercise, thus resulting in a lack of meaningful engagement with it on the part of some staff, as they did not see the relevance of it and made no clear links between the observation process and their own professional requirements. Now there seems to be more joined up thinking between the two processes. Besides, colleagues have found it helpful to have the opportunity to discuss and share ideas about their practice with each other. There have been many positive comments received about the peer observation process and how it has helped staff reflect on their own teaching practices.

The negatives of this system were that a small minority of staff did not believe that there was any benefit in going to observe teaching outside of their own subject area. This is an understandable concern and it is a challenge that those responsible for creating and managing the peer observation scheme need to consider when reviewing it. The original rationale for wanting to allocate peers from different subject areas to work together was that it would help to remove some of the familiarity and, in some cases, conflicts of interests associated with observing their subject specialist colleagues. It was also a belief that it was important to expose teachers to new teaching and learning experiences rather than the comfort of their own subject areas.

Reflections on the success of peer observation at Hilltop College

Initial feedback from staff on this new model of peer observation has been positive. They appreciated that the scheme was highly coordinated, individually focused and not too time consuming. A crucial component of this new process was that it prompted some members of staff who had become rather set in their ways to venture out of the safety of their department staffrooms and into the classrooms of colleagues from different subject areas, who were engaging in a range of innovative practices. Although the college is yet to see the full benefits of these peer observations, the scheme has clearly led to a change in attitudes and the wider culture of how some lecturers perceive the observation process. This can only be a positive thing and help to sow the seeds for future development.

Have there been any concerns about the current model? The biggest bone of contention was that only 'good' teachers were involved in the pilot. However, it has since been agreed that in the future all teachers will be involved in the peer observation scheme. It is the professional dialogue and reflection that is the important element and not necessarily shining a spot-light on the pockets of outstanding teaching practice. Moving forward this process needs to viewed by staff as an experience that they are equally involved in as both an observer and learner.

The concern about observing outside a member of staff's subject specialism will be addressed next academic year by conducting the formal observation timetable in subject clusters to allow for peer observations to then follow in areas that are more closely linked. This will help address the 'what am I supposed to learn watching a hairdressing lesson?' complaint that emerged this year from one member of staff in engineering. Although this teacher is consistently one of the best teachers in the college, they were unable to step outside of their own subject lens and see the excellent teaching taking place elsewhere.

This college is moving to an ungraded lesson observation process in the coming academic year. It is envisaged that the new model, with an emphasis on professional development and individual reflection, will further aid the peer observation scheme as it will remove the focus from a judgemental label and address the developmental needs of the teacher. To fast-track this process, all teaching staff will be joining an observer for one official college ungraded observation. The benefits of this new observation model will hopefully be extensive. Not only will the observer have a subject specialist with them, which was one of the concerns expressed by observees, but this will encourage professional discussion before, during and after the observation. As the conflict of having a grade attached is removed, then this will open the door to a more collaborative approach between the observation team and staff, which we hope will highlight the requirements of the observation process and crucially get staff talking about what really matters and that is what makes effective teaching and learning.

Conclusion

What lies at the very core of what it means to be a conscientious professional for any teacher is a conscious commitment to want to continue to learn, develop and to improve their practice so as to ensure that they are doing the very best they can for every student they teach. Being accountable for what you do is an important feature of the work of any professional these days and that is unlikely to change in the future. If teachers are to be held accountable in a meaningful and sustainable sense as professionals, then surely one of their key responsibilities must be to critically reflect on their teaching throughout their careers, with a view to the outcomes of such reflection feeding into enhanced and updated knowledge and skills. Peer-based models of observation can provide a useful springboard from which to begin to address such responsibilities, whilst simultaneously creating a community where reciprocal learning has the potential to flourish, leading to ongoing improvements in teachers' pedagogic knowledge and skills and from that a richer learning experience for students.

References

Adshead, L., White, P. T. and Stephenson, A. (2006) 'Introducing Peer Observation of Teaching to GP Teachers: A questionnaire study'. *Medical Teacher*, 28, 68–73.

Brookfield, S. D. (1995) *Becoming a Critically Reflective Teacher*. San Francisco, CA: Jossey-Bass.

Buskist, W., Ismail, E. and Groccia, J. (2014) 'A Practical Model for Conducting Helpful Peer Review of Teaching'. In Sachs, J. and Parsell, M. (eds.) *Peer Review of Learning and Teaching in Higher Education – International Perspectives*. Dordrecht: Springer Science + Business Media.

Gosling, D. (2002) *Models of Peer Observation of Teaching*. London: LTSN Generic Centre.

Hammersley-Fletcher, L. and Orsmond, P. (2005) 'Reflecting on Reflective Practices within Peer Observation'. *Studies in Higher Education*, 30(2), 213–224.

McMahon, T., Barrett, T. and O'Neill, G. (2007) 'Using Observation of Teaching to Improve Quality: Finding your way through the muddle of competing conceptions, confusion of practice and mutually exclusive intentions'. *Teaching in Higher Education*, 12(4), 499–511.

O'Leary, M. (2013) *Developing a National Framework for the Effective Use of Lesson Observation in Further Education*. Project report for the University and College Union, November 2013. DOI: 10.13140/RG.2.1.1751.7286. Available at: www.ucu.org.uk/media/6714/Developing-a-national-framework-for-the-effective-use-of-lesson-observation-in-FE-Dr-Matt-OLeary-Nov-13/pdf/ucu_lessonobsproject_nov13.pdf.

O'Leary, M. (2014) *Classroom Observation: A guide to the effective observation of teaching and learning*. London: Routledge.

Peel, D. (2005) 'Peer Observation as a Transformatory Tool?' *Teaching in Higher Education*, 10(4), 489–504.

Tilstone, C. (1998) *Observing Teaching and Learning – Principles and Practice*. London: David Fulton.

Innovations in observing classroom practice

10

VIDEO-ENHANCED OBSERVATION

Developing a flexible and effective tool

Jon Haines and Paul Miller

Introduction

We have been working on using readily available technology to create a new approach to lesson observation with the common goal of improving the outcomes for teachers, schools and learners for the past three years. Despite the prevalence of formal lesson observation systems, limited enhancement through the use of technology seems to have occurred to date. With an increased requirement for school leadership teams to have a sound understanding of the quality of teaching and learning within their schools (Wilshaw 2012), this has arguably given rise to observation systems in which teachers 'have seen their work and their worth become broken down and categorized into checklists of performance standards or competencies' (Hargreaves 2000: 152). As such, many teachers tend to view in-school observations as judgemental, punitive, superficial and stressful, rather than beneficial or developmental (e.g. O'Leary 2012; 2014).

Increasingly lesson observation, a potentially formative and valuable process, has become widely regarded as a tick-box exercise, more akin to Gosling's 'Evaluation Model' (Gosling 2002), engendering defensive attitudes and strained relationships. Power differences between teacher and line manager can be exacerbated when judgements over lesson quality are viewed and discussed purely from the observer's partial perspective. As with pupil learning, the tick in the box may be viewed as the most significant outcome, rather than any formative experience.

As trainee teachers, teachers, trainers, observers, mentors and coaches, we have both explored and experienced observation in multiple and diverse contexts, before combining our ideas to create VEO (Video-Enhanced Observation). Our intention has always been to help teachers and learners by repositioning lesson observation to promote professional dialogue between peers, stimulating professional development driven by authentic, easily accessible video and data. This neatly complements Gosling's peer review Model and the lesson study approach described by Wood in Chapter 13 of this book.

We aim to provide an intuitive, simple, but flexible tool which allows teachers to record, tag, review and share key moments of practice, to build upon and open up their learning. Supported by various communication technologies, the four walls of the classroom no longer need to act as barriers to broader dialogue and shared professional development. We envisage VEO as making observation a positive, practitioner-led experience so that large-scale and sustainable systems of continuous professional development can grow both within and between schools and educators.

This chapter describes our journeys before collaboration and since, interacting with the observation process and technology. In a world where educational goals are increasingly shifting, a professional social network supported by VEO's technology has the potential to help teachers learn from each other, pick their own path of continuous development, and ultimately improve the quality of teaching and learning.

Early origins

Having both worked in the commercial sector before undertaking a secondary Post-Graduate Certificate in Education (PCGE) programme at Newcastle University, VEO originated from our experiences in tackling comparable issues in very different contexts. After qualifying as a teacher, Jon moved on to become a curriculum leader of science, in a large urban second-ary school in the north-east of England, while Paul worked as an education consultant at Newcastle University, focusing on improving developing-world education, particularly in West Africa.

In his work in Ghana and Sierra Leone, Paul identified a need to help promote an under-standing of the importance of learner-centred pedagogy amongst teachers in the developing world, particularly as students remained largely passive in many classrooms and there was still a reliance on rote instruction as the main form of teaching (Akyeampong et al., 2006). In the contrasting context of the English education system, Jon gained first-hand experience of the pros and cons of conventional models of lesson observation and recognised that the potential for observation to stimulate personal and professional development was all too often under exploited. Paper-based lesson observation notes and feedback seemed to offer restricted opportunities to maximise the learning potential of these observations, partly because the ability to accurately describe and contextualise complex events occurring within the lesson after the event, was very difficult, if not impossible.

Over the last 15 years, we have participated in hundreds of lesson observations both as observers and observees. We have found that performance management observations can be stressful and time consuming and have little impact on the professional development of teachers or improved outcomes for learners. Speaking to many UK primary and secondary headteachers, it was clear that a substantial amount of senior staff time was being commit-ted to observation, though arguably this investment of time was not necessarily leading to tangible improvements in teaching and learning. Paper-based observation notes used dur-ing feedback seemed to have limited value and existing modes of capturing and reviewing video failed to provide an efficient means of managing the process. Addressing these issues, alongside the need to share good practice throughout teaching and learning communities, reducing the time needed for lesson debrief and increasing the availability of a resource that would enable this were key goals in the development of our ideas.

Whilst we recognise the need to be accountable for the quality of the teaching and learning in our classrooms, we believe that this should not be at the expense of a supportive climate for professional development and improvement. Indeed, it is a shift towards this sup-portive climate that we strive towards and that underpins our thinking for the use of VEO.

If undertaken in a supportive way, and particularly if assisted by video technology, we argue that observations can be one of the best ways to improve practice. In their *Best Foot Forward Toolkit*, Harvard University's Center for Education Policy Research highlight three key flaws in lesson-evaluation and reflection (Table 10.1), which can be overcome using video (CEPR 2015).

As an observer, Jon has always aimed to be supportive of his colleagues and trainees, and while recognising the importance of accountability for pupil progress, he became very conscious of the need to prioritise productive discussion that could potentially support and develop good practice and address areas for improvement without undermining the confidence, spirit and enthusiasm of his teachers.

In Paul's case, the challenge of sub-Saharan Africa was a captivating one; students eager to learn and improve their lives. Engaging with a different environment and set of values provided the conditions for Paul to experience Argyris' (American Field Service 2012) reflexive 'double-loop learning' (Figure 10.1). By being immersed in a vastly different environment, it became apparent not only *what* teaching and learning practices prevailed, but *why*, informing the conception of new approaches to change in the overarching educational and cultural context, ultimately manifested in the VEO system.

TABLE 10.1 CEPR's key flaws in lesson observation

Lesson observation flaw	*Solution provided by video*
The Omniscience Flaw	Observing self-taped lessons allows teachers the opportunity to notice challenges that are otherwise difficult to perceive while teaching.
Symptom-Treatment Flaw	Video allows educators to press pause and ponder the root causes of problems.
Recollection Flaw	Teachers can re-experience the specific details of what happened during a lesson, rather than rely on memory alone.

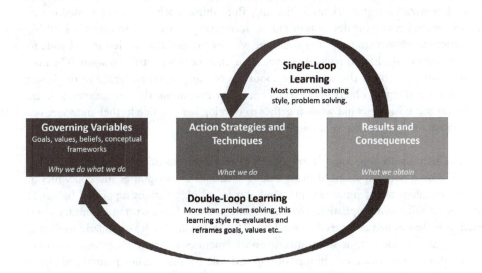

FIGURE 10.1 Double-loop learning.

Observation as an extended form of immersion, was critical to this enhanced understanding. Extensive observation and interaction illuminated thought processes and experiences that drove practice.

Assumptions about how learning could happen were thrown open, allowing Paul to question the educational status quo in low-income Ghana. For example, the majority of teachers had never experienced group work in their own school lives, let alone formal learning through doing. Exploring how and why things were done, in the context of pressing needs, made it clear that an innovative approach was required and this in turn triggered new ideas for building on widespread demand for learning and existing practice, observed as beneficial for pupil learning. Observation was critical to understanding and adapting, acting as a bridge between Paul and local trainee teachers (O'Sullivan 2006) and their different cultural backgrounds. Observation allowed the *what* and the *why* of the reality on the ground to be made apparent; discernible patterns in practice and interaction emerged. The next challenge was thus to help these trainee teachers see new possibilities in practice for themselves, beyond the limitations of their experiences as learners.

Ideas to extend these experiences into a holistic system for improvement seemed fine in theory, but we recognised that there were a number of factors that limited the effectiveness of observation as an improvement tool for participants. In order to exemplify the challenge observers face when trying to discuss classroom practice without the ability to re-play the events of a lesson, Jon often recalls an anecdote about feeding back to a colleague about what he perceived as the effectiveness of their questioning skills during a science lesson he observed, which he found difficult to encapsulate and express adequately in his feedback, as he only had his partial notes to rely on. His reflections on the experience highlight the limitations of relying on the observer's recall of the lesson and how it can lead to a missed opportunity for both parties:

> What made it great wasn't the question itself, but the way it had been presented, the enthusiasm and encouragement evident within the tone of the teacher's voice, the way she responded to her pupils' initial thoughts and suggestions, the way that suddenly the word came to life, illustrating that the word's origin is quite simple, and from here on in, few would forget its scientific meaning. But I think much of that was missed in our discussion, because the description and the accompanying scene wasn't readily available during the debrief. In truth, my colleague was just grateful that the lesson had gone to plan and that she had convinced me, yet again, that she was a capable teacher. The final questions, as is often the case, were about the overall judgement/grade of the lesson and when the next observation would be, rather than about the key moments of the lesson and how we could work together to develop her practice further and share her positive teacher-characteristics with others.

Neither of us consider this example or pattern to be unique to this particular occasion or school. We have both experienced many similar situations and responses and colleagues in other schools often tell of similar events. Paul also found observations supported by handwritten notes to be inappropriate in the Ghanaian context. There, written communication seemed to be less valued compared to the UK. Written feedback felt particularly unnatural when compared to life outside strict organisational structures and rigid classrooms, chiming with Davidson's explanation of a history of imposed colonial rules stifling natural and emergent societal change (Davidson 1992).

Paul set up procedures across schools to promote organisational learning through observation. Working across 35 different schools introduced the additional complexity of distance, not to mention issues of accountability. It soon became clear that there was little guarantee that observations would be carried out at all, let alone effectively. This was particularly important as sustainability of the process and outcome was needed at scale. As a Western consultant, Paul was conscious that his involvement was incredibly expensive compared to the incomes of the teachers and pupils' families he was aiming to support. In short, the success of implementing a schools-wide system of observation with teachers observing each other's practice was hindered by distance (physically and relationally), the quality of feedback and expense.

In both Ghana and the UK, the systemic issues and challenges associated with improving the quality of teaching and learning through lesson observation derived from the sum of the goals, capabilities and interactions of the individuals and organisations carrying out those observations. In other words, the effectiveness of the system depended on micro-level relationships, at the heart of which was the process of critical reflection and the willingness and capacity to engage in an open professional dialogue about practice. From the UK perspective, even within established regimes, support is needed to enhance these factors. As the observed teacher, even positive feedback, while gratefully received does little to help develop or facilitate unpicking the components leading to success for future replication. Equally, where recommendations are made for improvement, these can often consist of what could or should have been done. For example, advice to 'increase the amount of differentiation' or 'try (intervention x) next time', without the benefit of context, does little to help identify when, why or how this could be implemented, thus reducing opportunities for sustained and meaningful improvements in future practice.

Post-observation dialogue, framed (and perhaps in many cases limited) by a paper-based set of notes, leaves many questions unanswered and issues unexplored. Furthermore, the process is relatively time consuming and inefficient, especially given the lack of truly developmental outcomes. The key issues here are the missed opportunities to develop a better understanding of your own and others' practice, identifying what works well and most importantly why. Table 10.2 makes some helpful comparisons to illustrate the benefit of video-enhanced observations over and above the traditional paper-based approach:

Essentially, with the standard paper-based lesson observation process, what we were noticing was a mismatch between our view of desirable and actual outcomes (Figure 10.2). However, as indicated by McFadden *et al.* (2014: 460): 'Video annotation allows teachers to both observe and analyse classroom practice, supporting reflective practices as teachers' reflections are linked directly to evidence through video as documentation.'

As teachers, trainers and managers we both wanted to get more from these observations. As teachers we wanted to know more about what we were doing well so that we could refine and improve accordingly. As trainers and managers, we wanted to be able to illustrate more clearly the practice we had identified and open up opportunities for reflection and richer discussion about what we were able to co-observe. Furthermore, there was a growing demand and potential to share such examples, by developing a context-specific bank of recorded episodes of teaching which colleagues could draw upon to help improve their own practice.

In Ghana, Paul began experimenting with authentic video clips as a means to demonstrate and share new and good practice. Initially, these were set up and choreographed

TABLE 10.2 Paper vs. video observation

Paper-based lesson observations	Video-based lesson observations
Observer distracted by writing, takes eyes off the lesson for considerable periods of time.	Observer can remain focused on the lesson without the need to scribe notes of events. With VEO, the tags are overlaid on the screen so you simply keep watching while you tag.
One-sided account of events, often recalled with positive or negative bias.	Events are simply 'as they occur' and act as authentic objects for discussion and reflection.
Recall of events is incomplete: even if transcription of talk is accurate, intonation, enthusiasm and classroom atmosphere are impossible to capture.	Recall of events is thorough, in fact on review, often more is revealed than previously thought! VEO's unique tags also enables direct access to key moments and events at the touch of a button.
Feedback tends to be an observer-led lesson 'diagnosis'.	Feedback tends to be co-diagnostic and co-constructive, the events unfold for themselves and both parties are able to comment on what they see, reflecting on, reviewing and recapping complex events, multiple times if necessary.
Review and debrief tends to follow a chronological sequence covering as many aspects as were recorded.	By grouping together tagged events, VEO allows and encourages a focus on particular types of interactions, leading to meaningful and purposeful discussion.
Statements are often hard to validate due to lack of supporting evidence – for example 'there was a lot of teacher talk'.	The video provides a rich source of information which can clarify statements made by both parties.
Difficult to relay the pupils' engagement and learning.	Pupil engagement and learning can be seen and heard. With VEO, the observer can also specifically track pupil engagement and lesson focus, leading to simple graphical representation which can be used during the review/debrief and lead to well-informed discussion.
Sharing the observational outcomes with a wider audience is even more difficult than helping the observed party realise key moments within the lesson they just taught.	Video can be used to illustrate good and developing/changing practice to a wider audience. With VEO, the ability to share videos within (and if desired beyond) the organisation/school, search through the shared library for 'positive behaviour management' episodes (for example), and comment on shared clips is easy.

centrally by curriculum experts, incorporating visible practice with questions for reflection. Time and effort required meant that despite enthusiasm among the teachers, this was difficult to sustain.

Inspired by ideas in Christensen *et al.*'s work (2008) and by Africa's recent mobile technology success story, Paul shifted his thinking towards a network model of user-generated content. Peers and trainers filmed short extracts of actual lessons, building up a bank of clips that could be classified, discussed and re-used (e.g. as part of new teachers' induction). Trials demonstrated the benefits of this model for practitioner engagement and training efficiency. This proved effective when 'Lead Teachers', appointed for their dedication and openness to innovation rather than status, were given responsibility to manage the system locally.

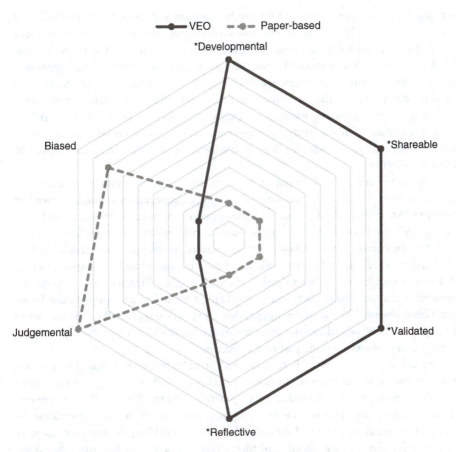

FIGURE 10.2 Lesson observation outcomes, paper vs. VEO.
★ = Desirable.

As an example, at a very basic level, Paul had noted many teachers regularly responding to only 5 per cent of pupils who would answer all of their questions during a lesson. For the majority of the teachers observed, this was the cue to move on to the next topic, leaving the remaining 95 per cent of pupils bewildered. By capturing this digitally and highlighting how the vast majority of the class were not ready to progress, it became clear that their needs could be much better served by simple pedagogical techniques that other teachers could recommend and demonstrate.

These videos were uploaded to an online video-hosting service, where comments could be made by both the teachers and their trainers. Local conditions began to intervene however, as patchy internet connectivity provided a significant obstacle. Nevertheless, on a local level, video proved very powerful in providing a shared focus for demonstration, discussion and change. For Ghanaian teachers, the chance to see others not only working in their environment, but achieving success there, which enabled growth in the perception of possibilities and provided practical assistance.

Video provided empirical, tangible evidence and the opportunity to more thoroughly unpick elements of practice, providing many other benefits too. Video recordings were able to capture a pupil's perspective, visible body language and movement, illustration of depth of subject knowledge, use of appropriate terminology, an overview of engagement and teacher-led vs pupil-led lesson time to name but a few examples. However, the use of video didn't come without its challenges. The main problem being the inconvenience of booking video resources, inexperience and difficulties of using the equipment provided, and most importantly, the time taken to review and discuss the video. Furthermore, independently reviewing lessons, while beneficial, seemed to have limited impact. Added value typically comes from supportive professional dialogue between colleagues causing cognitive and behavioural change, leading to development and self-improvement, or the improvement of others.

Reflecting on the hierarchical nature of conventional lesson observation processes, Jon envisaged a far more valuable conversation taking place between, for example, a head of department and a teacher in the department, if the conversation were to revolve around what they had learned from peer observation rather than direct observation by their line manager. Through peer observation, supported by video, Jon wanted to encourage and enable teachers to work together to identify and gather evidence of their own good and developing practice. The idea was to enable the teacher to gather video footage to illustrate their progress and development over time. Thus, rather than simply being a discussion about a particular lesson which had been observed by the line manager, this conversation would allow the teacher to identify their own professional development needs, undertake action and illustrate impact, leading to greater ownership on the part of the teacher.

This approach aligns well with O'Leary who argues that 'peer-based models of observation such as lesson study offer the potential to enhance pedagogic understanding and in turn contribute to the ongoing process of teacher development' (O'Leary 2012: 808). Furthermore, VEO's core functionality supports the key purposes and benefits of peer observation by stimulating professional dialogue and critical reflection and enabling the open exchange of ideas. Conversely, where many schools find themselves, is that a 'snapshot' paper-based lesson observation takes place, the senior leader provides feedback and agrees targets which feed forward into the teacher's annual appraisal. The teacher then acts upon these, often more by way of limited professional compliance than in the interest of personal and professional development, commonly referred to as the 'tick-box' approach.

The system-wide benefits of an efficient, affordable, intuitive video recording and feedback process should be enormous as Bill Gates recognised in his TED talk *Teachers Need Real Feedback* (Gates 2013). He estimated the cost, and therefore the potential value, of this system to be $5bn in the USA alone. Critically, through our work, we have examined and evaluated where that value lies. The result is in user-generated, *manageable* and shared video to support discussion – incontrovertible but *accessible* evidence of what is actually happening. Discussion of, and changes in, teaching practice leading to improved pupil learning then follows relatively conveniently.

The VEO concept

It was against this backdrop, fuelled by the increasingly widespread availability of handheld and connected technology that the concept of Video-Enhanced Observation came about, and coincidentally, the English translation of the Spanish word 'veo' is 'I see' – a rather fitting description of what VEO is all about!

The solution we arrived at was simple – so much so that neither of us could believe that nothing had been done quite like it before. The VEO App enables live recording of lessons, while pre-defined and customisable tag sets are overlaid onto the tablet screen so that key moments can be tagged and identified throughout (Figure 10.3).

This quickly categorises critical instances, building up a picture of the lesson characteristics through the data. Importantly, the tags also act as bookmarks, allowing both the observer and the observee to jump to (five seconds before) these key moments when reviewing the video (Figure 10.4).

FIGURE 10.3   VEO tagging key moments.

FIGURE 10.4   VEO lesson review timeline.

Looking back at a one-hour lesson can now take a matter of minutes rather than the full length of the recording. This fits better into busy teachers' schedules, with the confidence that important learning points have been identified and are accessible. Key moments are aligned with more continuous measures of engagement and classroom focus as controlled by the observer. These feed into line-graphs and pie-charts respectively, giving the observed teacher a view on how the profile of the lesson changed over time (Figure 10.5).

When aggregated, these can indicate patterns that teachers can work to change or build on. As the system is customisable, tags from any observation framework can be overlaid onto the live video, allowing for a different focus according to the lesson, teacher, occasion, school, setting or focus. These can be created or requested by the user, ensuring relevance to the teaching and learning environment in question. During a VEO session, the observer is now freed from writing copious notes. They have time to consider the impact of actions in the classroom, as well as to capture moments of pupil activity, which can provide valuable feedback to the teacher.

The secure VEO online portal (Figure 10.6) enables the collection and sharing of video and tag data. Designed to be as intuitive as any social network, it was important that searching and sharing of key moments would be as easy as possible.

VEO combines quantitative tag data with rich, qualitative video evidence, each supporting and adding to the strengths of the other. A good example of this is in the tracking of pupil engagement throughout a lesson, producing an interactive line-graph which allows the viewer to jump straight to moments in the lesson when engagement peaked or dipped. We have both used this feature to draw attention to transition points, reflecting with the teacher on the transition from one task to another and how different approaches to managing this transition can impact on levels of engagement. Video and data gathered over time significantly enhance the observation process by providing empirical evidence of both good practice and areas for development. Again, the simple graphical representation can highlight

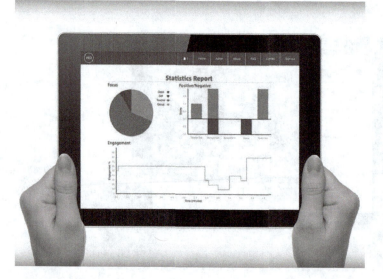

FIGURE 10.5 VEO data analysis.

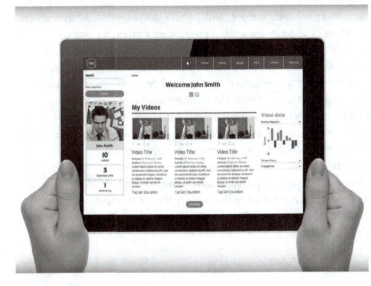

FIGURE 10.6   VEO secure online portal.

TABLE 10.3 The VEO development journey

Development stage	Summary of key functionality
Prototype App.	Live video tagging, app-based video and data review.
Refined App and Online Portal.	Upload to social network style secure online portal, allowing sharing and interaction at distance.
Flexible Tagging.	User-generated frameworks used to tag video, making data pertinent to the user and their context.
Retrospective Tagging.	Video can now be uploaded and tagged online from any web-connected device (extending the use of the VEO system to users without iPad access). Observers' perceptions of practice can be compared and consensus achieved.

these quickly and enable the viewer to quickly home in on particular aspects of practice. As these build up, not only do they become portfolios of practice for teachers to demonstrate active continuous improvement, they also form banks of authentic training resources that colleagues can share to enhance school and system–wide improvement.

VEO as a system has now evolved considerably from its early conception, as briefly summarised in Table 10.3.

Working with practitioners

Progress in VEO's development has been aided by close collaboration with colleagues working in schools and other training environments. The VEO prototype was trialled during one of Paul's large scale teacher training interventions in Ghana and, at a smaller scale, in Sierra Leone. This gave us early confidence over its usability, while indicating that convenient access to practice could be exceptionally powerful. Schools in the north-east of England also piloted VEO and their initial experiences fed into the app and portal's development, with teachers' ideas and innovative applications of the app expanding possibilities further. In one school, for example, teachers were using VEO to record pupils' reactions to lessons by asking them brief informal questions about their learning while it was in progress and recording their responses. Capturing student voice, was felt highly beneficial by the teachers involved, particularly in respect of quieter pupils, less visible to them during the ordinary course of class teaching.

Throughout the development of VEO, we were aware that positive user reaction would be vital to its success. Improvement in process and practice could only happen if end users were fully engaged, and their experiences were continuously improved upon. The key was to provide positive interactions with the technology and fellow users, which would support repeated use, and therefore consistently improve practice and its application. Preece and Shneiderman's (2009: 21) *Reader-to-Leader* framework was important in identifying 'usability and sociability factors', positive aspects to encourage contribution, alongside teachers' intrinsic and extrinsic motivations.

VEO: the future

We feel that we are just scratching at the surface of VEO's possibilities in education: our facilitated network model supporting our goal of affordably achieving real and scalable educational impact. At the micro-level, it is hoped that VEO can be used to enhance interactions around practice, whatever the context, supporting colleagues in reflective conversations that lead to practical and sustainable improvements. We have already seen and heard many anecdotal accounts of professional dialogue developing around behaviour management, questioning, explanation, balance of teacher-talk vs pupil-talk, independent work versus group work, all driven from key moments tagged within lessons using VEO. Within schools, a degree of control over and responsibility for improvement can legitimately be handed back to the teacher. This can be achieved by teachers actively demonstrating and sharing their improvement among peers and colleagues, rather than undergoing a number of staged observations per year in an enforced, top-down system. By freeing up such time, more effort and resources can be spent analysing and learning from real practice, with immediate benefits for teachers and pupils. The observation thus becomes a tool for the practitioner to support positive change and extend the boundaries and possibilities of good practice.

VEO also has the potential to inspire greater connections between schools and educators throughout the world. This has already started, in collaboration with Finnish, German, Turkish and Bulgarian institutions. With early adopters now present in the USA, Australia, China and the Middle East. The dream is to inspire cross-national and international collaboration, all driven by the very people who are best equipped to affect the pupils they are teaching – the teachers themselves. As communities of VEO users grow, skills and knowledge of the system can be supported from within the user groups, growing a network of advocates. This can open up practice to new audiences and allow teachers across the globe to learn from one another.

We are also excited by potential further applications of VEO technology. Recording and tagging pupils as they learn how to learn can help them acquire skills and behaviours to support their development into adulthood. Outside of compulsory education, VEO is already being used by Teesside University Undergraduate Paramedic students to refine and demonstrate their competence in practice (e.g. https:bit.ly/VEOTeesUni). In this arena, as with other vocational uses, the visual aid is critical to understanding and replicating successfully executed process and interaction. In medical and similar professions, human factors beyond the technical are being increasingly recognised as critical to standards of care. VEO is also exploring the use and sharing of video and tag-data across the medical and clinical fields, vocational competency assessment, legal communication practice, transport management, gap-year work placements and presentation skills. In all of these, there are cross-cutting needs for enhanced information, communication and organisational learning and education, review and reflection on interaction and process become powerful means to improve.

Conclusion

This chapter has described the origins and development of this new innovation in video recording technology, alongside the associated shift in methodology and process for improving practice through lesson observation. Deep engagement with this goal has led to an intuitive tool to support bottom-up professional development. It is hoped that this can truly reclaim observation through the power of positive participation from those on the ground. While the technologies themselves may not be revolutionary (i.e. the use of video and the sharing of data), this improved application, supported by practitioners, can lead to groundbreaking changes in the way that practice is owned, shared and nurtured – as identified in Lofthouse and Birmingham's (2010) study. Their experiences indicated that teachers benefited from video-based lesson analysis in ways that were not as apparent from participation in other forms of professional development, building confidence and supporting relationships with mentors. This suggests that the video format may provide better leverage for both engaging teachers in change towards 'the *object* of learning to teach' (Ibid. 16) and then enacting that change in the classroom.

We are both conscious that videoing professional practice, in any context, can present challenges and obstacles, particularly in terms of privacy and performance management. In our experience, schools and school leaders who engage in the process that we advocate, encouraging a supportive peer-led approach and allowing teachers the freedom to choose what to video and what to share, are those who benefit the most. They experience fewer challenges from staff and teachers, who are usually only too keen to try to improve their classroom practice and have been seen to develop a positive source of good practice in a relatively short timescale which can benefit the whole school.

By giving these tools to the teachers themselves, huge gains in the effectiveness and efficiency of observations can be realised, which along with a supportive institutional environment can enhance students' learning experiences and improve learning processes and outcomes. With VEO in the hands of teachers, continuous review, reflection, sharing and discussion can create a self-sustaining system of professional improvement. As teaching evolves across the globe to meet the changing needs of learners, VEO offers the potential as a flexible platform to enable and support development of innovative practice.

References

Akyeampong, K., Pryor, J. and Ampiah, J. G. (2006) 'A Vision of Successful Schooling: Ghanaian teachers' understandings of learning, teaching and assessment'. *Comparative Education*, 42(2), 155–176.

American Field Service (2012) 'Single-Loop and Double-Loop Learning Model: Adapted from interpretations of Argyris's writing'. Available at www.afs.org/blog/icl/?p=2653.

CEPR – Center for Education Policy Research (2015) *Best Foot Forward: A toolkit for fast-forwarding classroom observations using video*. Cambridge, MA: Harvard University.

Christensen, C. M., Johnson, C. W. and Horn, M. (2008) *Disrupting Class: How disruptive innovation will change the way the world learns*. New York: McGraw-Hill.

Davidson, B. (1992) *The Black Man's Burden: Africa and the curse of the nation-state*. New York: Three Rivers Press.

Gates, B. (2013) from TED Talk 'Teachers Need Real Feedback'. Available at: www.ted.com/talks/bill_gates_teachers_need_real_feedback?language=en.

Gosling, D. (2002) *Models of Peer Observation of Teaching*. London: LTSN Generic Centre.

Hargreaves, A. (2000) 'Four Ages of Professionalism and Professional Learning'. *Teachers and Teaching*, 6(2), 151–182.

Lofthouse, R. and Birmingham, P. (2010) 'The Camera in the Classroom: Video-recording as a tool for professional development of student teachers'. *TEAN Journal*, 1(2), December 2010 [Online]. Available at: http://bit.ly/tyfJ5M.

McFadden, J., Ellis, J., Anwar, T. and Roehrig, G. (2014) 'Beginning Science Teachers' Use of a Digital Video Annotation Tool to Promote Reflective Practices'. *Journal of Science Education and Technology*, 23(3), 458–470.

O'Leary, M. (2012) 'Exploring the Role of Lesson Observation in the English Education System: A review of methods, models and meanings'. *Professional Development in Education*, 38(5), 791–810.

O'Leary, M. (2014) *Classroom Observation: A guide to the effective observation of teaching and learning*. London: Routledge.

O'Sullivan, M. (2006) 'Lesson Observation and Quality in Primary Education as Contextual Teaching and Learning Processes'. *International Journal of Educational Development*, 26, 246–260.

Preece, J. and Shneiderman, B. (2009) 'The Reader-to-Leader Framework: Motivating technology-mediated social participation'. *AIS Transactions on Human-Computer Interaction*, 1(1), 13–32.

Wilshaw, M. (2012) 'Leading from The Front'. *Times Educational Supplement*, No. 5013, 5 October, 46.

11

OBSERVING WHAT MATTERS

Rachael Stevens

Why are lesson observations so problematic?

Sadly, the fear factor runs rampant when it comes to the use of observations in education. They are often high-stakes, linked to performance management and even pay in some schools. The traditional Ofsted-style performative observations have become the norm, with teachers feeling that the grade describes them as a professional, rather than a fleeting judgement on 30 minutes of one lesson. It is precisely because of this fear that some teachers understandably seek to minimise the time senior leaders spend in their classrooms. If they become the only opportunity leaders have to visit, evaluate and all too often grade teachers' work, they inevitably come with a disproportionate importance attached to them. But it doesn't have to be like this.

Ofsted (2015: 11) recently revised its approach to lesson observations stating that:

> Ofsted does not award a grade for the quality of teaching for any individual lessons visited and it does not grade individual lessons. It does not expect schools to use the Ofsted evaluation schedule to grade teaching or individual lessons.

Accordingly, the grade descriptors for the 2015 Ofsted framework for teaching and learning apply to criteria over time, so applying them to singular lessons does not make sense anymore. Ofsted has also stated that it is entirely up to schools how they choose to monitor and evaluate the effectiveness of teaching and learning:

> Inspectors must not advocate a particular method of planning, teaching or assessment. It is up to schools themselves to determine their practices and for leadership teams to justify these on their own merits rather than by reference to this inspection handbook.
>
> *Ofsted (2015:10)*

However, this apparent freedom only serves to highlight those schools and Senior Leadership Teams (SLT) that cannot imagine how teaching and learning can be evaluated without a number. All too often we hear of schools that still use Ofsted criteria that were simply not designed to judge single lessons or excerpts, or they mistrust the evidence that repeatedly tells us that graded judgements do not work (e.g. O'Leary 2013a, 2013b). They also seem to ignore Ofsted's declaration that they have 'no preferred teaching styles' and its accompanying rationale (e.g. Cladingbowl 2014), instead producing observation matrices that spread over several pages and imply that within them they carry the 'silver bullet' solutions to what makes an outstanding lesson.

Classroom observations do not give a definitive picture of a teacher's performance over time. Taking a traditional approach to teacher appraisal where lesson observations are infrequent, high-stakes and formally graded, for full-time teachers, three of these observations per year would represent about 0.4 per cent of their classroom practice. As such, they do not give opportunities to see the 'rapid and sustained progress' that inspections demand, yet the way in which they are used as high-stakes assessment in some schools means that their outcomes can have far-reaching consequences for the teacher and the school itself. It is unsurprising then that lesson observations still have the power to reduce perfectly competent, confident, effective teachers into quivering piles of nerves or walls of defensive suspicion. This inevitably raises the question as to what lesson observations can tell us about teaching and learning.

Using an 'observation classroom' as a window for teacher learning

Classroom observations can teach us a lot about practice, our students, their interactions and their needs. They can also teach us a lot about ourselves. It is a huge privilege to witness what goes on in our classrooms, to experience great teaching and support colleagues in their own learning. It does not have to be something to fear and it should certainly not be punitive. What is needed is a radical re-think, a change of mindset about what observations are for and what they can do to support classroom practice and students' learning.

At my school, we have been developing a range of observation approaches for some time. We have spent a lot of time refining and trialling these approaches. What we learn about classroom practice and colleagues' development constantly informs our thinking. Above all, though, we are attempting to put outcomes for students as our ultimate priority for all approaches. The professional and personal development of our fantastic staff is key to providing that and so our observations aim to dispel fear, move away from judgement and crude measurements and seek to give individual and useful means for all teachers to reflect on their practice.

One excellent tool we are lucky to have in helping us to develop a positive attitude amongst our staff is our *observation classroom* (Figure 11.1). Our headteacher is a keen advocate of Sir Tim Brighouse (2013), who in citing American professor of education, Professor Judith Little, maintains that in very good schools 'teachers talk about teaching, teachers observe each other's practice, teachers plan, organise and evaluate their work together rather than separately, and … teachers teach each other'. Our headteacher's philosophy was thus to create an environment and culture in the school that would actively encourage reflection on pedagogy. Hence the introduction of our observation classroom, which was installed six years ago.

The observation classroom consists of both a standard classroom and a built-in 'viewing room' with video recording and editing equipment (Figure 11.2). There is also seating for staff to watch lessons from behind the window, unseen when the lights are off from the other side of the two-way glass. The viewing room is soundproofed so whoever is observing can

FIGURE 11.1 Observation classroom.

FIGURE 11.2 Observation viewing room.

discuss it in this room without it disturbing the lesson in progress. We observe clear ethical guidelines about the room's use, a key aspect of which is the consent of both staff and students. Students always know they are being watched and permission to be filmed is included in our home/school agreement. Its use is not compulsory but operates on a voluntary basis.

Since our observation classroom was created, the way in which staff use it has evolved. At first, most teachers used it mainly to record themselves teaching, which they then watched in their own time. Since then, it has taken on a more communal focus and has become much more commonplace for staff to observe their peers teaching live. We refer to these as 'open lessons'. Teachers can book to teach a lesson in the room on a voluntary basis and invite their colleagues who aren't teaching during that period to view their lesson in the viewing room.

These observations are non-judgemental. There are no grades or assessment of the teacher's classroom performance at all and the use of the 'host' (see below) sharpens the focus on learning. All observers are there to discuss teaching and learning and a lesson can be observed and discussed freely without the dynamic of the room being altered by observers sitting in.

An important feature of our open lessons is that they are always 'hosted' from the viewing side of the glass. An experienced member of the SLT watches the lesson with the other observers. Before the observation, the observee will often ask their peer observers to concentrate on a particular aspect of their practice/the lesson. For example, how EAL (English as an Additional Language) students are coping with the work or the effect of questioning on learning. A key role of the host is therefore to steer the focus and discussion of the observers to the chosen area(s) of practice and remind them that they are not there to judge the teacher's performance. Most importantly, the observation becomes a collegial conversation about pedagogy, in real time, with an openness that can only come when there is a mutual trust and a belief that it is helping to develop professional practice amongst peers.

It works well in both a cross-curricular and subject-specific context. For example, in a recent open lesson for A level Religious Education, the whole RE department was able to observe an experienced colleague from one of our partner schools teach a part of the new syllabus, modelling the use of high-order discussion and questioning with year 12 students. This was followed by a discussion between the department and the teacher, with reassurance gained about methods as well as useful strategies being learned for teaching subject-specific content. Similarly, our Modern Foreign Languages department have used the room to share ideas about the impact of teaching for the speaking and listening examinations. The relatively new subject leader taught the lesson, which was not only beneficial in terms of opening up a discussion about specific pedagogy but also demonstrated to his colleagues that he was eager to practice what he preached!

Whilst the majority of schools do not have this facility, we know of two schools that have decided to create their own observation classroom as a result of having visited us and seen ours and the possibilities it offers. We have also built a second classroom in the past year at relatively little cost, as it only contains the sound system and not the recording and editing equipment that can be very costly. This means we have greater scope for more individuals and more departments to book the facility on a more regular basis, with the hope that every department in the school has experience of the open lesson and its benefits at least once during the course of the school year. However, if your school/college is not in a position to create an observation classroom, what can it do to accommodate 'live' group observations in order to develop this practice?

Using 'walk-throughs' as a window for teacher learning

One aspect of lesson observations that we have developed in recent years is the walk-through. Most staff in schools and colleges will be familiar with the concept of the walk-through or what is sometimes referred to as learning walks. Depending on the culture and ethos of teaching and learning prevalent in the institution, attitudes to walk-throughs can vary considerably. In some contexts, they have come to be viewed with an element of suspicion and scepticism by teachers, as they have been appropriated by some school leaders as an extension of performative observations with the added bonus of being able to fit three into an hour, where one may have been the norm with the 'traditional' performance management lesson observation. On the other hand, where they have been used in a low-stakes, supportive sense, then there is arguably a lot to be gained from the intelligent application of walk-throughs. But what can be learned about teaching and learning in such a brief snapshot?

'Open-door' policies to observation are becoming increasingly common in schools, with teachers used to having people calling in unannounced to see what is happening in their lessons. This is certainly the case in those departments where colleagues are used to sharing and subject heads make themselves available for impromptu visits, chats with students and praise. In contrast, in those schools and departments where an open-door culture is less common, classroom visits tend to signal formal observations, which can provoke feelings of guardedness and anxiety on the part of some teachers.

As a senior leader, it would be easy for me to state here that teachers have nothing to fear from walk-throughs, but that, of course, depends on the people walking through! It is therefore up to the SLT to create a climate of learning and sharing throughout the school and demonstrate this when conducting walk-throughs. Some headteachers might find this challenging, especially when they feel there are staff who are not trying their best for their students, but then I would argue that one of the hallmarks of a good leader is someone who attempts to tackle these issues on an individual basis rather than keeping the whole class in at break when only two or three have been disrupting the lesson! How then can schools use walk-throughs as a way to improve teaching and learning, that is supportive rather than judgemental, but which also creates a map that pinpoints where support and extra continual professional development (CPD) is needed and to what extent?

'Questions, Favourites, Feelings': a simple strategy for walk-throughs?

During my training as a Specialist Leader of Education, organised by the National College of Teaching and Leadership, I first encountered an approach to walk-throughs that I have used repeatedly since then because it is surprisingly powerful and in my experience has tangible impact. It uses a simple strategy known as *Questions, Favourites, Feelings* (QFF).

The first time I heard of this it was during a training session at a school none of the delegates had visited before. We were split into small groups and invited to walk-through three different lessons in an hour, each classroom visit lasting no more than ten minutes. We were actively distracted between each visit by the hosting deputy head, to discourage us from discussing and sharing what we'd seen, although we didn't realise this was a deliberate strategy on her behalf until after the event. In each classroom, where appropriate, we talked to students about their learning. Timing was strictly monitored and, despite there being six of us, our presence didn't seem to be obtrusive. As none of us were able to take notes, we didn't have the barrier or the potentially alienating clipboards between us and the teachers and students. This allowed us to observe, listen and to experience the atmosphere of the classroom.

We returned to our base room and were each given a side of A4 paper to write on for five minutes about what we had seen, but once again, without the opportunity to discuss with our peers. The paper had three equal sections and was headed: *Questions, Favourites,* and *Feelings.* We were asked to write comments under these three headings with no other prompts. I was immediately sceptical. Surely there wasn't enough room to write about what I had seen? I had visited three classrooms and there was plenty I wanted to comment on. I seriously doubted that these three simple headings would be able to capture what we had seen, certainly not enough to be able to provide useful feedback for the teachers we had seen. I didn't know where to start.

However, once I began writing about the section that seemed 'easiest', I found I was able to write quite a lot. I chose 'Favourite' first. What had I liked about what I had observed? What were the positives? My favourites seemed to fit each of the three lessons I had visited. Student behaviour was fantastic, the classrooms were bright and inviting, with stimulating displays of students' work throughout and there was lots of evidence of very good teacher/ student relationships throughout too.

So then, what about 'Feelings'? I assumed this was the atmosphere that we felt as we walked around. It felt positive, calm, ordered and safe. This was a good thing, wasn't it? Well … it felt secure, but if I was going to be honest, it also felt a bit *too* safe. Where was the excitement or the challenge? This felt a bit disloyal as my overwhelming feelings had initially been so positive. But the more I thought about it, the more it became clearer that there had been a distinct lack of energy in the learning. The students had not only been well-behaved, but they had been comfortable and very relaxed too. In actual fact, they had been quite passive.

So this made the 'Question' section much easier to complete. For each lesson, I thought it would be useful for me to ask these questions:

- Was this lesson 'typical' in terms of structure, student interaction and tasks?
- What were the students learning?
- How did I know?
- How were the ablest and the weakest students challenged and supported in this lesson?

We discussed what we had seen and written. Our observations and jottings were surprisingly similar considering we never had the opportunity to compare notes at any point. Spending only ten minutes in each classroom, we had all ended up praising the same things, experiencing shared feelings and asking the same questions. But what took us all by surprise was that a suited man whom we had not noticed in the room stood up after our discussion and thanked us all. He introduced himself as the school's headteacher. I immediately felt guilty and embarrassed. What had I said about his school that may have been unflattering? He told us that what we had fed back after just an hour in three classrooms were some of the key areas he had been attempting to address for the previous five years in post. Situated in a pleasant, leafy catchment area with supportive families, positive relationships between staff and students, results were good but had failed to get any better for some time. There was a relaxed atmosphere that according to the headteacher was bordering on complacency.

Reflecting on the experience, I had very much underestimated the power of those three simple focuses and the uncanny accuracy of the notes that we had all put together in what seemed like a very limited amount of time, but it certainly seemed to work. So I have used it many times since, both within my own school and also in some of my outreach work in partner schools. In some ways, it has made walk-throughs easier to manage. It has made feedback an altogether more supportive process. Interestingly, many of the teachers that the SLT might have predicted would prove the most difficult to work with in terms of improving their practice, have been very co-operative, which perhaps says something about the way this particular strategy is perceived by staff compared to a judgemental approach based on grading teacher performance.

As an observer, I have found it useful to allow the questions part to be addressed during feedback and recorded. This eliminates judgements being made on misunderstandings and gives the teacher being observed an opportunity to think in terms of why they choose particular tasks. Another really positive outcome of using this method for walk-throughs is that anyone can participate as an observer, regardless of their experience and that can be an empowering experience. Whenever anyone asks to observe one of my lessons, I now ask them to record what they see on these three-part forms. Colleagues of all levels of experience have told me that they have found the forms extremely easy to use and in turn I have found the feedback really useful. It is therefore great for peer visits within departments and with colleagues in other departments.

So, in summary, here is a list of pointers to remember when undertaking a QFF walk-through:

- Don't write as you observe; concentrate solely on observing.
- Try not to discuss what you see between classrooms and don't pre-empt or share your opinions with other observers.
- Allow ten minutes of quiet reflection and individual note-taking at the end of the observation before you discuss your comments.
- Always share feedback with the teachers involved and use this as an opportunity to discuss what you have taken away from the experience as well as things that they might wish to consider.
- Never be tempted to give the walk-throughs a grading: this is not what this type of activity is for. You are sharing experiences of a snapshot of teaching and learning, which is hopefully going to be the start of a reciprocal, developmental dialogue.

When you undertake a QFF walk-through for the first time, it might help to have some prompts to hand. It can help with that first committal of pen to paper! See Appendix 11.1 for an example of the QFF form we used originally, with prompts included. The following questions and answers may also help if you wish to set up a programme of QFF walk-throughs. Obviously every institution is different and you may choose to adapt this according to your needs and circumstances.

Q1. *How could QFF walk-throughs work as a whole-school focus?*
A1. We decided to focus on middle leaders first. We did some pilot walk-throughs first with departments that were having internal reviews, so when we introduced the model in one of our middle leaders' meetings, we already had some first-hand experience

from a couple of subject leaders who had been through the process, thus helping to add more validity and authenticity to the discussion.

Q2. *How does the feedback work? Is it just for individuals or for whole departments? Who gives the feedback and is feedback always given?*

A2. Yes, feedback is always given. Time is an issue though, and that's why to date it has been easier for the SLT member or lead teacher to give the walk-throughs. However, it is always valuable if one of the other observers can sit in, so it acts as a model for future walk-throughs, if time allows. It is important to discuss the forms with the observed teacher, particularly to allow opportunities for the 'Questions' section to be addressed. This could be seen as the trickiest section as it's the most developmental area and the questions could be seen as targets. However, they can often also be easily answered and thus eliminate areas of misunderstanding, something that critics of walk-throughs often cite: how much can you really gauge in ten minutes?

Q3. *Who sees the feedback?*

A3. This is an area that needs to be negotiated, and agreement reached between all parties beforehand. As this type of walk-through is a developmental and a supportive process, then the observer and the observed teacher should retain copies of the completed forms. Notes should NOT be passed to the teacher's line manager without their agreement.

As a lead practitioner, I keep copies for my own records – mostly to see how the forms are used by staff across the school. They can be easily anonymised, and I always seek permission from the observer and observee. In my experience, many teachers ask if they can put the forms in their CPD folders as evidence of ongoing in-school support, and the assistant headteacher with responsibility for CPD is offered a copy too, but that is only if the observer and observee agree.

Following on from walk-throughs

After we completed our first round of walk-throughs and middle leaders/responsibility post-holders had all had the opportunity to take part in the observations and the ensuing dialogue, many of them spoke about how it had given them more confidence to voice their thoughts and opinions and that it had been very useful to have non-specialists accompanying subject and pastoral walk-throughs to allow an objective viewpoint.

Many middle leaders have now introduced walk-throughs in their own departments, with a view to all teachers and support staff having the opportunity to take part in visiting others' classrooms and also being observed themselves. The trick is also to find a way to integrate walk-throughs into the fabric of the department, so that it is part and parcel of its regular practice and forms an essential part of the framework of support for its staff.

We have also developed the forms and the walk-throughs into what we call *Blink Reviews*, named after Malcolm Gladwell's book, *Blink: The power of thinking without thinking* (2005), which advocates the judgements the brain is able to process with relatively little information. These replaced the previous week-long, over-prepared departmental reviews that were in danger of becoming mini-Ofsted inspections, with all the stress and distraction from teaching and learning that came with the old-style inspection process. With *Blink Reviews*, they are often over in a day or two and each observation lasts no longer than 20–25 minutes. Over-preparation is positively discouraged, to try to promote a sense of normality. All members of the department are observed; all receive developmental feedback and the headteacher and his team gain an excellent insight into teaching across departments and the learning experiences of the students.

The observation forms are based on the QFF forms, this time with a section for what has been seen in the student books and also allowing the department members them-selves to define what they would like the focus to be, e.g. questioning or challenge (See Appendix 11.2).

Post-Blink, a short report is written, summing up what was seen across the department in terms of successes and good practice, together with areas for development. The subject leader has the right to reply and discuss before it is completed, and development points are agreed with realistic time targets in which to achieve them. Support is also offered where appropriate and when requested from the lead practitioner team.

Concluding thoughts

As an SLT we have learned that observations should be undertaken in pairs. Sharing with middle leaders and classroom teachers what we believe good practice to be can go awry if senior staff are not trained or are not consistent in their approach to observation and are not very sensi-tive to teachers' feelings about being observed. A good *Blink Review* will capture the essence of the class and the teacher. A poor review will be perceived as rushed and will be a wasted opportunity. Successful feedback that has impact is as essential for staff as it is for students.

It takes time to erase the damage and suspicion that has been caused by years of engrained practice where lesson observations have been used punitively, promoting prescription and an ignorance of what actually works in classrooms. But with increased understanding, informed leaders and an organic approach to change, it can be done. As with most things though, seeing is believing. Shorter, *Blink*-like observations; supportive walk-throughs and open les-sons are only part of the picture. Could SLTs use the time that used to be spent on longer, formal and judgemental observations to pair teachers up to plan together, to share strategies for subject-specific concepts, to observe learning behaviours and reflect together? Colleagues need to see for themselves how powerful developmental and supportive observations can be in growing cultures that trust teachers and encourage wider and more creative collegiate professional development at every level.

References

Brighouse, T. (2013) 'How Can We Continue to Raise the Quality of Our Teaching?' Article in *SecEd* magazine, published 7 February 2013, www.sec-ed.co.uk/best-practice/how-can-we-continue-to-raise-the-quality-of-our-teaching/. Last accessed 17 February 2016.

Cladingbowl, M. (2014) 'Why I Want to Try Inspecting without Grading Teaching in Each Individual Lesson', June 2014, No. 140101, Ofsted.

Gladwell, M. (2005) *Blink: The power of thinking without thinking*. London: Penguin.

Ofsted (2015) 'Ofsted Inspections: Clarification for schools', September 2015, No. 140169, *School Inspection Handbook: Handbook for inspecting schools in England under section 5 of the Education Act 2005*, June 2015, No. 150066, Ofsted.

O'Leary, M. (2013a) *Developing a National Framework for the Effective Use of Lesson Observation in Further Education.* Project report for the University and College Union, November 2013. DOI: 10.13140/RG.2.1.1751.7286. Available at: www.ucu.org.uk/media/6714/Developing-a-national-framework-for-the-effective-use-of-lesson-observation-in-FE-Dr-Matt-OLeary-Nov-13/pdf/ucu_lessonobsproject_nov13.pdf.

O'Leary, M. (2013b) 'Surveillance, Performativity and Normalised Practice: The use and impact of graded lesson observations in further education colleges'. *Journal of Further and Higher Education,* 37(5), 694–714.

Appendix 11.1: walk-through feedback sheet

Question

Are there any questions you would like to ask after the walk-through that might help the teacher reflect, or anything that would make your understanding better?

e.g.

At what stage of the lesson was this?
Is this a 'typical' lesson?
Are all students aware of their targets and how to achieve them? etc.

Feeling

What feeling(s) did you get about the walk-through as a whole?

e.g.

Exciting
Pacey
Calm
Passive
Challenging etc.

Favourite

What did you see that you especially liked?

e.g.

Displays
Student behaviour
Student learning
Methods of marking / assessment
Tasks/ resources etc.

Appendix 11.2: blink review form

Teacher:	Observer:	Dept. & Group:	Date:

Questions

Favourites

Books Adheres to school policy? Marked for Literacy?

Key focus from last Blink Review: (e.g. Questioning)

12

USING LESSON OBSERVATIONS TO PROMOTE TEACHER SELF-EFFICACY

Terry Pearson

Introduction

The lens of teacher self-efficacy is used to examine lesson observation in this chapter. A teacher's sense of efficacy is considered to make a major contribution to their proficiency in the classroom. Exploring lesson observation from the perspective of teacher self-efficacy has highlighted the potential of lesson observations to generate valuable information to support teacher professional learning which can foster the development of their self-efficacy. It has also raised doubts about the capacity of current observation practice in England's colleges and schools to produce the optimum conditions for developing and sustaining teachers' efficacy in their classrooms. A framework is presented and explained as a means of stimulating thinking and encouraging discussion of how lesson observation may be used effectively to develop teachers' perceptions of their self-efficacy.

Background

Over a period of almost a quarter of a century, graded lesson observation schemes have become the dominant model of lesson observation in many of England's colleges and schools and yet, according to the findings from two recent large scale studies, teachers don't gain much to support their professional learning from this type of lesson observation. A study of almost 4000 teachers in England's further education colleges found that close to three quarters (74.8 per cent) of respondents did not agree that their lesson observations had helped them to improve as classroom practitioners (O'Leary 2013). Moreover, although virtually all teachers in England's schools receive feedback from lesson observations, when compared with teachers in 33 other countries, fewer teachers in England reported that the feedback received about their performance led to positive changes in their teaching practices (OECD 2014). Clearly, there is considerable scope for improving lesson observation practice in England's schools, colleges and other organisations as these findings support the argument for moving away from contemporary lesson observation systems in order that England's teachers learn more from observations and find them more helpful in enhancing their classroom proficiency.

The outcomes from the above studies should not be surprising. The use of graded lesson observations has been problematised from a variety of viewpoints. This includes potentially damaging effects on professional relationships which can discourage teachers from taking innovative steps when teaching (Coffield 2012), conceptual and contextual difficulties surrounding the assessment of teaching practice (Cope *et al.* 2003), tensions created for teacher educators who often have to balance the effective facilitation of student teacher learning with the requirement to provide lesson observation grades for quality assurance purposes (Ollin 2009) and concerns about the trustworthiness and accuracy of the findings from graded observations (Pearson 2014a, 2014b).

So, what might be done to make lesson observations more useful to teachers so that the information they gain from them can be used more effectively to enhance their proficiency in the classroom? One common approach to advancing the use of lesson observations is to take on the challenges of addressing the elementary concerns of judgemental approaches by, for example, improving the accuracy of judgements made during lesson observations, standardising what is observed and recorded, removing grading schemes from the process, enhancing the post-observation dialogue between observer and teacher, and putting in place systems to support teachers in progressing the actions that emanate from observations. This chapter does not set out to provide illustrative exemplars of ways to address these concerns, nor does it attempt to provide solutions to other critical problems that arise when using judgemental lesson observations. Rather the purpose of this chapter is to pose, and go some way towards responding to a different and possibly more important concern: are lesson observations that require a third party to provide feedback the most effective way of using observation to help teachers develop their proficiency in the classroom?

This chapter outlines the beginnings of a process that sets out to establish an answer to this fundamental question. It reports on how an initial review of teacher self-efficacy literature led to the conclusion that a range of lesson observation approaches can be used to engage teachers in learning about their practice in the classroom and the practice of their colleagues. And what is more, these approaches have real potential to be more effective at building a teacher's sense of efficacy than the judgemental models which are currently prevalent in England's colleges and schools.

Theoretical overview

In a seminal paper by Bandura (1977), self-efficacy was presented as a means of determining the extent to which a person will respond positively in challenging circumstances. Bandura referred to his model as an 'integrative theoretical framework' in which he proposed that a person's perceived self-efficacy will have a direct influence on whether they will attempt a challenge, how much effort they will apply and how long they will persist in the face of adversity. According to Bandura, self-efficacy is a malleable phenomenon which develops and changes over time as new information and experience are acquired and adapted to fit changing conditions. Although research points toward a far from straightforward relationship between self-efficacy and personal performance in that, for example, self-efficacy's effect on performance may not always be positive (Powers 1991) and the strong positive relationships observed between self-efficacy and performance may at times be a function of performance's influence on self-efficacy (Vancouver *et al.* 2001), research has consistently shown that peoples' perceived self-efficacy is positively related to their achievements in a wide range of contexts. An early meta-analysis of studies of the relationship between self-efficacy and work-related performance confirmed that significant increases in performance can be due to high self-efficacy (Stajkovic and Luthans 1998).

Teacher self-efficacy, which has been defined as a teacher's belief in their 'capability to organise and execute courses of action required to successfully accomplish a specific teaching task in a particular context' (Tschannen-Moran *et al.* 1998: 233), has been researched extensively though this research has not been uncontested. Recent scrutiny has raised various queries about the meaning, interpretation and measurement of the construct as well as questions about some of the findings from its application in education settings (Klassen *et al.* 2011). Notwithstanding these concerns, a considerable amount of research suggests that teachers' self-efficacy is related positively to teacher performance and to important educational outcomes. It has been observed that teachers with reported higher self-efficacy demonstrate greater levels of enthusiasm and are more willing to experiment with innovative methods (Guskey 1988). It has also been reported that teachers who express greater self-efficacy work longer with struggling students, are less critical of learners when they make errors and provide more effective feedback. Moreover, studies of the relationship between teachers' self-efficacy and students' learning have at times shown a significant and strong positive association between teachers' sense of efficacy in the classroom and students' learning (Ashton and Webb 1986). Evidence has been garnered which shows the more efficacious teachers felt the more their students advanced their attainment in a range of subjects which includes reading, mathematics, language and history. Teachers' perceived high self-efficacy has also been found to be a significant predictor of increased students' academic achievement when final examination grades were aggregated at the school level to provide an overall indicator of a school's academic performance. In addition, there is substantial evidence to show that teacher self-efficacy is linked to students' development in aspects other than academic achievement. For example, higher teacher efficacy has been associated with enhanced student motivation, increased self-esteem, improved self-direction and more positive attitudes toward school. Nevertheless, it is important to recognise that teacher self-efficacy is both task and context dependent. Teachers may believe they are more capable of succeeding with some groups of students than others and they may have a higher sense of self-efficacy about one aspect of their teaching compared to another. While it is too early and hence misleading to suggest that teacher self-efficacy determines a student's success insofar as research into how teacher self-efficacy influences student outcomes has at times produced mixed and perhaps ambiguous results (Klassen *et al.* (2011), the research evidence shows overall that high teacher self-efficacy has been associated positively with teacher motivation and commitment and with successful student progress when learning.

Generating teacher self-efficacy information through lesson observation

In his model of self-efficacy, Bandura proposed that expectations of self-efficacy are based on four major sources of information: performance accomplishments, vicarious experience, verbal persuasion and physiological states, and these sources of information have been shown to have varying degrees of influence on a person's sense of self-efficacy. Little has been written about how these sources of self-efficacy information contribute to the formation and development of teacher efficacy. At present, it is unclear if some sources of efficacy information are generally more effectual than others and if the effectiveness of sources differs for different teachers in differing contexts. Moreover, it has been argued that teacher self-efficacy research in general has paid insufficient attention to examining the sources of information and further investigations are critical for advancing the theoretical understanding and practical relevance of the concept (Klassen *et al.* 2011).

Nonetheless, in the context of teacher self-efficacy in the classroom, the four main sources of capability related information identified by Bandura that are most likely to affect teachers' self-efficacy are information resulting from a teacher's experiences of teaching (performance accomplishments), information gathered by a teacher through watching other teachers teach (vicarious experience), information received by a teacher from another person or from other people about their capabilities to perform in the classroom (verbal persuasion) and the physiological states experienced by teachers when they are teaching and engaged in teaching related professional development. How these four sources of information are generated through lesson observations are illustrated in Figure 12.1.

Bandura identified information received from performance accomplishments to be the most influential of the four major sources as this is based on personal experience and thus provides the most authentic evidence of whether a person can pull together what it takes to succeed. Self-observation may therefore elicit the most influential teacher self-efficacy information. When teachers are able to see themselves at work in their classrooms the information they collect about their capabilities is the most authentic. There is no third-party involvement in interpreting the teaching situation or in gathering and analysing the information collected. In many ways, digital video technology provides opportunities for facilitating self-observation insofar as it captures naturally occurring classroom activities, some of which the teacher may

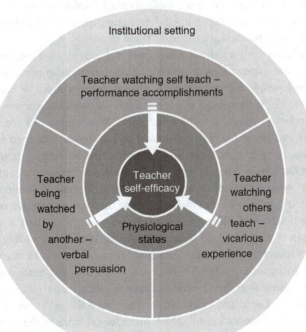

FIGURE 12.1 Sources of teacher self-efficacy information from lesson observations.

not have noticed at the time of teaching, fixes these in their time and place and makes them available for repeated viewing and manipulation which can, and often does, re-awaken the memories and experiences of the participants (e.g. Jewitt 2012). Nevertheless, video only records the material aspects of a lesson, presenting an extrospective view of the complexities inherent in what actually happened in the classroom. Self-observation is most likely to offer information that can be used effectively for judging self-efficacy when self-analysis and self-interpretation of classroom experience move beyond consideration of merely the visual elements of what happened in a classroom into an introspective study of what was also happening in the teacher's mind when these things occurred. While self-observation enables teachers to see themselves through their own eyes and to some extent 'relive' particular episodes of teaching, it is through the recollection and review of emotions, thoughts, ideas, perceptions and concerns as well as the evaluation of actions that give meaning to the situations teachers experience (Roche and Gal-Petitfaux 2015). Through this introspection, teachers can identify when they experienced setbacks, recall what they felt like at the time and what, if anything, they did to overcome the obstacles that faced them. In doing so teachers can judge to what extent they achieved, or failed to achieve, the standards they set for themselves. Comparing perceived differences between accomplishments and personal standards creates self-dissatisfaction when the accomplishments fall short of the standard. This can be either motivating or demotivating and the outcome is likely to be determined by the strength of an individual's belief in their capabilities to attain their personal standards (Bandura and Cervone, 1986). Teachers who doubt their capabilities tend to be demotivated quite easily by failure to achieve their self-imposed standards and those who trust their capabilities to succeed tend to increase their efforts and perseverance when their performance falters. Self-observation is thus a potentially powerful means of providing a rich seam of self-efficacy information to teachers that can be used to help them assess their capabilities, determine their own capability questions and explore their own routes to finding answers to those questions.

Vicarious experiences gathered from watching others carry out activities without undesirable consequences can engender expectations in observers that they too can perform those tasks successfully, while seeing people fail can reduce an observer's belief in his or her capabilities to achieve the same tasks. As vicarious experience relies on social comparison rather than direct experience, Bandura proposed it to be a less dependable source of information about a person's capabilities and hence likely to be weaker and more susceptible to change than that gained from personal attainments. Observing other teachers at work in their classrooms is consequently most likely to be a highly influential but less steadfast source of efficacy information. When teachers watch their colleagues teaching, they not only gather information about the abilities of their peers but they may also see their own teaching in that of their colleagues. This can lead to heightened self-awareness of who they are as teachers as well as the practice they use (Rosaen *et al.* 2013). Peer observation of teaching, most notably when the emphasis is shifted from 'observing to evaluate teaching' onto 'observing to learn from teaching', has been shown to increase teachers' confidence when they see others successfully using similar practice to themselves thereby reinforcing self-efficacy information gained from previous accomplishments (Engin and Priest 2014). They may also see others do well in situations where they have been less successful which provides evidence of the success of alternative ways of working in classrooms which may increase their willingness to explore these further (Hynes and Dos Santos 2007). Conversely, observing other teachers' fail in similar circumstances despite strong efforts to succeed is likely to diminish self-efficacy beliefs by leading the observer to the conclusion that the task is unmanageable or that they too lack the capability to succeed, unless the observer believes that they are more capable than the person being observed (Tschannen-Moran *et al.* 1998). Moreover, when observing others teach, teachers are inclined to consider how successful they might be if they were teaching in the same situation as people seek to evaluate their capabilities by comparisons with the abilities of others (Wood 1989). A teacher is much more likely to make an accurate evaluation of their capabilities through comparisons if the person they are observing shares similar characteristics with them and is working in similar circumstances as people do not tend to compare themselves with others who are significantly dissimilar to themselves.

Verbal persuasion occurs when one individual is persuaded by another or by others that they have what it takes to complete given tasks. Through verbal persuasion people are more likely to attempt a challenging task and persist than they would if they doubt their capability to perform the task and dwell on their personal inadequacies, nevertheless Bandura acknowledged that simply informing people that they are likely, or unlikely, to be successful does not mean that they necessarily believe what they have been told. Feedback received from being observed by another in the form of verbal persuasion is therefore potentially the least influential source of self-efficacy information. Information from previous accomplishments is wholly authentic as it is based on actual experiences of teaching and information from vicarious experience is substantially authentic as it is based on personal experience of seeing someone teach, whereas information about a teacher's capabilities obtained through a third party is almost entirely reliant on the credibility of the person giving the feedback and the trustworthiness of the information being presented. Nevertheless, this is not to suggest that receipt of feedback from a third party following an observation is unlikely to affect a teacher's sense of self-efficacy but simply to highlight that the influence the feedback has depends very much on what is said and who is saying it. Even though observers and teachers do not always interpret feedback in the same way, which can lead to each reaching different conclusions about the salient aspects of the feedback, when teachers engage in discourse exchanges during post-lesson observation feedback it has been shown to provide critical learning opportunities principally when the conversation supports reflection as well as promoting self-assessment for the teacher (Soslau 2015).

An important approach to reflection is the balanced focus on thinking, feeling, wanting and acting. Korthagen and Vasalos (2005) note that reflection in the education world has become alienated from the first three of these concerns because of the emphasis on external behaviours and therefore advocate a model of 'core reflection' to help teachers delve more deeply into the feelings, needs, beliefs and self-concepts that inspire them to teach in the ways that they do. They point out that this type of reflection does not entail the observer probing into the private lives of the teacher and it is possible to train observers to reach these more deeply rooted aspects of professional practice.

The framing of performance related feedback following an observation also needs consideration. Performance feedback that focuses on achieved progress underscores personal capabilities. Feedback that focuses on shortfalls highlights personal deficiencies (Bandura 1993). When the negative aspects of performance are accentuated e.g. a 25 per cent shortfall in expected progress, this undermines self-regulatory influences and is likely to result in a deterioration of performance. On the other hand, when positive aspects of performance are emphasised e.g. 75 per cent of expected progress already attained, self-efficacy is enhanced along with aspirations, efficient analytical thinking and self-satisfaction which often leads to enhanced performance (Jourden 1992). Feedback provided following a lesson observation therefore needs to be constructed in such a way that it helps the teacher to gain insight into the affective elements that underpinned their practice and also avoids stressing deficiencies in performance disproportionately or at the expense of highlighting attainments as this can have a debilitating effect on the teacher's self-efficacy and subsequent performance. Teachers consider teaching efficacy information received from a third-party to be more robust when it is perceived to be either affirming or clarifying (van Dinther *et al.* 2015). Feedback is seen to be an affirming experience when it corroborates the self-view and the self-evaluations made by the observed teacher prior to receiving the feedback information. When the feedback enhances the observed teacher's self-judgements of the capabilities that were brought to a particular teaching event and helps them to appreciate better the consequences of those capabilities this is regarded to be a clarifying experience. While a trusted colleague may provide feedback to a teacher which boosts or diminishes the teacher's sense of self-efficacy, it is likely that the motivating or demotivating effects of the feedback will be overturned if vicarious experience information or performance accomplishment information is encountered subsequently by the teacher which counters the third-party feedback.

Bandura recognised that people are also affected by their physiological states when judging their capabilities to deal with a situation. High arousal tends to be debilitating in that feelings of stress and tension are often seen by an individual as signs of weakness and indicators of potentially poor performance. The physiological states experienced by teachers when they are making judgements of their capabilities to complete teaching tasks provide emotional cues which can raise or lower their perceived self-efficacy to complete those tasks. If a teacher experiences excessively high arousal in the form of anxiety or nervousness when contemplating a particular teaching situation, the teacher may perceive this to be an indication that they will not perform as well as they might if they were less anxious or nervous. The effects of physiological states apply in a similar fashion in situations where teachers are receiving self-efficacy information from lesson observations. When teachers are observing themselves or watching others teach they tend to be less anxious about what they are doing at the time than on occasions when they are being observed by another, or by others. Edgington (2016) reported powerful tensions existing between a teacher's perceived requirements to conform to expectations and their personal values and experiences during formally graded lesson observation processes. The outcome from observations of this type in England's schools and colleges invariably casts the teacher on one side of a binary divide that provides for the affirmation or degradation of their professional status. They are deemed to have succeeded or failed, be competent or incompetent, act professionally or unprofessionally. The emotions inherent in being observed by someone can therefore induce levels of anxiety that have a deleterious effect on the teacher's performance. Furthermore, a teacher who sees their arousal as stemming from their personal inadequacies is more likely to lower their efficacy expectations than a teacher who attributes their arousal to certain situational factors. Moderate levels of arousal can improve performance by focusing attention and effort on the task in hand. Teachers who consider particular levels of arousal to be commonplace and necessary conditions of teaching are more likely to benefit from moderate levels of arousal when evaluating their self-efficacy than those who see arousal of this type as interfering with making the best use of their capabilities.

While these four sources of information are likely to have influence on teachers' perceptions of self-efficacy, Bandura acknowledged that information alone is not necessarily persuasive. The extent to which self-efficacy information becomes persuasive to a teacher depends upon how the individual processes it and their circumstances at the time of receiving it. For example, a teacher who was unsuccessful at controlling student behaviour during their first teaching session may process information about the event in a way that lowers their sense of self-efficacy. On the other hand, a teacher who over time has become accustomed to managing student behaviour well may process information relating to an instance of poor management of student behaviour simply as a blip in their capabilities with little bearing on their overall self-efficacy.

Although self-perceptions of teaching efficacy are personally constructed, a sense of self-efficacy is not formed independently of a teacher's surroundings. Bandura's view of self-efficacy is one of human agency that is closely aligned with social cognitive theory in that people develop their perceptions of how to think, feel and act in response to others around them (Bandura 1989). Teachers therefore develop a self-view of how to teach in their workplace that is shaped by their perceptions of how others teach and through feedback, which they believe confirms that they have earned the approval of those around them.

At times, teachers are inclined to model the beliefs and teaching approaches of others whilst equally being models for other teachers. Evidence shows a teacher's sense of efficacy is context-specific rather than universal and as such teachers' judgements of their self-efficacy are influenced significantly by their working environment. Several studies have confirmed that a supportive organisational climate that includes support from colleagues and leaders positively affects teachers' self-efficacy. Additionally, teachers who work in organisations that foster highly collaborative relationships and enable them to exercise control over key working conditions exhibit high levels of self-efficacy (Raudenbush *et al.* 1992). Within a teaching organisation, perceived collective efficacy represents the group members combined beliefs that they can work together to produce the desired outcomes. The more teachers have the opportunity to influence decisions that are teaching relevant, the more likely the organisation is to be characterised by a robust sense of collective efficacy (Goddard *et al.* 2004). The stronger the teacher's collective belief in their teaching efficacy, the better an organisation performs academically (Bandura 1993).

Implications

This brief introductory review of teacher self-efficacy research has shown that different forms of lesson observation can be used very effectively to generate a rich source of valuable information to promote teacher self-efficacy in the classroom. It also casts doubts about whether the one-size-fits-all approach of deploying judgemental, third-party lesson observations, which have been the mainstay of lesson observation practice in England's schools and colleges for more than 20 years, yields the most effective and meaningful performance and capability information to support the development of teacher self-efficacy. The effectiveness of information gathered from observations of this type to sustain a teacher's sense of efficacy in the classroom is potentially very limited and any changes in a teacher's practice accruing from feedback from third-party observations may be short lived.

Teacher professional learning clearly takes place from the 'double' perspective of being the observer as well as being the observed (Donnelly 2007) and evidence is emerging to show that the process of observing is just if not more valuable than being observed and given feedback (Hendry and Oliver 2012). If lesson observations are to be used in such a way that teachers find them helpful in building a high level and enduring sense of self-efficacy, which encourages and enables them to continually enhance their practice in the classroom, then teachers need access to a range of lesson observation opportunities that allow them to see themselves at work with their students and examine the classroom expertise of their colleagues. Self-referent information accumulated from frequent observations of seeing oneself teach and observing one's colleagues teach needs to be synthesised with self-efficacy information received from others watching oneself teach if teachers are to grow and uphold a high level of teaching efficacy. The more teachers are constantly on the lookout for opportunities to see themselves teach, to explore the teaching of their colleagues and to enable others to see them at work, the more likely they are to bring together fertile information about their capabilities and thereby foster their self-efficacy in the classroom.

Furthermore, examining lesson observation from a teacher efficacy perspective can help leaders in colleges, schools and other teaching organisations to design ways of moving away from simply using third-party lesson observation in judgemental ways to classify the quality of teaching or to identify the development needs of the individual being observed, and move more towards thinking about how lesson observation can be used more expansively to address the professional development needs of both the observer and the observee. Teachers can learn a great deal from using a variety of lenses to examine their own teaching and that of others, from watching credible practice being modelled during teacher education and staff development and from third-party lesson observations attuned less to evaluating performance and more to helping teachers find out about what they did in the classroom and the beliefs and values that underpinned their actions. Once the vista of lesson observations is opened up in this way, it becomes apparent that teachers need a greater say in how lesson observations are used in England's colleges and schools if this information is to better meet their development needs in the classroom. It also brings into the line of sight the need for leaders, managers and teacher educators to find ways of developing systems that enable teachers to access an eclectic range of lesson observation opportunities during their work and during their training.

References

Ashton, P. T. and Webb, R. B. (1986) *Making a Difference: Teachers' sense of efficacy and student achievement*. New York: Longman.

Bandura, A. (1977) 'Self-efficacy: Toward a unifying theory of behavioral change'. *Psychological Review*, 84(2), 191–215.

Bandura, A. (1989) 'Social Cognitive Theory'. In Vasta, R. (ed.) *Annals of Child Development*. Vol. 6, 'Six Theories of Child Development', 1–60. Greenwich, CT: JAI Press.

Bandura, A. (1993) 'Perceived Self-efficacy in Cognitive Development and Functioning'. *Educational Psychologist*, 28, 117–148.

Bandura, A. and Cervone, D. (1986) 'Differential Engagement of Self-reactive Influences in Cognitive Motivation'. *Organizational Behavior and Human Decision Processes*, 38, 92–113.

Coffield, F. (2012) 'To Grade or Not to Grade'. *Adults Learning*, Summer 2012, 38–39, NIACE.

Cope, P., Bruce, A., McNally, J. and Wilson, G. (2003) 'Grading the Practice of Teaching: An unholy union of incompatibles'. *Assessment & Evaluation in Higher Education*, 28(6), 673–684.

Donnelly, R. (2007) 'Perceived Impact of Peer Observation of Teaching in Higher Education'. *International Journal of Teaching and Learning in Higher Education*, 19(2), 117–129.

Edgington, U. (2016) 'Performativity and the Power of Shame: Lesson observations, emotional labour and professional habitus'. *Sociological Research Online*, 21(1), 11.

Engin, M. and Priest, B. (2014) 'Observing Teaching: A lens for self-reflection'. *Journal of Perspectives in Applied Academic Practice*, 2(2), 2–9.

Goddard, R. G., Hoy, W. K. and Woolfolk Hoy, A. (2004) 'Collective Efficacy: Theoretical development, empirical evidence, and future directions'. *Educational Researchers*, 33, 2–13.

Guskey, T. R. (1988) 'Teacher Efficacy, Self-concept, and Attitudes Toward the Implementation of Instructional Innovation'. *Teaching and Teacher Education*, 4(1), 63–69.

Hendry, G. D. and Oliver, G. R. (2012) 'Seeing is Believing. The Benefits of Peer Observation', *Journal of University Teaching & Learning Practice*, 9(1).

Hynes, M. M. and Dos S. A. (2007) 'Effective Teacher Professional Development: Middle-school engineering content'. *International Journal of Engineering Education*, 23(1), 24–29.

Jewitt, C. (2012) 'An Introduction to Using Video for Research' (National Centre for Research Methods Working Paper 03/12). Available at: http://eprints.ncrm.ac.uk/2259/4/NCRM_workingpaper_0312.pdf. Last accessed 28 March 2016.

Jourden, F. (1992) 'The Influence of Feedback Framing on Self-regulatory Mechanisms: A glass half full or half empty'. Faculty working paper no. 93–0117, Bureau of Economic and Business Research. University of Illinois.

Klassen, R. M., Tze, V. M. C., Betts, S. M. and Gordon, K. A. (2011) 'Teacher Efficacy Research 1998–2009: Signs of progress or unfulfilled promise?' *Educational Psychology Review*, 23, 21–43.

Korthagen, F. and Vasalos, A. (2005) 'Levels in Reflection: Core reflection as a means to enhance professional growth'. *Teachers and Teaching*, 11(1), 47–71.

OECD (2014) *New Insights from TALIS 2013. Teaching and Learning in Primary and Upper Secondary Education*. OECD.

O'Leary, M. (2013) *Developing a National Framework for the Effective Use of Lesson Observation in Further Education*. Project report for the University and College Union, November 2013. DOI: 10.13140/RG.2.1.1751.7286. Available at: www.ucu.org.uk/media/6714/Developing-a-national-framework-for-the-effective-use-of-lesson-observation-in-FE-Dr-Matt-OLeary-Nov-13/pdf/ucu_lessonobsproject_nov13.pdf.

Ollin, R. (2009) *The Grading of Teaching Observations: Implications for teacher educators in Higher Education partnerships*. Huddersfield: Huddersfield Consortium.

Pearson, T. (2014a) 'Lesson Observation: How trustworthy are graded lesson observations?' *FE News* [online]. Available at: www.fenews.co.uk/featured-article/lesson-observation-how-trustworthy-are-graded-observations. Last accessed 15 February 2016.

Pearson, T. (2014b) 'Should Colleges Still Be Using Graded Lesson Observations?' *Education Leader and Manager*. October 2014, 6–7. AMiE/ATL. Available at: http://issuu.com/atlunion/docs/elm_october_2014_low/7?e=9795814/9578273. Last accessed 15 February 2016.

Powers, W. T. (1991) 'Commentary on Bandura's "human agency"'. *American Psychologist*, 46(2), 151–153.

Raudenbush, S., Rowan, B. and Cheong, Y. (1992) 'Contextual Effects on the Self-Perceived Efficacy of High School Teachers'. *Sociology of Education*, 65(2), 150–167.

Roche, L. and Gal-Petitfaux, N. (2015) 'A Video-Enhanced Teacher Learning Environment Based On Multimodal Resources: A case study in PETE'. *Journal of e-Learning and Knowledge Society*, 11(2).

Rosaen, C. L., Carlisle, J. F., Mihocko, E., Melnick, A. and Johnson, J. (2013) 'Teachers Learning from Analysis of Other Teachers' Reading Lessons'. *Teaching and Teacher Education*, 35, 170–184.

Soslau, E. (2015) Development of a Post-Lesson Observation Conferencing Protocol: Situated in theory, research, and practice'. *Teaching and Teacher Education*, 49, 22–35.

Stajkovic, A. D. and Luthans, F. (1998) 'Self-Efficacy and Work-Related Performance: A meta-analysis'. *Psychological Bulletin*, 124(2), 240–261.

Tschannen-Moran, M., Woolfolk H. A. and Hoy, W. K. (1998) 'Teacher Efficacy: Its meaning and measure'. *Review of Educational Research*, 68(2), 202–248.

Van Dinther, M., Dochy, F. and Segers, M. (2015) 'The Contribution of Assessment Experiences to Student Teachers' Self-Efficacy in Competence-Based Education'. *Teaching and Teacher Education*, 49, 45–55.

Vancouver, J. B., Thompson, C. M. and Williams, A. A. (2001) 'The Changing Signs in the Relationship Among Self-Efficacy, Personal Goals, and Performance'. *Journal of Applied Psychology*, 86(4), 605–620.

Wood, J. V. (1989) 'Theory and Research Concerning Social Comparisons of Personal Attributes'. *Psychological Bulletin*, 106, 231–248.

13

LESSON STUDY

An opportunity for considering the role of observation in practice development

Phil Wood

Introduction

Lesson study has become an increasingly popular tool for investigating pedagogy across a number of countries particularly since the year 2000. The USA, UK, China, Singapore and Indonesia are just some of the international education systems that have developed the use of this technique in the last two decades. Yet this recent explosion of interest belies a long-term development which originated and has been evolving in Japan for well over 100 years. Why then has lesson study suddenly caught the imagination of so many in education and what can a consideration of the method add to our understanding and practice of observation?

Lesson study (kenkyuu jugyou) emerged as a grassroots movement amongst Japanese teachers in the 1870s (Nakatome 1984 cited in Fernandez and Yoshida 2004) and was intended as a means of sharing practice amongst teachers through the collaborative development of teaching approaches. From this early informal beginning, lesson study grew and eventually became a more formal process used by teachers and training colleges. In this way, collaborative approaches to pedagogic development became deeply embedded across much of the educational system of Japan over the course of the twentieth century. The collaborative nature of the approach has led to its adoption as a continuous school improvement activity in much of Japan, particularly in elementary schools (Takahashi and Yoshida 2004; Sarkar Arani, Shibata and Matoba 2007).

Lesson study remained a largely Japanese methodology until researchers and practitioners from other countries were exposed to it towards the end of the twentieth century. The work of Stigler and Hiebert (1999) and Lewis and Tsuchida (1997) laid the foundation for the translation of lesson study into parts of the USA system, with take-up across East and Southeast Asia, Europe, Canada and through the initial work of Dudley (2012, 2014) into the UK. As a consequence, lesson study is rapidly becoming an established technique for interrogating and developing pedagogic practice in many parts of the world and in all phases of education from primary to higher education.

In this chapter, I will firstly outline the basic lesson study approach, before considering the role and issues surrounding the use of observation as a methodology for understanding and developing support for learning. I will then go on to suggest additions to the lesson study model which might help to extend its potential for questioning and understanding the process of learning in relation to classroom practice.

The lesson study approach

Lesson study is underpinned by an iterative process involving a collaborative approach to planning, executing and observing and evaluating a lesson. This approach is exemplified in Figure 13.1, which outlines a five-step process for completing a single cycle of lesson study.

The process begins with a group of teachers coming together through mutual interest or concern relating to an area of student learning. The size of the lesson study group is determined by the context in which teachers are working, but has to be collaborative in nature. This means that two teachers could carry out the lesson study process together, although the fewer the number of individuals involved, the greater the potential there is to have a relatively narrow number of ideas coming to the fore in planning to meet the learning challenge which the group decides to focus on. For those new to lesson study, the use of a triad (in other words, a group of three teachers) can be useful as this allows for a relatively easy management of the process itself, whilst ensuring a variety of views.

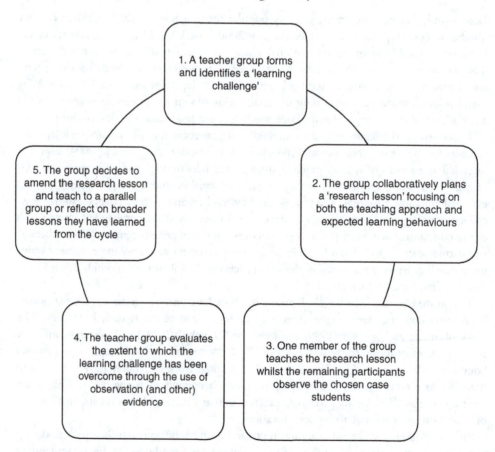

FIGURE 13.1 A basic lesson study cycle.

Once the group has been formed, it begins by identifying a learning challenge with which it will grapple (see step one above). The identification of the learning challenge is central to the process and should focus on an aspect of student learning that the teachers identify as giving rise to a particular concern. The learning challenge should be relatively specific and concerned with an element of curriculum content, competence or skills development. An example of a clear and appropriate learning challenge would be the difficulties that some students have in mathematics when attempting to convert between decimals, percentages and fractions. It is important that the learning challenge does not focus on either very general issues, for example learning about coasts in geography, as this covers a whole element of the subject rather than a specific learning challenge, or on issues which are themselves either outcomes or epiphenomenal. An example of this latter category is the notion of *engagement*. Whilst it may be tempting to focus on an issue such as this, engagement is actually an outcome rather than a learning challenge. It is through successfully helping students to understand difficult content and pitching that content at an appropriate level that engagement results. Therefore, the learning challenge should focus on the development of knowledge or skills, with engagement being a positive by-product of meeting these demands. It is also important that the lesson study group does not resort to identifying and discussing a particular *teaching* approach that they would like to try to improve, the discussion of *student learning* should be at the heart of deciding what will be investigated as a process for emerging pedagogic innovation and practice.

Once the learning challenge has been agreed, the group then collaboratively plans a lesson – known as the research lesson – which is designed to make the learning challenge explicit and begin to overcome it. (See step two in Figure 13.1). This is achieved by the group pooling their experience and pedagogic knowledge to discuss and plan the lesson. In some contexts, particularly in Japan, this collaborative planning process makes use of the presence of a 'knowledgeable other', such as an expert in the given academic field and/or an expert in the chosen area of pedagogy. They act as guide and devil's advocate to challenge and extend the discussion of the group in considering new approaches. However, in many contexts, the presence of such an individual is not practicable and the teacher group operates alone to plan the lesson. As with the case of the knowledgeable other, different contexts will allow different time frames to be used in planning the lesson. In some systems, it may be possible to spend a considerable amount of time in planning a single lesson, leading to a very fine level of detail in the plan. However, in many systems, such as that in England, there is a huge time pressure relating to the everyday work of teachers and therefore collaborative planning has to be carried out more rapidly. The experience of members within the University of Leicester lesson study research group is that it should be possible to complete the planning phase in between one and two hours, with extra time given over to associated resource development.

The planning process should include two basic phases. The first phase centres on the planning of the *teaching*, discussing each element of the lesson and why they believe that its inclusion will help students in overcoming the selected learning challenge. Once the teaching elements of the lesson have been completed, the group then needs to go back over the lesson in the second phase and attempt to predict student learning behaviours they believe they will observe over the course of the lesson. Discussion can focus on the learning behaviour of all individuals in the group, but there is concern that by attempting to observe everyone the observers may actually miss important aspects of observable learning. With this concern in mind, Dudley (2014) developed an amended approach to lesson study which relies on the identification of 'case students', who can be loosely thought of as indicative of a subgroup of students within the wider group. Subgroups should relate to the particular focus of the learning challenge and may include characteristics such as levels of attainment, language competence, or special educational need. Our experience suggests that each observer should only attempt to observe two students over the course of the research lesson, as to observe many more individuals can lead to the loss of detail in the observation. Therefore, if the lesson study cycle is being undertaken by three teachers, the group will identify four individuals for observation. The group considers what they believe will be the observable learning behaviours of the four chosen students during each element of the lesson, and these predictions are collated on the lesson plan as part of the planning process. In summary, the collaborative planning process focuses on a discussion and development of the teaching approach (phase 1), and leads to a prediction of student learning behaviours in response (phase 2).

Once the lesson has been planned, it is then taught by one member of the teacher group (step three in Figure 13.1) while the others observe the designated students. One major difference in lesson study observation is that it is vital for observers to be able to see the work and discussions being undertaken by those they are observing (Lewis 2002). Therefore, research lessons are characterised by observers sitting either on the side or at the front of the classroom so that they are able to clearly observe the students involved. It is also preferable for the observers to be able to sit close to those they are observing so that they are able to listen to any discussion the students undertake over the course of the research lesson. Because observation is focused on the learning taking place within the research lesson, observers do not attempt to observe and comment on the activity of the teacher; the focus is on the activity and behaviour of students. As such, observers should attempt to sit in a position close to the students being observed to allow more detailed analysis. Observations will attempt to note the activities undertaken by students, such as notetaking, involvement in whole-class question and answer, discussion activities or the completion of group work. The observation can be general in nature, i.e. noting down what is observed, but can also include the development of comparative notes linking the behaviours that are actually observed in relation to those that were predicted during the planning process. The use of observation in this way, to gain insights into the process of learning, is one feature of the lesson study methodology that will be discussed below as I would argue that much of this process occurs in ways that do not allow for direct observation, therefore calling into question the degree of accuracy and completeness which observation allows.

Once the research lesson has finished, the teacher group reconvenes to discuss and evaluate what has been observed (see step four in Figure 13.1), and the degree to which they believe the learning challenge has been overcome. There is an important cultural aspect to this process, as in some systems such as that in England, there is a strong tendency to begin evaluative discussions by focusing on an overall assessment of the teacher's effectiveness in the classroom. This is not the purpose of lesson study which instead focuses upon the learning experience of students. With this in mind, lesson study evaluation meetings should centre on questions such as:

- What did the case students do at each point during the lesson?
- How did this compare to the planned intentions?
- What learning was observed at each key point and what was the evidence for this?
- To what extent and in what ways do we believe the learning challenge has been met?
- How might the lesson be amended to better meet the needs of students through the learning challenge?

These questions emphasise that the focus of the evaluation meeting should be on the experience and learning of students rather than the performance of the teacher. Towards the end of the meeting the teachers must decide whether or not the lesson should be repeated with a parallel group in an amended form in an attempt to gain better and further insight into the issues surrounding the learning challenge, particularly where they feel that the initial learning challenge has still not been overcome (see step five in Figure 13.1). Where no such opportunity exists, the group should consider if they have been able to identify any wider lessons relating to pedagogy that they can take away from the process to apply in similar contexts.

The pros and cons of lesson study

Hargreaves and Fullan (2012) introduced the concept of *professional capital*. They argued that to enable the development of a high-quality teaching profession it was necessary to provide a conducive environment in which teachers were able to develop their professionalism, what they call their *professional capital*. They characterise professional capital as being the amalgamation of three elements: human capital, social capital and decisional capital. Human capital relates to the development of the knowledge, understanding and skills which teachers need to allow them to work with practical skill and, eventually, expertise in the classroom. However, Hargreaves and Fullan also argue that to develop individuals' human capital, the use of collaborative development (social capital) is also extremely important. This collaborative work needs to be authentic and driven by the needs and professional curiosity of the teachers rather than being driven externally by managers and leaders imposing development foci and working practices upon them. Finally, decisional capital relates to the need to give teachers a degree of autonomy in undertaking planning for their own development. Where each of these three aspects of professional capital exist, Hargreaves and Fullan believe it is possible for successful teacher development to occur. Lesson study, as outlined above offers just such opportunities, and therefore whilst Hargreaves and Fullan do not explicitly comment on lesson study, I would suggest it is an ideal vehicle for developing the professional capital of teachers.

Whilst lesson study can offer positive opportunities for pedagogic development, it is, however, not without its problems. First, it does require a considerable investment of time, including the need for collaborative planning, the presence of several teachers within a lesson and evaluation by the group beyond the end of the research lesson. Given that lesson study relies upon sustained incremental changes in practice, the time requirement can be seen as problematic if the process is to be carried out properly. However, the more important, and deep-seated problem that lesson study might be identified as having is the very role of observation itself. Lesson study relies upon the observation of the learning process; indeed, student learning is at the centre of the methodology. However, it is important to consider the extent to which learning, as a process, is an observable action.

In contexts where observation focuses upon teaching and teachers, much of the practice of interest is external. For example, if an observer is interested in a teacher's practice relating to whole-class questioning, it is possible to observe facets of this activity, such as the questions asked by the teacher, the degree to which questions of varying challenge are asked to particular individuals, the degree to which answers are provided by the students and whether or not all students present are involved in this activity. Learning is, however, a far more complex and difficult process to observe than many people realise; even for those who work in education.

Nuthall (2007) argues that the process of learning occurs at three levels; one being wholly visible, the public- and teacher-led elements of learning; the second a semi-visible layer that is characterised by student interaction; and the third an invisible layer constituted of mental processes including prior learning and working memory. As a consequence, any attempt to observe the process of learning will only ever be partial, as important elements of the process will, according to Nuthall, not be open to observation. This can result in somewhat vague descriptions of how learning is observed within lesson study or leads to a reliance upon the external behaviours associated with the process. For example, Lewis (2002) highlights the need to watch students' faces and to capture their discussions. Cerbin and Kopp (2006) advocate the development of approaches to teaching which begin to make students' thinking visible, again, in part through the use of discursive pedagogies. However, as Nuthall (2007: 158) states:

> How students learn from classroom activities is not simply a result of teacher managed activities, but also the result of students' ongoing relationships with other students and of their own self-created activities or use of resources.

Therefore, whilst observation is important in capturing elements of the learning process, these insights strongly suggest that on its own it cannot capture the breadth and complexity of student learning. Underlying much of our use of lesson study has been the learning theory of Illeris (2007). He argues that there are three dimensions to learning. At the individual level, the acquisition of learning is an interplay between a cognitive dimension and an emotional dimension, which together lead to the acquisition of new learning. However, the vast majority of any individual's learning is also the result of their interaction with the social and material environment. Therefore, a social dimension is also central to the learning process involving interaction and collaborative learning. Using this simple conceptual framework as a basis for understanding the observation of learning, we have to accept that observation will only ever provide a partial perspective, predominantly based upon observation of interaction between the individual and social, with some ability to estimate the role of emotional processes. However, the degree to which we are able to accurately distinguish and record an emotional state is very doubtful. For example, our own use of lesson study has demonstrated on a number of occasions a clear disparity between students' actual engagement in learning activities and our interpretations of their actions based upon observation. Finally, the cognitive dimension of learning remains hidden, being synonymous with the invisible layer described by Nuthall (2007).

What this reflection on the restricted potential of observation in capturing an understanding of learning suggests is that, whilst central to the process of lesson study, observation needs to be supported with other strands of evidence. Reliance on the use of observation as a single method of capturing the complexities of the classroom may well result in restricted and mistaken interpretations, which in turn restrict the potential utility of the process. However, if other forms of evidence can be captured and used to triangulate and extend the insights gained from observation, a fuller and more critical interpretation of students' interaction with planned activities is possible.

Extending the lesson study process

Observation should remain at the centre of the process of lesson study, but as argued above it requires additional evidence if it is to help the teacher team to gain a clearer and more accurate understanding of the learning process that case students have undergone during the course of the research lesson. There are a number of different additional evidence sources that can be used as part of the lesson study process and the degree to which any of these are used will depend upon resources, particularly time, available to the teacher team. One obvious additional evidence base is the artefacts produced by the case students over the course of the lesson. These artefacts might include written work, calculations, the drawing of diagrams or use of images, to name but a few. In addition to observation, these artefacts will give further insights into levels of understanding and perhaps even student thinking, although this will depend upon the degree to which students were autonomous in creating the artefacts, as opposed to copying or setting down predetermined information. If observers have attempted to link their wider observations of student behaviour to the artefacts created, it begins to be possible to link student work with their learning behaviours. This can be achieved by noting when certain elements of writing etc. were completed in observation notes. In this way, it may be possible to begin to ascertain the focus or process of student thinking at a given point. However, it must always be remembered that the artefacts are only a partial proxy too and do not lay open the complete thought processes of the student at a particular point in time. One of the main advantages of using this source of evidence is that it does not add to the overall time resource needed for the evaluative process, but merely acts as another perspective within the evaluative discussion after the end of the research lesson.

Where time is available, another evidential strand that can offer a great deal of insight is the use of interviewing with some or all of the case students who were observed during the research lesson. General interviewing techniques can be used, focusing on asking students what they believe they learned, how they believe they have learned it and how useful they found the lesson. Although it is important to be mindful that such interviewing may often lead to very general responses that add little to the analysis of the learning process during the research lesson. A more useful interviewing method worth exploring is the use of stimulated recall interviewing. Here students are asked to bring any artefacts they developed over the course of the lesson, such as notes or diagrams and the interviewer then asks a series of questions using these artefacts as a focus and stimulus for discussion. Thus questions become focused on asking students to reflect upon what they were thinking about and what they were doing at particular points during the research lesson using the artefacts as a stimulus. This allows a partial view of the cognitive dimension of student learning over the course of the research lesson. However, as with the other strands of evidence, this approach does not allow for an exhaustive or wholly accurate recollection of the thought processes undertaken by the student. On the other hand, it does offer some insights which can then be compared with the artefacts themselves as well as the observation. In our experience, it is stimulated recall interviewing which often adds different, or even dissonant, perspectives concerning student learning over the course of the research lesson. This is particularly the case in relation to attention and engagement. On a number of occasions, we have found that students can appear to be disengaged from particular activities, offering little or no attention to the teaching focus, but on the completion of a stimulated recall interview demonstrate well-developed and acute understanding in the particular area of learning.

Where it is possible to undertake stimulated recall interviewing and add artefacts from the lesson to a consideration and evaluation based on observational reflections, the understanding and discussion relating to how students have interacted with the focus of the learning challenge can be far fuller and more critical than considering observation data alone. Nevertheless, it should be noted that the complexity of teaching and learning environments means that however much evidence is collected, the view of learning will always remain incomplete. It is impossible to get a wholly accurate and comprehensive record of the process of learning that has been undertaken over the course of the lesson. Yet this does not prevent us from gaining useful and critical insights into the learning process by the use of this method.

One additional approach which can be used within lesson study is the use of group interviewing at the start of the process. This is called participatory lesson study (Wood and Cajkler 2016) and involves the teacher group, or one of their members, discussing with a group of students what it is within the chosen subject that they struggle with and find difficult to understand. This approach challenges the assumption that the teachers have the best and most complete view of what it is the students are actually struggling with and argues that direct discussion with the students themselves may help identify the areas which can most usefully be researched. This early group meeting can also focus on asking students how they believe the challenge might best be overcome. Having gained these early insights, the teacher group then meet to collaboratively plan the research lesson, as would occur in the normal approach to lesson study. However, they are able to engage with reflections and opinions given by students and are able to critically consider and enfold any insights they believe might be useful into the planning process. On the completion of the research lesson, the student group can be reconvened and asked questions about the degree to which they believe the research lesson helped overcome the learning challenge. This approach can be used instead of, or in addition to, stimulated recall interviewing, depending upon the available time for the teacher team.

These additional strands of evidence, as with the observation, are partial and incomplete in the narrative they provide about the learning of students during the research lesson. However, by triangulating them to identify similarities and differences in the evidence, useful insights can be developed concerning the degree of student learning, the processes involved, and the degree of success or otherwise of the chosen activities. In this way, the broadening of the activities used to interrogate learning processes beyond, but in support of, observation add a great deal to the overall process.

The potential of lesson study: concluding thoughts

Lesson study has become increasingly popular across a number of countries over the past two decades. There is a growing body of evidence, much of it perceptual, that the process can help teachers gain a greater understanding of the difficulties inherent in areas of student learning and also develop new and more reflective pedagogic approaches. However, to develop and ensure a critical and well-evidenced approach, I would argue that it is dangerous to rely wholly upon observation as the only medium for capturing evidence of learning. The approaches used within lesson study need to be consciously and explicitly linked to an explanation of the theory or process of learning on which data capture is being based. Therefore, the insights of researchers such as Illeris and Nuthall call into serious doubt the validity of using observation as the only method for capturing the student learning process during the course of the research lesson. Having said this, observation should not be discounted as a useful technique in its own right but should, instead, be supported through the use of other forms of data capture as outlined above.

What is certain is that by re-orientating observation towards the investigation of student learning within lessons, supported by scrutiny of artefacts and the use of interviewing, a great deal more can be learned about classroom pedagogy than is the case through the use of external, often unannounced, accountability observations (O'Leary 2014). In addition, the collaborative, formative and potentially iterative process of lesson study is an obvious vehicle for encouraging the development of professional capital, as described earlier in this chapter. Lesson study is not the only technique which can be used to reclaim observation as a positive, professional tool for teacher growth, but it is certainly a good starting point!

References

Cerbin, W. and Kopp, B. (2006) 'Lesson Study as a Model for Building Pedagogical Knowledge and Improving Teaching'. *International Journal of Teaching and Learning in Higher Education*, 18(3), 250–257.

Dudley, P. (2012) 'Lesson Study Development in England: From school networks to national policy'. *International Journal for Lesson and Learning Studies*, 1(1), 85–100.

Dudley, P. (2014) *Lesson Study: A handbook*. Retrieved from http://lessonstudy.co.uk/wp-content/uploads/2012/03/new-handbook-revisedMay14.pdf. Last accessed 14 March 2016.

Fernandez, C. and Yoshida, M. (2004) *Lesson Study: A Japanese approach to improving mathematics teaching and learning*. London: Routledge.

Hargreaves, A. and Fullan, M. (2012) *Professional capital: Transforming teaching in every school*. New York: Teachers' College Press.

Illeris, K. (2007) *How We Learn: Learning and non-learning in school and beyond*. London: Routledge.

Lewis, C. (2002) *Lesson Study: A Handbook of Teacher Led Instructional Change*. Philadelphia, PA: Research for Better Schools.

Lewis, C. and Tsuchida, I. (1997) 'Planned Educational Change in Japan: The case of elementary science instruction'. *Journal of Educational Policy*, 12(5), 313–331.

Nakatome, T. (1984) *Konaikenshu o Tsukuru: Nihon no konaikenshu keiei no sogoteki kemkyu [Developing Konaikenshu: A comprehensive study of management of Japanese konaikenshu]*. Tokyo, Japan: Eidell Kenkyusho.

Nuthall, G. (2007) *The Hidden Lives of Learners*. Wellington: NZCER Press.

O'Leary, M. (2014) *Classroom Observation: A guide to the effective observation of teaching and learning*. London: Routledge.

Sarkar Arani M. R., Shibata, Y. and Matoba, M. (2007) 'Delivering Jugyou Kenkyuu for Reframing Schools as Learning Organizations: An examination of the process of Japanese school change'. Nagoya University *English Journal*, 3, 25–36.

Stigler, J. and Hiebert, J. (1999) *The Teaching Gap: Best ideas from the world's teachers for improving education in the classroom*. New York: The Free Press.

Takahashi, A. and Yoshida, M. (2004) 'Ideas for establishing Lesson-Study communities'. *Teaching Children Mathematics* (May), 436–443.

Wood, P. and Cajkler, W. (2016) 'A participatory Approach to Lesson Study in Higher Education'. *International Journal for Lesson and Learning Studies*, 5(1), 4–18.

CONCLUSION

Matt O'Leary

How can observation best be used to stimulate and support excellence in teacher learning and improve the student learning experience in the classroom? This is a question that underpins the very *raison d'être* of this book and it is a question that has been explored in every chapter from start to finish. And rightly so! For if we choose to invest time in using a particular method or approach in education, whether it be with students or teachers, we need to know that it is time well spent and that ultimately it adds value and meaning to the educational experience.

A recurring theme illustrated throughout this book is how observation has huge potential to offer as a formative and supportive method for helping teachers to improve their pedagogic knowledge and practice. Yet for too long the use of observation in our education systems has been colonised by deficit approaches that have been more concerned with attempting to measure and judge practice in an isolated, episodic manner rather than genuinely seeking to exploit its rich potential as a tool for collaborative teacher learning. Each chapter in this book has emphasised the importance of placing the professional needs of practitioners at the heart of any successful and sustainable approach to observation instead of the production of performance management data. In doing so, there are a number of benefits to be gained for the individual, the institution and the profession as a whole.

Some of the *expansive approaches* to the use of observation discussed in this book clearly have an important role to play in helping to increase teacher agency and professionalism as they provide opportunities for teachers to take ownership of what they do and how they do it, as opposed to simply performing reactively to satisfy the monitoring demands of a top-down agenda set by others. As Phil Wood argues in his chapter on lesson study, such approaches offer an important means of encouraging the development of teachers' 'professional capital' (Hargreaves and Fullan 2012). But increasing teacher ownership need not mean that they are somehow less accountable for what they do. If anything, there is a strong case for saying that by giving teachers' greater ownership of their practice and professional learning, they become more accountable to their employers, students and themselves. If teaching staff are engaged in ongoing reflection of their practice as one might reasonably expect any conscientious practitioner to be, then they are often best placed to self-reflect on the strengths and areas for improvement in their own practice and thus identify their specific professional needs at any given time. But what if a teacher is not predisposed to do this or even demonstrates signs of professional incompetence? How might observation help in such cases?

The importance of cultivating cultures of collaboration between staff, particularly via peer-based approaches to observation that draw on aspects of coaching is another common theme to emerge from this book. These have the potential to redress some of the power imbalances associated with top-down, hierarchical approaches and can encourage a greater sharing of practice and dialogue that can be of mutual benefit to both the observer and observee. Equally when underpinned by mutual trust and respect, they provide the foundations for challenging yet supportive professional dialogue about practice. As Fullan and Hargreaves (1992: 19) maintained in their use of the term 'interactive professionalism', teacher improvement is much more likely to prosper when there is a culture of collaboration and collegiality rather than 'punitive appraisal schemes'.

So, what are the key messages from this book and its implications for the future use of lesson observation in an educational context? A rich range of contextualised examples are provided throughout for readers to consider in terms of pursuing different or 'alternative' approaches to observation. But whatever alternative approaches may look like, it is clear that in order to maximise the potential of observation they need to be underpinned by a supportive and collaborative ethos of teacher learning and growth. Professional trust must be at the core of any such approach rather than suspicion and distrust.

If observation is to continue to be used as a core element of teacher evaluation, it needs to be part of a teaching and learning system that supports continuous improvement for teachers individually and as a collective community of practice. Fostering collaborative learning amongst teachers is much more likely to support student achievement than divisive, ranking exercises. Expansive approaches to observation offer the opportunity for creating open, collegial spaces in which to discuss teaching and learning; spaces where teachers not only feel safe to discuss, analyse and critique their practice without fear of being judged, but that they should want to and feel excited about doing so. But inevitably this takes time. It is important for teachers, leaders and policy makers to accept that there are no quick fixes, one-size-fits-all solutions or instant results when it comes to developing and applying successful and sustainable strategies to promote teachers' professional learning.

The time has come for observation to no longer be seen as a predominantly summative assessment tool or disciplinary mechanism, but instead as a method of systematic inquiry that has an important contribution to make to educators' analysis, understanding and improvement of teacher thinking, learning and practice. Only with such developments can the profession truly begin to reclaim observation as an empowering tool in the future growth of teachers. But this will only happen if teachers are encouraged to experiment and to expose their practice to the eyes of others without fear of punitive surveillance systems.

References

Fullan, M. and Hargreaves, A. (1992) *What's Worth Fighting for in Your School*. Buckingham: Open University Press.

Hargreaves, A. and Fullan, M. (2012) *Professional Capital: Transforming teaching in every school*. New York: Teachers' College Press.

INDEX